D1433399

Also available at all good book stores

9781785316272

9781785315466

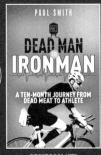

9781785316173

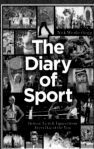

9781785316289

9781785316197

9781785316821

9781785317248

9781785315619

9781785314315

Dead Man Running

Dead Man Running

One Man's Story of Running to Stay Alive

Kevin Webber
with Mark Church

First published by Pitch Publishing, 2021

Pitch Publishing
A2 Yeoman Gate
Yeoman Way
Worthing
Sussex
BN13 3QZ
www.pitchpublishing.co.uk
info@pitchpublishing.co.uk

ISBN 978 1 78531 988 4

Typesetting and origination by Pitch Publishing
Printed and bound in Great Britain by TJ Books, Padstow

Contents

For my children, Hayley, Ben and Ollie, if nothing else I hope this book shows you that when you get knocked down you get up and go again, as I like to think I have done.

Preface

I NEVER had any desire to write a book at any stage of my life, probably because I never thought I had anything new or different to say that had not been written before.

I started writing email blogs in 2014 because of my life-changing situation and within a few months people started asking me if I was going to write a book about my experiences. I was flattered and assumed they were just being nice, but the question about writing a book about my journey never went away.

Finally, when my friend Mark Church asked me if I had ever thought about writing a book about my story it made me stop and think seriously. Mark thought the journey I have been on would be of interest to people and he said he would help put my words on paper. Mark's offer plus my mantra of living for the day was enough to convince me to set out on my writing debut.

I hope that you enjoy sharing the highs and lows of my journey and if nothing else my story might help you become a better and kinder person because I know that is what has happened to me.

Thank you.
Kevin Webber, June 2021

Introduction

KEVIN WEBBER'S story was one that needed to be told. But who should tell it? There was only one person for that job. The man himself.

But writing about yourself is a difficult thing to do. That is where I came in. I had spent time with Kevin and was amazed by the journey he had been on. I always thought there was a book in there and one afternoon I asked Kevin if he had ever thought about putting pen to paper. He said he had but he wasn't sure how to get started. I offered to put his words in print, and I was delighted when he said yes, because I wanted to give something back to him. Kevin does so much for other people, and I thought he should have his story told as a way of saying thank you for everything he has done.

I also wanted to help write the book for his family. I think Kevin would agree that without their love and support he would never have achieved everything he has. It makes me happy to think they will always have his book, no matter what the future holds, and I hope Sarah, Hayley, Ben, Ollie, and Ian are happy with how the story has been written.

Kevin is an inspirational fella and I will always be grateful he trusted me to help him write his story.

Mark Church, June 2021

'What will I think of me
the day that I die?'

'Saltwater', Julian Lennon
1991

As you read through my six-year journey you may feel that you, like me, want to support Prostate Cancer UK. If you are able and want to help keep families together for longer, please do sponsor me as it all goes to the charity, at

www.justgiving.com/fundraising/kevin-webber9

Thank you

Chapter 1

When life changed

MY NAME is Kevin Webber. I am an ordinary 56-year-old guy who loves his family, loves his job, loves his friends and loves a pint. I also love running.

My life changed seven years ago. Everything was going great. I was working hard and doing well in my job at NatWest Bank. I had no financial worries, all my family were healthy and life was good. I was living my life the best way I could. That involved a bit of running, the odd marathon here and there but nothing too serious.

Then, in the summer of 2014 we took a family holiday to America. My kids were 16, 14 and nine and I thought it might be the last chance we would get to have a holiday together. I can remember not wanting to go away with my mum and dad after I was 16, so this was going to be a special family holiday.

We decided to go to America and stayed at my brother-in-law's in South Carolina, then drove to Florida to spend a week at Disney World and Universal Studios. No matter what people say, you cannot help getting wrapped up in the magic of Disney and I was no exception, having my photo taken with Tigger and Winnie the Pooh and enjoying having time with the kids and my wife Sarah.

Whilst we were staying in Florida, I started to notice that I was waking up in the night, desperate for a wee. I would suddenly be wide awake, having to rush to the toilet but would only urinate for a couple of seconds and that would be it. An hour later the same thing would happen. I would wake up bursting for the toilet, rush to the bathroom and only go for a couple of seconds. This was happening two or three times a night and, in my mind, there was no reason for it because I wasn't really drinking alcohol in the evenings as I was the one that was doing all the driving.

I didn't think too much about it because we were having a fantastic time and I thought it might just be the heat or the water and it wasn't uncomfortable. I just put it to the back of my mind. We left Florida, had another week in South Carolina and came home having had the wonderful family holiday that I had desired.

The following week I returned to work and after a couple of days I noticed that when I sat down it felt like I was sitting on a golf ball. I would have this uncomfortable feeling for a couple of minutes but it disappeared when I got up and had a walk around the office. My job with NatWest was to look after a portfolio of commercial banking clients and I had to give them my full attention during meetings. But the feeling of sitting on a golf ball was starting to niggle and I was not able to concentrate. Some days the feeling wasn't there, but on others it would last for an hour and I was really starting to notice it.

I was still being woken up two or three times a night desperately needing to urinate then finding nothing really happened and, in the words of Bill Clinton, it was much the same when I had 'relations' with my wife. So now I had three noticeable problems all in the same area and I had no idea what any of them meant.

I then did what most men never do and booked an appointment with the doctor. I honestly thought he would tell me that I was being silly and there was nothing to worry about. I hadn't really mentioned how I was feeling to my wife Sarah and I thought it was better to be on the safe side. A week later, I was off to the surgery and the only thing I was nervous about was wasting my doctor's time.

I told the doctor the three symptoms I was experiencing, and he told me that he wanted to do a prostate test. Suddenly, I had gone from worrying I was wasting his time, to having the doctor's finger up my bottom doing an examination of my prostate. It wasn't the most comfortable experience of my life and a couple of days later I had to go back and have a whole range of blood tests. They told me they would have the results in a week, and I went back to work and got on with my life.

A week later I went back to the surgery to get my results. I wasn't nervous because, like most people, I believed you told the doctor your problem and they sorted it out because they always knew the answer.

I sat down with the doctor and he looked at his computer and said, 'Mr Webber. Your PSA, or prostate specific antigen, score is 341 and we will have to do a range of other tests.' Alarm bells started ringing in my head. My dad had had prostate cancer a decade earlier and even though he never really discussed it, the one thing he did mention was his maximum PSA score, which was 12. His prostate cancer was curable, and he needed radiotherapy to sort it. I had just been told my PSA score was 341! The doctor gave me a form and told me to take it to reception and an appointment at Epsom Hospital would be made for me in two weeks' time. As I got up to leave my doctor said, 'I recall your father had prostate cancer too,' and as I was walking out the door his final words were, 'Good luck.' I walked to reception to hand in my form thinking to myself, 'is this down to luck now?' and I had the words prostate cancer firmly in my mind.

I made the journey home and the alarm bells were still ringing loudly. I went straight to my computer and searched 'prostate cancer'. The first thing that came onto my screen was a link to the Prostate Cancer UK website. I discovered they had a forum and even though I hadn't been officially diagnosed, I decided to post on the forum and see what advice I might get. So, I wrote, 'I am a reluctant newbie,' and stated that my PSA score was 341 and asked what happened now. Almost immediately I got some lovely responses from a range of people saying it was treatable and most people get cured and continue to live their lives. All the responses were very positive, but I was still worried.

All I said to my wife at this stage was the doctor thought there might be a problem with my prostate, and I was having another appointment in a couple of weeks. The date for that appointment arrived in the post and I was booked to see a urologist at Epsom Hospital. From my research, I knew a urologist dealt with bladder problems but also dealt with prostate cancer and now I was extremely nervous and worried.

Two weeks after being told my PSA score by my doctor, Sarah and I were making our way to Epsom Hospital for my appointment with the urologist. This was the first appointment Sarah had been to with me and when we met the urologist my first thought was, 'He has got chubby fingers'. I was right to be worried because five minutes later he was using those fingers to do a proper examination of my prostate, which was very uncomfortable, and he then consulted his notes which included my PSA score. He looked at me and said, 'I wouldn't normally diagnose anything from the examination I have just done and your PSA score, but in your case Mr Webber I am sorry to tell you that you do have prostate cancer.'

The fact he was telling me at this point meant I knew it was bad. He gave me some tablets and told me I would need to have several scans and a biopsy in the coming weeks. Sarah and I went home, and I immediately went back on the Prostate Cancer UK forum and explained what my diagnosis had been.

Again, the responses were all very positive, telling me it was curable. I also spoke to Hugh, a colleague at work who been diagnosed with prostate cancer in 2013 but had been treated and was now fine. Hugh told me what happened to him and suggested I would have six months of uncomfortable treatment, but then life would get back to normal. Everyone was telling me it was curable, but I was now facing the prospect of more scans and a biopsy in October. Even though I was worried, I didn't want to burden Sarah with how I was feeling because I didn't think that was fair on her, plus I was being told by everybody it could be treated.

The biopsy was a horrible and undignified experience. From the moment I walked into the room I just felt embarrassed; I know that may be a strange word to use but just the thought of me face down with something being put where the sun don't shine was bad enough. What was even worse was that this was to be done by two female nurses in their late 20s. Then from what I understood I was going to have 18 needles individually fired through my bowel and then have the needles pulled back, ripping out a sample of my prostate. And this was going to be done through my backside via what looked like a policeman's truncheon. They were shooting 18 needles because it was difficult to be precise with each one even though they use a basic scanner and they wanted to conduct an overall inspection of my prostate to see where the cancer was.

The first six needles were fired into me by the specialist, pulled back out and each one was more painful than the last.

It felt like an elastic band was being flicked hard against my testicles (not that I actually knew what that felt like but you get my drift). After six needles the specialist stopped. My first reaction was relief, but then I asked the specialist why he had stopped firing. He replied, 'Mr Webber, to be honest with you I couldn't miss.' As I was getting dressed, I started to realise that the reason he had stopped firing the needles was that everything in my prostate was cancerous.

The specialist told me I would be given another appointment to get the results of the biopsy and the scans. I was beginning to realise this was serious. My backside was now bleeding too and continued to do so for the next few days.

Next, I had to have an MRI and bone scan, but I was still going to work. I told a few people at the bank that I had been diagnosed with prostate cancer. As well as Hugh, who had been diagnosed the year before, I also told my boss Stuart and his boss Neal, who were both incredibly supportive. I guess in some ways they thought, 'There but for the grace of God go I'. At that stage, I hadn't told anybody else, including my kids and wider family, because I didn't want to be asked questions that I didn't know the answers to and I didn't want them to treat me differently.

On 23 October I picked up the paper and read that Alvin Stardust had died from prostate cancer. When I was a kid Alvin Stardust was the 'glam rock' star and seemed indestructible. I hadn't thought about people dying from prostate cancer and here it was staring me in the face, making me realise this was potentially more serious than just getting diagnosed, getting treated, getting cured and getting on with my life. I was now really scared and was no longer sleeping at night.

A letter arrived saying I would get the results of my biopsy and scans at an appointment on 6 November back at Epsom Hospital. By a quirk of fate, the urologist I was seeing this time was the specialist who had treated Hugh. When I told Hugh who I was seeing, he said he was a brilliant doctor and that filled me with confidence.

The day of my appointment to get my test results arrived and Sarah and I made our way to Epsom Hospital and the MacMillan Butterfly Centre. We arrived and sat in the waiting room. I was nervous and scared. My name was called, and Sarah and I were told which room to go to. I opened the door and the first person we were introduced to was a MacMillan nurse and a man who said he was doing some research, and would it be ok if he sat in on the meeting. I had no problem with that, but as we sat down the alarm bells were ringing in my head because I was wondering why there was a MacMillan nurse there.

Before the appointment I had done some research and I knew the specialist was going to give me a Gleason score based on my biopsy. The score would fall somewhere between six and ten with six being the lowest form of cancer. The specialist looked at me and said, 'Good morning, Mr Webber. I am looking at your test results and your Gleason score is between nine and ten, but let's say it is a nine.'

I sat there trying to make sense of what he had just told me. With a score of nine we had just moved, in one sentence, from bad to dreadful news. I immediately asked him for a prognosis, hoping he would say I could be cured. He looked at me and said, 'Mr Webber, you have between two to ten years, but you should realistically think you have between three to four years to live. Definitely don't think ten.'

When you get told news like that you immediately just hear the words 'two years' and Sarah and I burst into tears. In the space of a minute my world had come crashing down and I just clung on to Sarah. The MacMillan nurse came and put an arm around us both and I realised why she was in the room. She was there because she knew I was going to be given the worst possible news.

The specialist then said, 'Mr Webber, I am so sorry, but we are going to get you an appointment with an oncologist who will form a plan for your treatment. (I now know only 30 per cent of men with my diagnosis live past five years and some only live a few months.)

Sarah and I were taken to a small waiting room where we just held each other and cried. I think we were both in shock because this was a diagnosis we had never considered. We were then taken to see Professor Chris Parker, an oncologist who sat with us and told us that even though the prognosis was very serious there were still things that could be done. He told us he would come up with a plan of action and book us an appointment to see him again.

And that was it. Sarah and I went home and tried to take in what we had been told. We did a lot of crying and I decided to write and send the following email to work:

Hi Guys

I am afraid it could not have been much worse.

I have Metastatic Prostate Cancer (I am in esteemed company as that is what Alvin Stardust had), I will leave you to Google it but there is no cure and they can only try to stop it for a while or slow it down, bit of a bummer.

Needless to say, I won't be in tomorrow as I have to sort out loads of stuff and arrange bits with the quacks and I also have another scan on Monday just to see how far it has gone round my other lymph nodes plus another session on Tuesday as they need the results of Monday's scan and are talking about putting me on some experimental trial drug.

As you can imagine I have to get the courage to tell my family and I am not looking forward to that much, as it's hard enough to cope with my emotions right now let alone someone else's, although Sarah has been great.

I would be grateful if you could keep this to yourselves until Monday as there are people I need to tell over the weekend who have to hear it from me first rather than third hand, I am sure I can trust you in that regard but between the six of you say what you like!

Finally, you have all been so supportive since I first told you, thank you so much, sorry to bring bad thoughts to your day. When you see me next don't ask how I am though, as I will just burst into tears.

Kev

I also knew I had to tell my brother and my dad. We had a light that needed fixing in our hall and my brother is a bit of an expert handyman, so I asked him to come around the next day to look at the light. When he came, I didn't say anything to him, but I suggested we both go and see Dad who lived ten minutes away. We went to Dad's and I sat them down and told them my prognosis, which was bloody difficult. My dad was very upset because one of the deals when you are a father is you die before your kids and now that might have changed.

So, I had told my dad, told my brother and told work. And now the worst bit. I had to tell my kids. Sunday was Remembrance Sunday and Ollie, my youngest, was in the cubs who were part of our local Service of Remembrance. My other two children from my previous marriage, Hayley and Ben, would be with us, so I decided to tell them all together after the service. Saturday was tough, not being able to tell Ollie, but I wanted to tell them all together. I had read that telling them all together is important because that way they hear the same news, the same way, can hear each other's questions, don't feel that there is any favouritism and finally can start to be that support network for each other, as sadly they will need it in time to come.

Telling my children was one of the hardest things I have ever done, but I didn't say anything about only having two years left to live. I just told them I had incurable cancer. Hayley, my eldest, cried, Ben had tears in his eyes, and I think my youngest Ollie cried because everyone else was crying and he didn't understand. And then we went to the park and played football, which might seem a strange thing to do after telling your children that you are dying. But in my mind, it was important that they saw I felt fine that day. I didn't want my children to see me as a victim and treat me differently.

The following day, Sarah and I went back to Epsom Hospital and saw Professor Chris Parker who was now officially my oncologist. He told us that I was going to be given a course of chemotherapy followed by a course of radiotherapy. The treatment would start on 13 January, had asked if it would matter if it was delayed so I could perhaps have one last good Christmas before the chemotherapy started, and maybe worse. Professor Parker was absolutely fine with that and understood the reasons.

I went back to work and effectively made sure everything was in place before I started my chemotherapy and the bank were fantastically supportive. I managed to get through the work Christmas festivities, but in my head, I was thinking that I didn't really have two years to live. I had been told that I was going to have around a year of treatment so realistically I only had a year left and I had no idea how I would be feeling by then. I felt as if all my dreams had been taken away from me and I was incredibly sad. But Christmas was coming, I had my family to think of and I was determined to try and enjoy myself.

The other person it was important for me to tell was my best mate, Jim. Jim and I were drinking and occasionally running buddies and we had run 100k from London to Brighton together earlier in 2014. I arranged to go for a run with Jim one evening and told him my prognosis. I think we both spent the next mile or so running in the dark with tears rolling down our cheeks.

When you get a prognosis like mine it takes away your ability to dream. No kids' 18th or 21st birthday parties, no graduations, no first cars, no weddings, no grandchildren, no driving round Europe with Sarah in a camper van when I retired. All these dreams had been taken away from me forever.

Sarah and I have always loved Woolacombe Bay in Devon, so we decided to hire a house there for New Year. I paid for 11 of us, including my children and our best friends, to go to Devon after our Christmas at home and we had a wonderful New Year celebration. I somehow managed to put everything to the back of my mind for a few days, but then it was time to go home and face the reality of starting my chemotherapy.

On 12 January I had my last day at work. The bank had been brilliant, and I worked hard to try to be in the frame of mind that I was going on holiday and needed to get everything tidied up and finalised before I left. I wasn't thinking about starting chemotherapy the next day, but I knew my clients would have noticed that I hadn't been myself since my diagnosis. I hadn't told them that I had prostate cancer, so the last thing I did before I left the office was to send an email to my clients, some of whom I was very close to. This is what some of that email said:

Dear All,

I just wanted to say thank you for your compassion and understanding of my personal situation. As you can imagine at a healthy 49 the last thing I expected after some minor symptoms was to be told that I may only have a few years to live, so it has been a bit of a struggle to be honest to hold it together some days.

I have no idea how long I will be off for; I may be back briefly in a couple of weeks or you may not see me for six to nine months it just depends on how 18 weeks of chemotherapy and six weeks of radiotherapy does me in and how long I need to recover.

Have a healthy and successful 2015

Kevin

Sending that email made me sad because it made what was happening to me very real after a day when I was too busy to think about the reasons why I was going. The fact that I was leaving my clients and work colleagues and I didn't know when I would see them again really made it hit home.

Although I had not left the office until after 6pm, clearly some customers were still at work too and as my train pulled into my home station I had already received a few supportive and shocked emails from them and it had me in tears. As I walked from the train to my home, all I was thinking was how much I was going to miss work and whether I would ever go back. I went for a long run and felt very sad. I thought I might never run again after the chemotherapy started and that would mean the end of my favourite hobby and something I loved doing.

The next morning, I woke up with a knot in my stomach. Today was the start of my chemotherapy. Six courses over 18 weeks and I was very nervous. I was most worried about having a canula put into my vein because this was one of my biggest phobias. Bizarrely, I was more scared about that than the chemotherapy. Sarah drove me up to the Royal Marsden Hospital in Sutton. I had decided to have my treatment done privately because I would see the same oncologist on every hospital visit and this is what I wanted. I had been told that by going privately, it would be a much nicer 'waiting experience' for chemotherapy. There was mention of a coffee machine, comfy chairs and carpeted floors and that was good enough for me. But most importantly I learnt that the Royal Marsden only survives through donations and private patients and I was happy for them to make money through me and my treatment to help others.

We arrived at the Royal Marsden, I had a blood test and we were taken to a very nice waiting room (they weren't lying). I was then taken to what is known as the 'chemo room'. There were already five people in the room all receiving their course of chemotherapy. I was immediately overwhelmed by a feeling of doom. I was entering a joyless, airless place and it felt like the life was being sucked out of me. There was no hope in that room, and I was terrified. I sat down and a canula was inserted into my arm. I just wanted to rip it out as a cold saline solution was injected into me and I could feel the freezing liquid going into my veins. The nurses brought out my 'bag of chemo' which I looked at and realised that bag of poison was going into me. It was the most horrendous feeling. The chemotherapy started and Sarah sat with me as I tried to distract myself. My iPad was on my lap, but all I kept doing was looking at the bag and praying it would be over soon. After 90 minutes it was over, and Sarah drove me home.

Sarah parked the car and I shuffled up the driveway towards our front door. I didn't feel any worse than I had before the chemotherapy, but I was behaving how I thought I should behave after having chemo. I slumped in a chair and Sarah made me dinner and I went straight to bed. I was sad about everything and it felt like the beginning of the end. I desperately wanted to go to sleep and forget it all for a few hours, but I was wide awake. I had been given a ton of steroids during the chemotherapy and they are like having double espressos. It was a horrible night as I lay there thinking my life was over and all my dreams had been taken away. It had been a horrific day and I had another five courses of chemotherapy ahead of me and I honestly couldn't face it. I eventually cried myself to sleep for an hour or so.

The next morning, I woke up and everything hit me again. I shuffled over to our bedroom window. A typical cold, grey, miserable January morning greeted me. I stood there feeling like my world had come to an end. And then I suddenly thought, 'I'm going to go for a run.' I dressed in layers of running gear to keep out the cold, went downstairs and put on my trainers. Sarah saw me at the front door and asked me what I was doing. I told her and she said I couldn't because of the chemotherapy. I told her that the doctor hadn't said I couldn't go for a run and she quite rightly told me that I hadn't asked him!

I decided I was going to run to the park which was half a mile from our house and come straight back. I set off and it was bitterly cold, and I was slow. My legs felt like they didn't want to move, but I was telling myself to keep lifting them and move forwards. I felt sick and tired, but I managed to get to the park, do a couple of laps, turn around and run home. I managed three miles and collapsed in a chair feeling nothing but pure elation. I had done it. Everything hurt, I felt sick and I was exhausted. The thing is, you see, I had proved that I could still run; a slow, shorter, different run, yes, but run none the less, and for the first time since my diagnosis I had a bit of hope and joy about the short term.

I decided that I was going to run every other day and I now had something to focus on other than having cancer and feeling ill. I had a purpose which was good, but four or five days after my first course of chemotherapy I started to notice its effects. Over the next few weeks, my tongue turned black, my hair started falling out, my nails cracked and I was sore all over my body. But I kept running every other day to the park for a few laps and back.

Now, I should explain how a three-week cycle of chemotherapy works. You have your course at the hospital and then feel awful for a few days. You then have a week where your immunity is extremely low, and you feel tired and lethargic. And you have a final week when you start to feel a bit better. And then you have your next course of chemotherapy and start the cycle again. During that first cycle, I kept running and I was starting to feel fitter. Three miles had turned into five miles and I was running with a backpack that contained all my details, extra clothing and water in case I collapsed. By week three, I was doing loops near my house but making sure I was never more than a mile away in case anything went wrong.

It was time for my second course of chemotherapy, but I was feeling more positive. I saw Professor Parker for a blood test and told him that I had started running. I also explained to him that I had entered the Brighton marathon before I got ill, and I now wanted to run it in eight weeks' time. I had run it the year before and had immediately entered for 2015. As I said at the start of the book, I had always been a keen runner and had done quite a few marathons, including London twice. If I'm honest I don't think I would have been considering running the Brighton marathon if I hadn't already entered but it had now become my goal and was giving me something to aim for.

Professor Parker told me that nobody with my cancer could run a marathon on my kind of chemotherapy, but he could tell I was serious. He suggested I try and find someone else who had run a marathon on chemotherapy. I searched and searched but couldn't find anyone. I told Professor Parker and despite that he said it was my choice if I wanted to run the Brighton marathon and he would be slightly happier if I could train properly for it to prove it to myself and, I guess, for his peace of mind. This was the news I wanted to hear and now all my focus was on training and running the Brighton marathon. I had less than two months to train properly and be ready whilst still having my chemotherapy.

Every time I went out for a run it felt like jeopardy. I was always scared that this would be the time I was going to collapse and not be able to get home. Anyone who has ever trained for a marathon will tell you that once you are running over ten miles it gets hard. You are out there for a long time, but I stayed local so I was never too far from home. I was training by doing six-mile laps from our house and I was now trying to run almost every day. I was feeling fitter, but one day I stopped under a railway bridge and burst into tears. I felt weak, tired and I was worrying about my family and how they might cope without me, but I turned that sadness around by visualising what it would actually be like to finish the Brighton marathon and I saw myself, arms in the air, going across the finish line. That was enough right then to get me running again. Overall, I didn't feel too bad; training was going ok and I had got through three courses of chemotherapy. I had somehow managed to run 18 miles during a training session, so I felt I could finish the marathon. I was also taking my diet seriously, reading loads of running magazines and buying lots of expensive running gear. I had a focus, a goal, all the gear and no idea, but right then that was enough.

The first chemo sessions had really bashed my body and my blood was in a bit of a mess, so they decided I needed to do daily self-administered injections in my stomach to increase the platelets. Now I know some people have to do this every day forever with some conditions, but for me it just added to the misery of life on a short prognosis and I remember sitting on my bed at home looking at the needle wishing I was dead, so I didn't have to go through all this rubbish that I could only see getting worse.

With a few weeks until the Brighton marathon, Sarah and I went to my brother's for dinner. I suddenly started to get shooting pains down my spine and when we got home, I decided to have a bath to try and take the pressure off, but the pain was getting worse. I was in agony. The pain in my lower back was unbearable and we took my temperature. When you start chemotherapy, they tell you that if your temperature ever gets over 39 degrees Centigrade you must go straight to hospital. My temperature was well over that and Sarah immediately drove me to Epsom Hospital after calling them and saying I was on my way.

The pain was now so bad I couldn't sit down, so I had to prop myself up in the car for the journey. They rushed me in for a scan because they wanted to make sure I wasn't infected in some way or having a spinal cord compression, which is common for those suffering from prostate cancer. The cancer can cause your spine to contract and can lead to paralysis, but it is preventable if they catch it quickly. They pumped me full of antibiotics and morphine during the scan, but I was still in agony and I felt terrified that I was going to be left paralysed. I was still in great pain but I suddenly fell asleep and when I woke up, a few hours later, I felt alright. The hospital did some more checks and then let me go home. It had been an awful experience, but I felt ok, so we decided to go and do some shopping. Sarah and I were in Waitrose when my phone started ringing. It was the Royal Marsden to check how I was feeling. They then asked me where I was, and I told them. They immediately told me to go straight back to hospital because I shouldn't have been sent home.

Back to the Marsden we went, and I ended up spending a further three days there, being pumped full of drugs. I was in a room on my own, lying in bed and worrying that I might not be able to run the Brighton marathon. Being on my own there was nothing to distract me so my head was full of worst-case scenario thoughts. I was missing training and felt awful but did not mention to any of the doctors or nurses that I was planning to run the marathon. I didn't want them to tell me I couldn't, and I hadn't seen Professor Parker, so I said nothing. One thing that they decided, though, was that I should not self-inject anymore as they concluded that those injections were what had caused my bad reaction as they were effectively forcing my bone marrow to make more of a type of cell that clearly my body did not like. I just had to hope that without the injections and only a couple more rounds of chemo my blood would self-repair, so to speak.

I was discharged from the hospital ten days before the Brighton marathon. I felt tired and weak, but I immediately started training again. Having already run 18 miles in a session before going into hospital, I took it gently, but I was determined to be on that start line. Getting there had been the goal that had kept me going over the last few weeks and now it was just around the corner.

I had been in touch with Prostate Cancer UK to tell them I was running the marathon on chemotherapy. I wanted to support them because their forum had been so important to me and I wanted to raise awareness that one in eight men will get prostate cancer during their lives. I spoke to Gary at the charity, who was really encouraging and sent me a t-shirt to run in. I set up my Just Giving Page and nearly £15,000 had already been raised for Prostate Cancer UK before I set foot on the start line of the Brighton marathon. This included an incredible donation of £5,000 from one of my customers. I remember looking at the donation and feeling guilty. I knew the customer well, but this was an enormous amount of money to be donating. I decided to ring him to make sure he had put the decimal point in the right place. And he said, 'Kevin, you are one of the nicest people I have met, and you don't deserve to have cancer.' This gave me a massive boost because it made me realise that I was touching people and making them think about prostate cancer and possibly their own lives.

The night before the marathon I was in race mode. Before any long race you are wondering if you will finish, worrying you will get an injury and realising you have got to run 26.2 miles. I had got through the training on chemotherapy, I felt ok and I was ready to run the Brighton marathon.

Chapter 2

Running the London and Brighton marathons on chemo

I TRAVELLED down to Brighton with Sarah and Ollie in convoy with Jim, my training partner, who had entered the Brighton marathon with me as he was desperate to run a sub four-hour marathon, something I had only ever done once, in Brighton the year before. Jim was also running for Prostate Cancer UK and his family had come to support us. We parked on the outskirts of the seaside town and then waited for the official bus that would take us to the start. The queue for the buses was horrendous and I was starting to panic that we were going to miss the start of the race. A bus finally arrived that we could get on, but once we got to its destination, we still had to make a mad dash to the start line. It wasn't the ideal preparation, but Jim and I managed to find the Prostate Cancer UK crowd and we had a team photo with everybody running for the charity.

I was excited and felt pretty good as we arrived at the start line. I had been worried that some of the side-effects of the chemotherapy might hit me today, but thankfully they hadn't. I was completely caught up in the atmosphere of the marathon, the buzz was incredible, and my adrenaline was pumping. The weather was perfect, blue sky with the sun shining, as Jim and I crossed the start line to get our marathon under way.

For the first six miles we ran through the streets of Brighton with the crowds on either side of us cheering all the runners. I was being sucked along by the atmosphere and felt tremendous. We then got to the seafront and faced an uphill climb. Things started to get harder, but we were going at a reasonable pace and I still felt good. We got to the top of the hill leading out of the town, went around a traffic cone and came back down the hill. You could see the pier, Brighton Marina and the big wheel and I was buzzing. For the six miles out of the town, there were no crowds and a couple of times I needed a wee. As I explained earlier, because of the cancer the urge hit me very quickly and I had to quickly jump into a bush to relieve myself, feeling very self-conscious. My knee had also started to hurt, which slowed us down, but we kept running.

After 12 miles, we arrived at the pier and suddenly the crowds reappeared. The adrenaline started pumping again. I was looking for Sarah and Ollie because the pier was one of the places we had agreed they would be standing during the race. I saw them, gave them both a quick hug and Ollie shouted, 'Love you, Daddy,' which gave me a huge boost (I still have a video of that moment on my phone). Then I saw two familiar faces in the crowd. Andy and Liz were work colleagues who had come to support me, and I was blown away. I hadn't seen them since I started chemotherapy in January and it was very emotional seeing them. I wanted to stop and speak, but they waved me on, and Jim and I kept running.

My knee was now hurting lots, but the crowds and the adrenaline kept me going. Our pace had dropped, and it was getting tougher with every mile. I felt guilty because I knew I was slowing Jim down. He had always wanted to run a marathon in under four hours, but he had promised to stay with me and get me through the race. He was as good as his word and that took lots of pressure off me, although I did feel guilty.

We got to Shoreham which was the 20-mile mark. Jim and I were both wearing our Prostate Cancer UK t-shirts and we kept seeing another runner wearing the charity's colours. We got chatting to Greg and he told us this was his first marathon and he was running it because his dad had prostate cancer. Greg ran with us as we hit the last couple of miles of the marathon. We were running along Brighton seafront; the crowds were not held back by barriers, so it felt intimate as they shouted encouragement. I had 'Kev-Laaa' on my shirt and I could hear the crowd shouting my name. I knew I was going to finish the marathon and I was ecstatic. With a mile to go we saw the Prostate Cancer UK stand and all the volunteers were clapping and cheering Jim, Greg and me. The charity must have been delighted to see three of their runners together nearing the finishing line (you can see the photo of the three of us later in the book). All the hours of training, all the pain, all the tears and all the doubts had been worth it because all the people I was running for were stood cheering me on and you couldn't get the smile off my face.

The final half a mile really hurt. When I could see the finish line, I grabbed Jim and Greg's hands and we crossed the line together. I was elated. As I said earlier, I had visualised this moment during my worst times in training and it was everything I wanted it to be. I had my arms in the air, a massive smile on my face and I felt on top of the world. At that moment, I had achieved the impossible. I had accomplished what I set out to do and shown I wasn't a fraud. I had proved to Professor Parker, my family and all my sponsors that I could run a marathon on chemotherapy. Most importantly, I had proved it to myself. And I had recorded a time of four hours and 38 minutes, which was 50 minutes slower than the previous year but not bad for a bloke on chemotherapy.

I quickly dropped from a massive high to a feeling of anticlimax, which happens to most runners when they finish a marathon. Jim and I said goodbye to Greg and went to get our bags. I was feeling sad that the race was over. We went to the athletes' village and my spirits were lifted when I saw Ollie and Sarah. I went to the Prostate Cancer UK stand and said hello to a few people, but I was exhausted. We got on the bus that took us back to our cars and I said goodbye to Jim. Sarah drove us home and I was tired, sore and completely knackered. But I had done what I set out to do and I don't mind telling you I was proud of myself.

Two days after Brighton I got a phone call that changed the next couple of weeks for me. A friend said she might be able to get me and Jim last-minute places in the London marathon. To cut a very long story short, we were being offered the chance to replace a celebrity runner if they decided to drop out. She explained we wouldn't be given a timing chip, but we would get a number, although officially we were not supposed to do that. It was an unbelievable opportunity to be given, but I initially felt guilty about taking the place if it came up because I knew how many people wanted to run the London marathon. After chatting with Sarah and Jim, we decided to say yes because it might be the last chance I got to run London or any marathon for that matter. The problem was Jim and I had to wait to find out if any celebrity runner had decided to drop out. The marathon was just 12 days away and it fitted in with my chemotherapy, so I was desperate to get the opportunity to run.

The waiting was hard. Because of my illness, if something good was offered to me I wanted it to happen. I was still exhausted after the Brighton marathon so I wasn't training. All I was doing was sitting by the phone waiting for the call to tell me if I had a place for London. With three days to go until start day, I got the call to tell me I had a place. I put the phone down feeling ecstatic and relieved. Jim had a place, too, so we would be able to run it together. But then I started to worry. I had run one marathon on chemotherapy and I was about to attempt another, two weeks later, having done no additional training. My knee, which had flared up in Brighton, was still giving me problems and I didn't know if it would stand up to another marathon. As a wise man or a dentist once said, had I bitten off more than I could chew? There was only one way to find out.

Three days later, in the early hours of the morning, Sarah dropped Jim and me off at a hotel in Greenwich to pick up our running numbers. All the celebrity runners who were running the marathon for the organisation that had given us the places were there and we found the right person who had our numbers. They told us we wouldn't get the timing chip that goes in your shoe because that would record the time of the celebrity who was meant to be running the race and it would be pretty obvious that we were not them. We were not told which celebrity we were replacing, and I felt like a naughty schoolboy who had sneaked under the fence to run the race.

We dropped off our bags at the right place and I was feeling excited. There was still a fear in the back of my mind that someone was going to tap me on the shoulder and say, 'That number belongs to Gemma Collins (or some other celebrity) and you are definitely not Gemma Collins.' We got towards the start and my prostate cancer urge for the toilet hit me. I didn't want to run the first half a mile and then have to stop, so 20 yards before the start line, I nipped to the side of the starter's gantry and did my business. Not the textbook way to start a marathon but when you have to go, you have to go: well I do anyway! I had mentioned to Jim that we should give running at a four-hour marathon pace a go and that was how we started. Jim still wanted to run a sub four-hour marathon and I was determined to give him the chance to achieve that goal after he stuck by me at Brighton.

We found a sub four-hour pacer and stuck to them. I felt great, had that buzz again and the adrenaline was pumping. Then, just before Tower Bridge and the ten-mile mark, I realised that I wasn't going to manage the rest of the marathon at the pace we were running. I told Jim not to worry about me and to keep going and break his four-hour barrier. I would be ok because there were medics all over the course in case anything went wrong, and it wasn't like I could get lost. Plus, I would enjoy the experience more if I wasn't busting a gut to keep up with Jim's pace. Jim headed off and I ran my own race. As I was going over Tower Bridge someone called my name. It was a friend called Carole, who used to work with me at the bank, and she was watching the marathon with her husband. She waved, took my photo and that gave me a real lift because I hadn't seen Carole for many years.

I felt ok as we entered Docklands and I chatted to anyone who was wearing a Prostate Cancer UK t-shirt. Having met Greg during the Brighton marathon and heard his story, I felt it was important to thank anyone who was running for the charity. I got talking to a father and son who were running for their uncle and hearing their story gave me a real sense of purpose. I spotted a runner in a Prostate Cancer UK t-shirt, sitting on the pavement. I thought he might be struggling, so I stopped to check he was ok. He said he was just tying up his shoelaces and I asked him why he was running for Prostate Cancer UK. He told me that he worked for the charity and I discovered it was Gary, who I had spoken to when I decided to run the Brighton marathon for the charity. I ran a few miles with him, and I was still feeling good. People in the crowd were shouting, 'Kev-Laa' (it was on my shirt again, so thank you, Gavin and Stacey) at me and their encouragement was keeping me going. Gary left me as he had paced himself better, but I was pleased to have met him.

With six miles left I was starting to feel tired, but I was in a nice groove and running freely. I got to the final mile and entered Birdcage Walk, running straight past Sarah who was waiting for me. She called my name and I turned back, gave her a quick cuddle and headed towards the Mall and the finish line.

For anyone who has run the London marathon, you will know the finish can be very quiet because it is lined with hospitality tents and by the time I got there nobody was watching. Suddenly a thought entered my head and I couldn't shake it. I wasn't wearing a timing chip and I knew, having run London before, when you finish, they take your official time off the chip. I started panicking that the officials were going to discover that I had taken the place of a celebrity and I was going to get into serious trouble. At the start I didn't care but, now I was about to finish, all sorts of thoughts were running through my head. I even worried that I would cross the line and see Jim being escorted away by the police! I could see the finish line and I felt like a criminal that was about to get caught. And then an announcement I'll never forget came over the tannoy. 'As this is the 35th year of the London marathon all runners can keep their timing chips as a memento.' I couldn't believe my luck. They were not going to check the chip and all my worries disappeared as I crossed the finish line. Two weeks after finishing Brighton, I had run London and I was ecstatic.

Jim was waiting for me and he gave me the brilliant news that he had finished in under four hours. I was so pleased for him and I then realised that my time was 12 minutes quicker than Brighton, which made me feel even better. We found our wives and decided to head straight home. We got to Waterloo and just missed our train, so we went to the nearest bar and had a celebratory pint. I sat with Jim and it was a wonderful feeling to be with my mate, having run two marathons in two weeks. On the train journey home, I started thinking about keeping my sponsorship page open for a year and seeing what other events I could enter. I didn't want to run another marathon. I wanted to do something bigger. When we got home, I sat down with Sarah and told her what I was thinking. And she said to me, 'Kevin, you should do the one race that is the only thing on your bucket list.' So that's what I did.

Chapter 3

The only thing on the bucket list

WHEN I was at school, I enjoyed playing sports but wasn't particularly good at any of them. Every year there was a sports day with a mile race which I always ran and I loved that. I had a bit of staying power and never gave up, so the mile race suited me. In my final year, when I was 16, I won the race and I think it was because of my tenacity that I crossed the line first.

After leaving school, I gave up running because other things like work, sailing and chasing girls came into my life, but in my early 20s I started playing rugby and joined Sutton and Epsom Rugby Club, more for the social side than the rugby. One day someone mentioned that the club organised a half-marathon every year and that I should run it. I paid my entry fee, did no training and ran the half-marathon in a few seconds under two hours. It was the first time I had done any running since winning the mile race at school and it completely wiped me out, but I really enjoyed it. I decided running was going to become my new hobby and I wanted to do it properly. Of course, there was no internet in 1985, so I did the old school trick of going to the newsagent and buying a running magazine because I was going to take my new hobby seriously.

I sat down with the magazine and started reading an article about a crazy race across the Sahara Desert called the Marathon des Sables. The previous year had been the first time the race had been run and I was fascinated by the challenge of running six marathons in six days across the desert, with a rucksack on your back. I had images of me as Beau Geste, but I knew I would never be able to run that distance in those conditions and there was no way I would be able to afford to enter the race or be fit enough to run it. But the Marathon des Sables had sowed a seed in my mind, and I looked at it as the Everest of running. I got on with my life, continuing to run as a hobby, including some half-marathons along the way. But the Marathon des Sables was always there, nagging at me, feeling like an unattainable goal.

In 2012, Olympic gold medallist James Cracknell ran the Marathon des Sables. He finished 12th in the 251 km race, which at the time was the highest placed finish for any Britain who had entered it. A documentary about his incredible effort was made called 'The Toughest Race on Earth' and Sarah bought the DVD for me for Christmas. I made the whole family sit down to watch it with me on Christmas Day. It was a powerful and emotional story and I would describe his effort as that of an inspirational, driven nutter.

Seeing the race on the television reignited my passion to run it and I turned to my family and said, 'I'm going to do this race,' which was greeted with looks of disbelief and horror. They had just watched a double Olympic champion almost kill himself and now I was saying I wanted to do it. But it had been my dream since reading that article back in 1985.

I chatted to Sarah and she was encouraging but also realistic. She pointed out that it would cost the price of a family holiday to enter and fitting in the training around my full-time job would be impossible. She explained that she didn't want me to enter, then not be able to train properly and ultimately not be able to complete the race, because she knew how much that would annoy and frustrate me. As always, my wife was spot on, so I sadly put the race to the back of my mind.

Sarah and I had that conversation in our kitchen which is exactly where we were sitting three years later, the evening after I had run the London marathon on chemotherapy. She looked at me and said, 'I don't know what you are thinking of doing next, Kevin, but I think you should do the one thing on your bucket list.' And that was running the Marathon des Sables. I couldn't believe what I was hearing. My wife was encouraging me to go and chase my dream at a time when I had a terminal illness and it might not be the most sensible thing to do. The most important person in my world had given me the thumbs-up and that meant everything.

On the train back from the London marathon I had been thinking about the Marathon des Sables, but I was worried that it would be a selfish decision to run it, with the amount of training I would have to do, and it would probably be impossible for me to take part anyway. Now Sarah was encouraging me to go and do it, and I felt even more love for her.

Even though Sarah was telling me to do the race, I had to be realistic. In my head I only had 18 months left to live and the Marathon des Sables was in a year's time. I didn't know if my treatment would keep me alive to be able to run the race. Would I be in a hospice, be an invalid or maybe dead by then? I just didn't know.

Two days later I had my fifth course of chemotherapy. I saw Professor Parker for a blood test and as I sat with him, he asked me, 'Did you run the Brighton marathon?' I replied, 'No. I ran the Brighton and the London marathon.' He nearly fell off his chair. He smiled and asked me what I was going to do next. I explained to him that I wanted to run the Marathon de Sables and what the race entailed. I'm not sure he thought it was a great idea. In fact, his words were, 'Why would anyone want to do that race, let alone somebody in your condition?' But, he could tell how determined I was and said if I could train for it then I could do it. It was exactly what he had said to me before the Brighton marathon and again it was exactly the response I wanted to hear. I went and had my course of chemotherapy and I sat with the canula in my arm, pumping poison into my veins, and I was smiling. I felt good about myself. Since I had last sat in the chair in the room that sucked the life out of you, I had run the Brighton and London marathons and now

I was going to attempt to run the Marathon des Sables. Cancer takes everything away from you, but I had grabbed something back through running and I knew I could push myself, despite having this awful thing inside me.

So now I had Sarah's permission and had told Professor Parker, all I had to do was enter next year's race. I went on the Marathon des Sables website to register and was greeted with the worst possible news. The only entries they were taking were for the 2017 race and there was a waiting list for the 2016 race. I had to get a place for next year because I didn't think I would be alive in 2017. I was panicking and decided to ring Prostate Cancer UK and explain that I wanted to run the race for them and would they be able to pull a few strings to help me get a place for 2016, but I would pay for it. They said they would see what they could do and a couple of hours later they rang back and told me they had managed to get me a place for next year's race. I paid the entry fee and filled in the entry form immediately. The dream was alive and I was ecstatic.

Reality kicked in. My goal of running the race was based on a magazine article and a James Cracknell DVD. I had no idea what training I needed to do, what my diet should be and how I should tackle the race. I didn't know anybody who had done the Marathon des Sables and unsurprisingly I had no experience of running an ultra-marathon across a desert in April. I did some research and kept reading about a guy called Rory Coleman who was apparently the man to go to if you needed a coach for the Marathon des Sables. I didn't think he would have any interest in coaching me, but I found an email address for him and sent him a message. Rory replied and said he would be happy to meet me for a coaching session. But before meeting him I still had to have my last course of chemotherapy. The horrible thing about chemotherapy is you do feel worse after every session. I had lost my sense of taste, my body continually ached, and I was sore everywhere. Even though I had run the two marathons, I still felt very ill, but all I was thinking about was getting the chemotherapy finished. I went into that horrible room for the final time, had the poison put into me and left knowing that was the end of it.

I always worried about whether the chemotherapy was working, but my PSA scores had gradually been coming down from my starting point of 341. After the final course, my score was 3.4 which was extremely encouraging. The other good piece of news was I now had a month off treatment before I started six weeks of radiotherapy. The day after finishing chemotherapy, I was running across Epsom Common listening to my iPod with the playlist of my favourite songs in my ears. One was 'Saltwater' by Julian Lennon which I had listened to hundreds of times. That morning it came on and I suddenly heard the lyrics, 'What will I think of me the day I die?' I stopped and played the song again and when I heard those words, they made perfect sense to me. When the day inevitably arrived and I was lying on my death bed, I didn't want to look back with any regrets. From now on I needed to do the right things, say the right things, be proud of everything I did and be a better person. That morning on Epsom Common the words of Julian Lennon became one of my mantras.

I drove to Cardiff to meet Rory for my coaching session, having no idea what to expect. We sat at his kitchen table and Rory explained what it was like to run the Marathon des Sables. Rory had run the race 13 times and the previous year he had coached Sir Ranulph Fiennes. Sir Ranulph had heart issues when he ran the MDS, so I knew Rory had experience of working with people who had health problems and I had told him about my prostate cancer in my original email. We sat and chatted for the whole day and Rory gave me his way of training for and completing the MDS. This involved me losing 10kg, which would be the amount I would be carrying every day, training like a madman and having a diet of 'lightweight' foods that were full of calories, like nuts and granola. The training included something called the 'power hour' which I had to do once a week on a treadmill. Rory explained that I would sprint for 90 seconds, jog for three and a half minutes, sprint for 90 seconds and repeat this for an hour. He also suggested I enter three races, the Race to the Stones (a two-day 100km ultra-marathon in July), the Druid's Challenge (a three-day 120km ultra-marathon in October) and the Pilgrim Challenge (a two-day 106km ultra-marathon in February). Rory told me everything I needed to know, from where I would be sleeping to what I should wear.

On the journey back from Cardiff I had a much better idea of what I needed to do to complete the Marathon des Sables.

I immediately entered the three races Rory had suggested and started training like a madman. I followed Rory's plan and was running between six and ten miles every other day, doing his 'power hour' once a week and following a weights programme at the gym. It was hard work, but I was feeling fit and strong, my PSA score was low, the side-effects of the chemotherapy were wearing off and I was feeling good.

I then started six weeks of radiotherapy. Professor Parker had explained that normally if you have incurable cancer like me, you do not have radiotherapy, but there was some evidence that 'blasting the mothership' could help. I was going to be blasted once a week and for my first appointment I was told to go to the Royal Marsden Hospital with a half-full bladder. As you have probably gathered, doing this with prostate cancer is difficult because when you want to go, you desperately want to go. My first session of radiotherapy was a scary experience. I had no idea what I was walking into. First, they gave me two small tattoos on my groin so each week they could line up the scanner. Then they loaded me in, bursting for a wee, left me on my own and blasted me. This was the routine for the next six weeks and my only side-effects at the time were feeling nervous before each session and worrying I was going to wet myself!

I continued following Rory's training plan and in July I ran the first of the three races that he had suggested. The Race to the Stones crosses the North Wessex Downs and the Chilterns and you have two days to complete the 100km course. This was a chance for me to see if the training was working. I didn't think I knew anybody who was doing the race and I was nervous but also excited to run my first multi-day ultra-marathon. As instructed, I parked my car at the finish and a coach had been organised to take us back to the start at Lewknor. As I was getting on the coach, I bumped into a guy called Mike Julian who I had played rugby with at Sutton and Epsom back in the 1980s. It was great to see him, and it turned out that Mike had run the Marathon des Sables, so I spent the coach journey picking his brains and catching up with him.

We arrived at the start and there was a real buzz amongst all the runners. The weather was lovely and I felt good over the opening 10km. I arrived at the first checkpoint and two runners appeared that I knew. Mark and Perry were both work colleagues and it was great to see them. We chatted for ten minutes and I discovered they were also doing the Marathon des Sables next year and this race was also part of their training. They were running the whole 100km in one day, but seeing them and Mike earlier gave me a real boost. The rest of the day went well. I got through the first 50km without any problems and I arrived at the halfway point after seven hours. I was given my own tent for the night and I went off to get some food and immediately bumped into Rory in the canteen. Rory was with a chap called Richard, who was also running the Marathon des Sables next year and I spent the evening chatting with them. I went back to my tent feeling pretty good about myself and the world. I had started the day not knowing anybody but now knew several people who were also doing the MDS next year.

I woke up the next morning and I was sore everywhere. Every part of me ached as I got ready for another 50km. I set off at 6.30am and it was a tough day. The pathways were rocky and pitted, not easy to run on especially when you are feeling tired and stiff. It was extremely hard work, but the scenery was spectacular, and I found the route fascinating. You pass the prehistoric Uffington White Horse figure and the Liddington Castle, and you are following the steps of the Vikings and the Romans because the Ridgeway is one of the oldest routes in the country. Eventually the iconic Avebury stone circle came into sight and I was delighted. I could see what I assumed was the finish and even though I was tired, aching, muddy and sore, I was going to complete my first ultra-marathon with cancer.

I got to the stones and felt fantastic. I had my photo taken but then noticed some runners going past me back down the hill. The horrible realisation hit me that 'The Stones' wasn't the end of the race and there was still 2km to run. I somehow managed to find enough energy to get myself to the actual finish and I crossed the line in just over seven hours. I had completed my first two-day ultra-marathon and was extremely happy with my efforts. I got my medal, had a photo with Rory, grabbed something to eat, found my car and drove home. I had completed a race that was part of my preparations for the Marathon des Sables, which was a big tick in the box, and I was proud of myself. Everything was looking positive but that was about to change.

Chapter 4

Getting to the start line

A FEW days after completing the Race to the Stones, I went back to the Royal Marsden and got my latest PSA score, which was 0.42. This was great news. I always look at my prostate cancer as PSA-driven. By having a low score, I had fewer tickets in the 'cancer raffle' and the chances of one of those tickets attaching itself to another organ in my body and killing me were much less than at the start of my journey. I'd got through chemotherapy and radiotherapy, run two marathons and an ultra-marathon and my PSA score was the lowest it had been. Life was good.

I continued training like a madman, following Rory's programme. I was meeting a group of runners every Saturday to run two laps of Richmond Park. Like me, they had all entered the Marathon des Sables for the first time and it was great to pick their brains and run with them. I also went regularly to Epsom Downs racecourse which had a sand track for the horses to train on. The track is a mile long and goes uphill and I would sometimes spend three hours going up and down it to get used to running on sand.

Worryingly, I had noticed my right knee was starting to give me a pain and it was gradually getting worse. I had to stop doing the 'power hour' and the pain got so bad that I had to stop running. I tried the cross-trainer in the gym and swimming, but both were uncomfortable and even walking was giving me pain. I was worried that the cancer had got into my bones and that was causing my knee to hurt. I had gone from running an ultra-marathon to struggling to walk. Mentally I was in a very bad place. The anniversary of my cancer diagnosis was fast approaching and in my head that meant I only had a year to live. Running the Marathon des Sables was the dream that was keeping me going and now I couldn't run, which meant I couldn't train, and the cancer was taking the one thing I had left away from me. Without training, my life had no structure and I was just sitting at home feeling more and more depressed. I was desperate because the clock was ticking, and I felt my time was running out. I wasn't sleeping and found myself in a very dark and deep hole.

I had always intended to go back to work and I felt that would give me the structure I needed. Plus, I needed to find out what was wrong with my knee and whether I had any chance of getting to the Marathon des Sables. My GP had been signing me off from work every three months and I went to see him at the end of September. The appointment was at six in the evening and the weather was miserable. I walked into his office, sat down and burst into tears. I explained how I was feeling, told him about my knee and explained that I wanted to go back to work. I wasn't sleeping at night because I was so worried about Sarah and the kids and dying scared me. My GP prescribed three weeks of sleeping tablets and then looked at my knee and referred me to a specialist in Wimbledon. He also agreed that I could go back to work if it wasn't full time. Having been off sick for nearly a year I knew I was still entitled to my annual leave, so I got in touch with the bank and suggested to them that I came back for three days a week with the other two days being treated as holiday. I didn't care about my holiday entitlement because I only had a year left to live and going back to work was better than just sitting at home trying to fill in time.

A week later, I went to Wimbledon for an MRI scan on my knee and saw the specialist. He explained the scan was possibly showing the onset of arthritis and there was lots of other damage. Basically, I would need an operation. I sat there and thought my dream of the Marathon des Sables was over. I only had a year to live and if I had the operation there would be two months of recovery and that wasn't an option. The news was a devastating blow. The specialist then told me we had one other chance to get the knee better. I had to rest it for nine weeks, which meant no running, swimming, gym or any physical exercise. The only thing I could do was walk. The specialist could give me no guarantees, but I knew I had to take this chance because it was the only one I had.

I returned to work just after seeing the specialist. I was nervous about seeing my colleagues for the first time since January. When you are ill, it is difficult for people to know how to treat you and I didn't want them treading on eggshells. The first morning I was up early, putting my suit back on, walking to the station and catching the train to London. When I had left the office in January, I hadn't been sure if I would ever go back and I think some of my colleagues were pleasantly surprised to see me. The bank gave me some projects to work on, but in the nine months I had been away there had been quite a few changes. I was finding it hard to take things in and I was exhausted. The cancer, the lack of sleep and worrying about the Marathon des Sables were making my return to the bank difficult and I didn't want to be a burden. I was also concerned the bank had let me come back out of sympathy because I wanted to be an asset to them. But I had some structure back in my life and it was nice to be with my colleagues again.

I had been back at work for a week when I was walking across Trafalgar Square one morning and noticed a piece of pavement art. It had a slogan that said, 'You only have two lives and the second one starts when you realise you only have one.' I stood there and kept reading it. It summed up perfectly where I was in my journey and that morning when I had gone for a run after my first course of chemotherapy had been when my life really started. Up until then I had always put things off until tomorrow. Now I had one life left and I couldn't put anything off anymore because there might not be a tomorrow.

The slogan on the pavement in Trafalgar Square summed up how I was going to live the rest of my 'one life'. I now know, of course, that we should all think that way in any case and not wait for an epiphany to make us value every day.

I was sticking rigidly to the no-exercise plan from the specialist. One evening, I was late for the train home from work. I got to Waterloo and could see the train sitting on the platform about to depart. I knew if I ran, I could make it, but I stuck to what the specialist had told me and let the train leave without me. The Marathon des Sables was more important than the train home.

The second race Rory had recommended as part of his training programme was a three-day ultra-marathon at the end of October called the Druid's Challenge. I had already paid my entry fee, but I knew I couldn't run it because the specialist had told me to rest my knee so I decided to offer to be a volunteer. The organisers were happy to use me, and I spent three days as a marshal at the race. It was a great experience and I met other runners who were doing the Marathon des Sables. At the finish, I handed out medals and I felt part of the race even though I hadn't been running it. It did me good to be back in that environment and I went home on a high. I continued to go to work and rest my knee. The worry about getting to the Marathon des Sables was always at the back of my mind, but I was starting to come out of the dark place that I had found myself in.

At the end of November, I had another MRI scan on my knee and went back to the specialist in Wimbledon. This meeting would make or break my chances of getting to the Marathon des Sables. The specialist put the scan on the screen and said, 'Well, that's the power of rest. I wouldn't believe what I was seeing if it wasn't in front of me.' All the dark areas that were causing me pain on the first scan had disappeared. The specialist suggested the drugs I was on for the cancer might have caused the joints to become inflamed but with nine weeks of rest the knee had gone back to normal. I was ecstatic. The dream of the Marathon de Sables was alive again and I slowly returned to training. I had to ditch Rory's training schedule because I had missed nearly three months of the programme and all I wanted to do now was get to the start line of the Marathon des Sables. I started running three miles every other day and combined that with some gentle swimming and the odd gym session. I did not want to put too much pressure on the knee and if I had to walk across some of the desert then bugger it, that was what I would have to do.

In early December I was back at the Royal Marsden to get my latest PSA score. It had gone back up to 1.6. This was terrible news. The cancer was starting to grow again. It was a year since my diagnosis, I had endured stomach injections, chemotherapy and radiotherapy, but now the bloody thing was growing again. Despite this worrying news, I continued training and we returned to Woolacombe Bay in Devon for a family New Year with Jim's family again. At the end of January, I went back to the Royal Marsden and Professor Parker told me my PSA score had gone up to 4. My cancer had doubled in size in a month and if that continued, I worked out I would probably be dead by the end of the year. Sarah was with me and I broke down in tears. It felt like we were back where we started. It had been a tough year, but my PSA scores had been dropping and the bad news had gradually been getting less bad. Now my PSA scores were about to run out of control and the bad news was getting worse again.

Professor Parker discussed what we should do next. He explained that he wanted to put me on a drug called abiraterone, but it was expensive, costing around £36,000 a year. I had private medical insurance, so I rang the insurers and they informed me they would only pay for one year because it was a life-extending drug and not a cure. I told Professor Parker and he said he would try and get me on the Cancer Drugs Fund. This enabled NHS patients to get expensive cancer drugs that were not cost effective for the NHS to provide. It also meant if the drug worked I could have it for more than one year. Professor Parker worked his magic and managed to get me the drug via the fund. I knew from my research and others on the PCUK forum that if the abiraterone didn't work, I would have to go on drugs that were like old-style chemotherapy. These were likely to have more horrible side effects and might not keep me alive very long. It was also clear that for a lot of men abiraterone never works at all.

Time was of the essence and Professor Parker wanted to get me on the abiraterone as quickly as possible. Two days before I started taking the drug, I had the third of Rory's ultra-marathons to run. The Pilgrims Challenge is a two-day, 106km run across the North Downs of Surrey. Despite the news that my cancer was growing, I was determined to complete it. I arrived on the first day of the event and the weather was awful. It was a typical February day, cold and wet, a complete contrast to the weather when I had run the Race to the Stones the previous summer. Despite the weather, I was delighted to be there, and I managed to complete the first day in seven hours. About halfway through the day, I got to Box Hill and there were Ollie and Sarah, which was a lovely surprise and gave me a real boost. At the finish I was shattered, and we stayed the night in a school hall. The evening was great fun because I chatted to lots of people who were doing the Marathon des Sables and I saw lots of familiar faces from the Druid's Challenge where I had been a marshal. People were becoming aware of my story and the challenges I was facing, and it felt great to be part of the ultra-marathon community.

I woke up on the second day cold and stiff, having slept on the school hall floor. I had been surrounded by snoring runners so hadn't had much sleep. My kit had dried overnight but my trail shoes were still wet and putting them on was not a nice experience. My feet were immediately soggy, my body ached everywhere, but I got started and managed to get through the day. The Pilgrim Challenge is an 'out and back' race, so you redo the route of the first day back to the start line. It was a tough day, but I got over the finish line and felt fantastic as my medal was hung round my neck. My time was similar to the first day and I had completed my second multi-day ultra-marathon, this time in the winter, and it did my confidence the power of good. I also felt part of the ultra-marathon family.

Two days later I started taking the abiraterone. Was this drug going to work and what would the side-effects be? I had no idea, but after a week I went back to the Royal Marsden for a blood test. My PSA score had gone down to 2.3 which was amazing news. The drug was working but my liver scores were not good, which was a side-effect of the drug. This was a concern because I would have to have a medical examination before the Marathon des Sables and needed my liver scores to be normal. But it was encouraging news after a week of the drug. I continued training and I was now going to work four days a week. My next blood test was on 7 March and my PSA score had come down to 1.2. The abiraterone was still working. And two weeks later my PSA score had come down to 0.96 and my liver score was heading back to where it should be. It was all good news, and it seemed the planets were aligning to enable me to go to the Marathon des Sables in a month.

One of the provisions of being allowed to compete is you must have an ECG and be passed medically fit for the race. I travelled to Southampton to have my medical with a doctor, who was also competing in the Marathon des Sables that year. I was very nervous that my prostate cancer might prevent her signing me off, but I passed the ECG with flying colours and she signed the piece of paper that said I was medically fit to do the race.

Prostate Cancer UK then gave me a day I will never forget. They invited me to Wembley for the League Cup Final between Manchester City and Liverpool as their guest of honour, which included the extra treat of being introduced to the teams before kick-off. The charity said I could bring somebody, so I took my son Ben because the day of the final just happened to be his 16th birthday. After a fantastic lunch, we were allowed on to the pitch to soak up the atmosphere. Ben suddenly got nervous and I looked at him and said, 'I promise you, in years to come you will never say, "I wish I hadn't gone on the pitch at Wembley," but you might say, "I regret not going on the pitch when I had the opportunity",' and he got it and there we were in front of 80,000 fans loving the moment. When I was formally introduced to both teams, I could not believe I was shaking hands with the likes of Vincent Kompany, Raheem Sterling and Jordan Henderson. The last person I met was Jurgen Klopp, the Liverpool manager, and the Sky cameras were right next to us. As I walked off the Wembley turf, my phone went mad with family and friends sending messages saying they had seen me on the telly and I had given the camera a cheeky grin after shaking hands with Jurgen that they all saw. It was a day I will never forget and to share it with Ben was very special; thank you, Prostate Cancer UK.

I had increased my training and was back every Saturday at Richmond Park with the other MDS runners and was using the sand track at Epsom Downs again. And then I started to get a pain in my hip. It got worse and the dark thoughts started entering my head. Had the cancer got into my bones and was I going to be physically able to get to the Marathon des Sables? The pain got so bad that I couldn't run and even walking was painful. I had to stop training and it felt like my dream was being taken away from me again. I went back to my GP and he referred me to another specialist in Wimbledon. The specialist scanned my hip and the only option available to get me to the Marathon des Sables was to have a cortisone injection. There was no guarantee the injection would work, but it was my best chance. I was booked in to have injection three days before leaving for the race and the specialist explained it might take a week before I noticed any improvement, but it was a gamble worth taking because I was determined to be on that start line.

Obviously, it was going to be hot in the desert. Even I had worked that one out. I needed to acclimatise and one of my training group at Richmond Park suggested doing an intensive course of Bikram Hot Yoga to get used to the heat of the Sahara. Two weeks before getting on the plane, I had my first session of hot yoga in Wimbledon. It was like an oven in the room and the session lasted an hour. I wasn't very good at the yoga, but I gradually got used to the heat and by the end of the course I was quite enjoying it.

The hip was still painful and even though I was trying to rest it I had a prior engagement that I was determined to honour. Prostate Cancer UK had asked me to join Jeff Stelling of Sky Sports fame, to walk the final marathon of his challenge to walk from Hartlepool United's ground to Wembley

Stadium. Jeff had already done nine marathons in nine days and I joined him at AFC Wimbledon's ground for the final leg a week before leaving for the Sahara. Even though my hip was still painful and it was a risk, I had decided to walk six miles with Jeff to Griffin Park and see how it felt. The atmosphere was wonderful and I walked with Jeff, Matt Le Tissier and Mark Bright amongst others; it was good to see that so many people cared. We got to Brentford's ground and the hip felt ok, so I carried on. I ended up doing the whole day and met some wonderful people, including a guy called Lloyd Pinder who had also been diagnosed with terminal prostate cancer. Straight away we had a mutual respect and immediately formed a strong bond. We reached Wembley and even though the hip was sore, I had proved to myself that I could walk a marathon and the hip might get me across the desert.

Three days before getting on the plane, I had the cortisone injection in my hip. It was still painful, but now nothing was going to stop me getting to the Sahara. The night before leaving for the desert I packed all my equipment. During my training, I had practised with the kit needed for the race, including eating the dehydrated food that was going to keep me going. This was my first experience of running in a desert and I wanted to make sure there were no surprises when it came to my kit. My backpack, which I would carry every day, weighed 11kg, including all my drugs which took up lots of room plus all my other kit, including a venom pump in case I was stung by a scorpion or a snake. My mother-in-law had sowed the Prostate

Cancer UK logo on to my backpack and the charity had given me one of their flags, which I attached to a telescopic fishing rod in the back of my bag, so it would fly proudly above me in the desert. I think the charity saw the value in me running the race with prostate cancer and I was extremely proud to be supporting them.

I went to bed early and woke up at 4am because I had to take my cancer drug on an empty stomach an hour before I ate anything. This was something I was going to have to factor into the race. Sarah and Ollie drove me to Gatwick Airport. At the check-in desk there were 300 other British runners and I was nervous and excited. I was given an official race wristband and a Union Jack badge for my bag. For the first time, I realised I was competing in an international race and representing my country gave me a huge sense of pride. I then had an emotional goodbye with Sarah and Ollie as I went to passport control. Luckily for my emotions I soon met Rory to have some breakfast and get the excitement going again. A month earlier an email had arrived from him inviting me to be in his tent with six others for the race, which was an immense honour. Seeing Rory helped me settle down and we boarded the plane and found our seats for the flight. As the plane took off for Morocco, I thought to myself, 'Right then, Kev. No turning back now. You are going to the Marathon des Sables.' The dream was on.

Chapter 5

The Marathon des Sables 2016

THE FLIGHT to Morocco was like no other I had been on. As soon as we took off, everybody was out of their seats and chatting. We were on a chartered plane and all the passengers were running in the MDS, so the atmosphere was fantastic and there was an amazing buzz. I was like a sponge, soaking up as much information as I could about the race, and I realised there were lots of first-time runners like me who were also feeling scared and nervous. It felt like I was heading off on a proper adventure with no idea what was going to happen, and this was being magnified by all the conversations I was having on the plane.

After four hours, we began our descent into Ouarzazate airport, a small affair shared with the military. Looking out of the window all I could see was sand, which I was expecting, but it was still thrilling to be landing for the race. I made my way down the steps from the plane and the heat hit me straight away. It felt like opening a massive oven door, but the hot yoga sessions had done the trick because the heat wasn't unbearable. As I stepped on to the tarmac another plane full of runners landed behind us.

I was in unknown territory and followed everyone else to the arrivals hall. We were given a form to fill in, which was written in French and would allow us to enter Morocco. I had to guess what most of the questions meant and I realised why Rory had told me to bring a pen because once I had answered the questions on my form, my pen disappeared as it seemed to be the only one amongst all the runners. We had had our kit bags with us on the plane and our other bags, which would be taken from us at the start of the race, were picked up from the baggage carousel.

On leaving the airport, I was greeted by a convoy of about 20 coaches that were going to take all the runners on the six-hour drive to the start of the race in the Sahara Desert. I picked the nearest coach, climbed onboard and sat down near the front. Other runners started getting on and an Irish lad called Will sat down next to me. We introduced ourselves and chatted about the race as we waited for the coaches to leave the airport. Finally, over 1,000 runners from all over the world were on the coaches and the journey to the start line began. We drove through the town of Ouarzazate and made our way over the Atlas Mountains. Looking out of the window, I felt like an extra in *The Italian Job* as the coach made its way up narrow roads with sharp corners and dramatic drops over cliff edges. The view was breathtaking, but I was wondering if we were going to survive the coach journey never mind get to the Sahara. Eventually the coach made it to the top of the mountains and we came down the other side, through Moroccan villages where the locals stared and waved at our convoy. I was soaking up the excited atmosphere on the coach whilst trying to take in the view from the window. We stopped after three hours for lunch. We were given a bag of food, which included bread and cheese, and I sat in the sand with all the other runners and it felt like we were on a school trip to the desert. This was everybody's first taste of having no proper toilet facilities and I think it was a shock for lots of people, but it didn't bother me and any inhibitions I did have went out of the window as I squatted in the sand.

After lunch, I chatted with Will on the coach and we were given the Marathon des Sables roadbook. This had all the information for the race including each day's start times and maps of each of the routes, which were confusing. But it was exciting to see the race in black and white and everybody had their heads in the roadbook. People who had run the race before were telling first-timers like me what to look out for and it felt like I was part of a big family who were all in it together. Even though my journey so far had only been on a plane and a coach, it felt like I was part of the Marathon des Sables team and the camaraderie on the coach was wonderful. There was a little part of me, though, that wondered if we were going to be lambs to the slaughter.

It was getting dark when the coach turned off the road and drove down a single dirt track. All I could see were the coaches in front, but suddenly there were bright lights everywhere. We had arrived at the start of the race and I was officially in the Sahara desert. I followed Will off the coach, collected my bag and there were tents everywhere. To my left were hundreds of dark tents and to my right was a collection of white tents. Everybody was walking towards the white tents, so I followed the crowd. I realised this was the information point where we would find out where the tent we would be sleeping in was located. I started to panic because I knew I was in Rory's tent, but I had not seen him since we had breakfast at Gatwick Airport. How was I going to find my tent at night in the middle of the desert? I felt a tap on my shoulder and there was Richard who I had met with Rory at the Race to the Stones. Richard was also in Rory's tent, so I followed him to Tent 105 which he informed me was in the best location. Rory greeted me and I made myself at home which meant unrolling my sleeping mat in my designated space, putting my suitcase at one end of the mat, my kit bag at the other and lying my sleeping bag down. The tent was very small with walls but open ends and the eight of us would be sleeping packed together like sardines.

I introduced myself to the other inhabitants of Tent 105 as they arrived. They were Selina, Nick, Jeff, Phil and Chris and everyone spent the time organising themselves into the very small space. I quickly realised there was no privacy in the tent, which didn't bother me, and it was exciting to meet everybody. It was getting cold, so I put on my fleece and followed the others towards the bright lights to get something to eat. Before the race started, the organisers provided food in some huge catering tents. I got my dinner and sat with the other members of Tent 105 and after eating we went back and settled in for the night. We still had our suitcases, so I found a pair of tracksuit bottoms, climbed into my sleeping bag and lay there in the desert. Everyone was tired after a long and exciting day, but getting to sleep was difficult because the tent next to ours was very noisy. Eventually they did quieten down after a bit of encouragement and I fell asleep.

I woke up early the next morning to take my abiraterone. It was just before dawn and out of the end of our tent all I could see was sand. I carefully made my way out from the shelter to have a proper look around. It was cold and the vastness of the desert immediately struck me. I felt very small and the sand dunes looked very big. I sat and watched the desert come to life as the sun came up. It was the most beautiful sight and I lapped it up. The other members of my tent were slowly waking up and we chatted about what would happen today. I saw a couple of camels being led on foot by Berbers and Rory told us to always keep in front of those camels during the race because if they overtook you that was your race over. Pace-setting camels – only at the Marathon des Sables!

We made our way back to the catering tents for breakfast and we then had to officially check in for the race. This meant having all our kit checked and handing back everything we were not going to carry. Everything we didn't need would go into our suitcases which we would not see again until the finish. Rory was telling Tent 105 what we did and didn't need. For example, I had a large roll of surgical tape and Rory told me to get rid of half of it to save some weight in my kit bag.

Check-in was alphabetical, so I was at the end of the day. I spent the morning organising my kit and chatting to those in our tent who had checked in and been given their race number. I had some lunch and then it was time for me to go and have all my kit checked. I changed into my race gear which I would now eat, sleep and run in and made my way to another set of tents with my kit bag, suitcase and all my paperwork. I got rid of my suitcase and then joined a long queue to be officially checked in by the race organisers. I realised how hot it was in the desert, waiting for my turn and after an hour I reached the front of the queue. They weighed and checked my kit and then I handed all my paperwork to a French doctor. She looked at my medical forms and asked me why I was taking a steroid called Prednisolone. I explained that I had prostate cancer, but that seemed to get lost in translation. The doctor took my papers to another doctor and I was left standing watching them in deep discussion. I had no idea what they were saying, but they looked very serious and I started to panic that they were not going to let me do the race. Eventually the doctor came back, gave me my papers and pointed me to another volunteer who gave me salt tablets and my checkpoint card. I still didn't know if I was going to be allowed to do the race, but I was handed my official race number which was 1201. The relief was overwhelming because I was convinced the doctor who had looked at my papers was going to find a spurious reason not to let me do the race. But I had officially been given the all clear and I proudly had my photograph taken holding my race number.

I was the last back to our tent and there was now a bit more space because we had got rid of the suitcases. We went back to the catering tent for the evening meal, which was the last food we would be given by the race organisers. They gave us five litres of water that had to last until the first checkpoint tomorrow and then Patrick Bauer, the founder of the Marathon des Sables gave a briefing. It was the first time I had seen all the other runners gathered and the size of the race was mind-blowing. Seeing over 1,000 other competitors, from all over the world gave me an enormous sense of pride to be stood amongst them representing Great Britain.

It was getting cold and all I was wearing was my race kit, which consisted of socks, shorts, running shirt and a windproof top. I realised my nights were going to be freezing and I got into my sleeping bag back at the tent with a mixture of excitement and apprehension. This was the final sleep I would have before the race and I lay there looking at the stars, imagining what was to come tomorrow. I eventually dropped off but woke up at 4am shivering and horribly cold. I didn't want to move, but now I was awake I needed to go to the toilet. I checked my shoes for sleeping scorpions and crept out into the desert. I didn't go far from the tent to do my business and then lay in my sleeping bag trying to get warm. Eventually I gave up, took my abiraterone and quietly started preparing for the day. The tent slowly started to wake up and the sense of excitement began to build.

As it was race day, we were now in charge of preparing our own food and that started with breakfast. I sat on a large rug, just outside our tent and cooked porridge on my little paraffin stove. I felt amazing, cooking my porridge, watching the sun come up over the Sahara on the opening day of the race. Suddenly our tent disappeared as six Berber helpers dismantled it in a matter of seconds, to transport it to the finish line. I ate my porridge watching the tented village vanish from the landscape and with no shade I started to feel the temperature rising. After breakfast, we all sat on the rug and prepared our kit for the start of the race. I placed my hat and sunglasses next to my kitbag and decided to visit the toilet one more time before we made our way to the start. When I got back my sunglasses had gone. I asked everyone if they had seen them, but nobody knew where they were. It was time to make our way to the start line and I was in a panic. Without my sunglasses I wouldn't be able to see where I was going, and I could go blind staring into the sun. On top of that, they might throw me out of the race for not having them as they were a mandatory piece of kit. I was in a real state, but Jeff from the tent gave me a pair of tinted goggles that were his spare pair. He said I could have them for the race and I stopped panicking that my race was over before it had started,

Walking to the start I felt incredibly proud. The bloke with terminal cancer had made it. There had been times when I had thought I wouldn't get to the start line, in terms of being alive and being fit enough to do the race. But here I was, and it was the best feeling in the world. A photo was taken of all the runners from a helicopter and then I joined the queue to start the race. With over 1,000 runners I was a long way back, but the atmosphere was electric. Patrick Bauer gave another speech and then 'Highway to Hell' by ACDC started blasting across the desert. I was feeling pumped up and the adrenaline was flowing. I 'elbow bumped' (this was four years before Covid but nobody shook hands because there was nowhere to wash them properly) some of the other runners, including Perry and Mark from the Race to the Stones and the doctor who had done my ECG and was also competing.

And then the 31st Marathon des Sables started. Well, it started for the elite runners at the front of the queue, but it took a couple of minutes for me to get across the start line and begin the race. I was in a tightly-packed mass of people and I spotted a helicopter hovering above us. As I took my first few steps into the desert, the helicopter, with a cameraman hanging out of the door, flew low over our heads, spraying sand into our faces and making a tremendous noise. It was incredible and I, like everyone else, was waving, shouting and smiling with the widest grin as the adrenaline kicked in.

I followed the crowd of runners in front of me, moving slowly between 50ft of inflatable barriers and then there was nothing but desert. The runners started to spread out and I found some space and got into my rhythm. I was feeling great, caught up in the emotion of the start but I started to realise we were heading straight towards the enormous sand dunes I had been looking at for the past two days. The sand we were running on was firm and I could see the elite runners going up the first of the Erg Chebbi sand dunes. After a kilometre, we reached the base of the first dune and the sand got softer. As I started to run uphill, it felt like I was running in treacle. Every time my foot hit the sand it sank two inches and I quickly realised I wasn't going to be able to run up the dunes. People around me were trying but finding it impossible to run and were getting frustrated. There was no point using up my energy this early on the first day, so I got my walking poles out of my kit bag and started walking slowly. It didn't bother me that I wasn't running. During my training I had done lots of walking because of my cancer and my injuries, so I was happy to walk. I pulled down Jeff's goggles and got on with it. I quickly learnt that a good trick was to put your foot in the print someone else had made in the sand because it made it easier to grip, but my feet were still sinking with every step.

The race was already tougher than I had ever imagined. It was getting hotter, the powder-dry sand was stealing my energy, the dunes were steep, and I had 12kg strapped to my back. There was no way my training could have prepared me for all of this, but I got to the top of the first dune, ran down the other side and then started slowly walking up the next one. Even though the race was already exhausting I was soaking up the view which was incredible. The sand was a golden yellow and there was a line of runners stretching into the distance making their way up the dunes like ants under a clear blue sky.

I was in a good rhythm and one of my training partners from Richmond Park called Mark overtook me and shouted, 'See you at the finish, old boy.' I was happy walking at my own pace and conserving my energy and I wasn't going to try and keep up with anyone. It was getting hotter and hotter as I went up and down the sand dunes and the desert was like a furnace. The sand was scorching and I could feel the heat through my running shoes every time I put my foot down. The sweat dripped off the front of my cap like a waterfall and my head felt like it was in an oven at gas mark five with the door shut. The conditions were getting harder by the minute and I was hurting. But this was why I had come to the desert to compete in the toughest race on earth. And it wasn't disappointing me.

After another four miles of walking, I came to the end of the Erg Chebbi sand dunes and I knew from the roadbook that after the first checkpoint at the bottom of the dunes there was a long stretch of flat sand that I would be able to run on. It was a wonderful feeling getting to the bottom of the final dune, but as I got to the checkpoint the wind picked up. My race card was stamped, and I was given two bottles of water with my race number on the lid and bottom of each one. This was to stop you dropping your bottle in the desert, because you would get a one-hour time penalty if it was found.

I was shocked by the scene of carnage at the first checkpoint. There were runners in a complete mess, who had obviously gone off too fast and were already paying the price. I was tired and my legs were aching, but I drank some water, filled up the bottles on the front of my kit bag and had a handful of peanuts. I decided not to have my salt tablets and went straight back into the desert, but the conditions had changed dramatically. I was in the middle of a sandstorm, being blasted by sand coming directly into my face and I could only see 20m in front of me. Thankfully, I had Jeff's goggles to keep the sand out of my eyes but there was no chance of running in the conditions. I left the checkpoint but immediately needed to get rid of the porridge and nuts I had consumed during the day. Thankfully, there was a solitary bush that I could squat behind, but I had to put my backside into the wind so passing runners wouldn't see me doing my business. My backside was being sandblasted and I genuinely had a bottom as smooth as a baby's after I had finished thanks to the exfoliation!

I felt a kilogram lighter as I headed straight back into the sandstorm and walking was extremely hard work. It felt like you were pushing against a brick wall and the only good thing was the wind had made it feel cooler. The excitement of being in the race had worn off and it was now just hard work. As I plodded along, the only thought in my head was getting through the sandstorm and after six miles of battling the wind, I arrived at the final checkpoint. I was exhausted and had a look at my roadbook as I drank my water. Surely the final few miles of the day would be easier. Not a chance, as I saw we were heading straight into more sand dunes. I got my head down and started walking toward the dunes which were not quite as daunting as the Erg Chebbi dunes.

I reached the top of the first dune and was greeted by a small abandoned village. I was incredibly tired and needed a rest, so I decided to sit on the village wall. The first day was proving so much harder than I had ever imagined it could be and the severity of the conditions was a massive shock. As I sat on the wall thinking about how hard the rest of the race was going to be, I looked up and saw Jeff. We decided to do the rest of the route together and help each other get over the finish line. We set off again, but Jeff was struggling and had to keep stopping. He told me that he had had two knee replacements and said I should go on without him. I told him that we were going to finish together, and we kept going up and down the dunes. It was brutally hot and eventually we got to the top of the last dune and saw the finish. We walked to the bottom of the dune and together we ran the final quarter of a mile, very slowly. We crossed the line together and gave each other an enormous hug. I had done it. Somehow, I had got through the first day of the Marathon des Sables and now I knew what the race was all about.

We were directed towards a Berber who was serving cups of sweet tea. It was the greatest drink I had ever tasted, but I was feeling weak, sick and had a splitting headache. The adrenaline of getting to the finish had kept me going, but now that had worn off and I wasn't feeling very well. I was given four bottles of water and then had to find my tent. Thankfully, it was only

100 yards from the finish and Jeff and I were the final ones to arrive back at Tent 105. Everyone was delighted to see us and as we put our kit down, Rory told us they had been worried that we might have dropped out of the race. The camaraderie of our tent meant they wanted us to complete the first day and they were all delighted for us. I sat in my space, but I was still feeling sick and unwell. Rory asked me if I had been taking my salt tablets during the day. I told him that stupidly I hadn't, and he explained that I should be having them at every checkpoint because they helped my body retain the water and kept me hydrated. Lesson learnt, I took a couple of tablets, sat quietly and started to feel better. From our tent you could see the finish and I watched as runners came back from the desert in pieces. The Marathon des Sables could destroy you and there were rumours going around the tents about how many runners had dropped out on the first day. The chat in our tent was all about the conditions we had encountered, and Rory told me it was one of the toughest days he had experienced during 13 years of doing the race. Everyone agreed it had been a brutal day and I took an enormous amount of satisfaction from knowing I had got through it.

During the day I had been dreaming of my evening meal: dehydrated sweet and sour chicken. I sat in the shade of the tent, boiling my chicken, feeling exhausted. As I ate my dinner, I realised there was another five days of this torture to come but I was loving the sensation of being in the race and felt extremely calm. As I looked across the desert, there was nowhere else I wanted to be. I could have been in a hospice waiting to die but here I was, more alive than I had ever felt and having the most incredible experience.

After dinner, I went to the 'email tent' where you could send one email a day to one person to tell them how you were getting on. I queued up until a laptop was free and sent an email to Sarah. Before the race I had started sending updates on my treatment to about 400 people, including work colleagues. I had asked Sarah to forward my emails from the race to everybody and I enjoyed writing about the first day and explaining how I had managed to get through it.

Back at Tent 105, there was more discussion and rumours about how many people had dropped out of the race, but we were all shattered and needed to sleep. I was lying on my mat when one of the race volunteers came into the tent with printouts of messages sent from home. Anybody who knew your race number could send you a message and I was in tears reading all the supportive words from loved ones and friends. I even got a message from a gentleman who had had my race number the previous year, wishing me all the best.

I fell to sleep very quickly but after an hour and a half my cancer woke me up, needing the toilet. This became a regular pattern throughout the night because I had been drinking so much water. I would wake up, put my head torch on, check for scorpions, creep out of the tent, relieve myself and get back into my sleeping bag. After waking up at 4am I was freezing cold and couldn't get back to sleep. I started thinking about the day ahead, took my abiraterone and watched the sun come up over the desert. All my muscles were aching. I felt stiff and sore, but I was so happy watching the desert come to life again.

I cooked my breakfast as the rest of the tent started to wake up, got my kit together and started preparing for the second day of the race. I looked at the roadbook and saw the route started with more sand dunes, but they didn't look as bad as those on the first day. Before we left for the start line, I noticed a group of people making their way towards some Land Rovers. I asked Rory what was going on and he told me that was the 'walk of pain'. It was the runners who had dropped out being taken back to Ouarzazate to wait five days for the race to end or make their own arrangements to get home. I watched them leaving and felt for all of them because their dreams had been shattered by the MDS. I was determined the only time I would be making that journey was with a medal round my neck.

I had been wearing my kit for three days, hadn't had a wash and was feeling very grubby as I made my way to the start line. 'Highway to Hell' was being blasted out again and the helicopter was hovering above us. The atmosphere wasn't quite as excitable as the first day, but the adrenaline was pumping. And I wondered what the rest of the Marathon des Sables held in store for me.

Chapter 6

Beating the desert

I NO longer had a fear of the unknown. After the brutal opening day of the MDS, I was expecting more of the same: horrendous sand dunes, unrelenting heat and more blisters. The good news was the first few kilometres of day two were flat and I was able to run them. It was nice getting into my rhythm and even though the temperature was rising, I was enjoying myself. We approached some massive sand dunes, but thankfully we could run between them rather than having to climb up them. The flat scrubland turned into a dry riverbed which was tough to run on because of the cracked earth and rocks. I was getting acclimatised to the heat, but the sweat from the peak of my cap was still cascading like a waterfall. We ran past a small village and some of the locals waved at the lunatics running across the desert and after 12km I reached the first checkpoint. I remembered to take my salt tablets with my water, had a handful of peanuts and went straight back into the desert. The rest of the day was hard work but nowhere near as punishing as the first day. I kept plodding along at my pace as we went through the valleys between a range of mountains called Jebel el Abeth. The scenery was spectacular, with the mountains leaning over us and I was in my own head space. Even though I was tired, hot and in pain, I felt part of the race and part of the desert. I got through the second day with no alarms and crossed the finish line having ticked off another 41km in seven hours.

I made my way back to our tent feeling satisfied with my efforts. A tough day but not a brutal one. I put my kit down and discussed the day with my 'tent family'. Everyone agreed they were getting beaten up by the desert. Chris had a problem with blisters, Nick was constantly hungry and everyone had been battered by the conditions. I didn't feel too bad but was still completely knackered. We heard rumours that another 20 people had dropped out of the race and would be doing the 'walk of pain' in the morning.

I decided to get a blister that was on the ball of my foot looked at, because it was starting to get uncomfortable. I hobbled to 'Doc Trotter's', which was a tented area with 80 French doctors. I was given a ticket with a number and had to wait until my number was called. I saw a couple of runners on the verge of collapse and they were rushed into the tents to be treated. Eventually my ticket number was called, and a doctor looked at my foot, gave me some tape and told me to treat it myself. I realised that a doctor was only going to patch me up if I had a more spectacular injury. There were runners in the tent who couldn't stand up and some whose feet were in a dreadful state. As I left, I saw the tent where runners were taken if they needed to be put on drips and it was a stark reminder of how brutal the MDS was.

Back at Tent 105, I taped my foot, had my dinner, sent an email to Sarah, and settled down for the night. Tent 105 was starting to feel like my lifeboat. I felt safe in it and we were all there for each other. Anything we had achieved before the race counted for nothing and the respect and camaraderie under that roof was amazing. I fell asleep and my normal night-time routine took over. Wake up freezing cold, need a wee, check for scorpions, creep into the desert, get back in my sleeping bag and repeat an hour and a half later.

I won't bore you with what I had for breakfast and watching the sun come up over the desert again, but I was stiff and sore everywhere. I was tired and knew what the desert was going to throw at me on the third day. More sand dunes, more riverbeds, more sand, more heat and another 37km that were going to test me to my limit. It was tough and relentless, but I got through it and was pleased with how the day went. Back in the tent, we all discussed what the desert was doing to us and looked ahead to the legendary fourth day of the MDS. Tomorrow was a double marathon and I was dreading it: 84km across the desert would be brutal and the tent was very quiet as we prepared for what lay ahead. I was exhausted and went to sleep extremely nervous about the 'hell' that was coming my way in the morning.

After another cold night, I woke up and there was a tense atmosphere in the tent. After my normal routine, I made my way to the start line at 8.15am knowing I had until 3pm the following day to complete this stage of the route. The top 50 placed runners were leaving three hours later, so with fewer people and a staggered start, I was nearer the front of the queue. The conditions were cooler at that time of the morning, and I set off with an army captain that I had met on the start line. I knew after 11km we would be tackling the fabled Jebel el Oftal mountain and Rory had warned me it could become a bottleneck with runners trying to get over it. I was determined not to get held up, so I ran at a steady pace to the first checkpoint.

After a drink, salt tablets and a handful of nuts, I got going again and could see the Jebel el Oftal mountain getting closer. There was a sand dune to negotiate before I even reached the rocky climb. Just like the first day, my foot kept sinking every time I took a step in the soft sand and after 20 minutes, I finally started making my way up the rocky face of Jebel el Oftal. I was already knackered from the sand dune and now I was part of a 'snake' of runners going up the mountain. Everybody was walking and the climb got steeper and steeper. I was using my hands to scramble up and over rocks and there was nothing to hold on to. We were 40ft above the ground, and it was frightening. Some of the runners were suffering with vertigo and I just kept following the person in front of me. Despite the fact we were meant to be in a race, everyone was helping each other up the mountain. Around 200m before the top a couple of ropes were screwed into the rock and we needed them to help pull us up because the climb was now so steep. I dragged myself towards the top, hanging on to the rope for dear life. I was incredibly hot and tired as I finally reached the summit of Jebel el Oftal. We were 3,000ft up and the view of the desert was incredible, but psychologically and physically the climb had been a killer. I had to sit down because I was exhausted. Thankfully, because we were so high there was a cooling breeze, the first one of the race, and it was very welcome.

I then had to make my way down the other side of the mountain. Trying to run was impossible because the ground was smooth and very slippery. I didn't want to go head over arse, so I took my time and carefully negotiated my way to the bottom. I was greeted by more sand dunes and I started to realise all the horror stories I had been told about day four were true. I trudged up and down the dunes and thankfully the desert started to flatten out. I was able to run, reached the second checkpoint, did a quick, 'splash and dash' and headed straight towards two enormous jebels (mountains). The route took us between them, and I suddenly hit civilisation for the first time since landing at the airport. It was surreal because in front of me were palm trees, street signs and even a hotel. I had no idea where I was, but there were a few locals cheering us on and a young boy spraying us with water from a hose as we ran past. It gave me a real lift to get a brief glimpse of normality as

I kept plodding along. I could feel someone on my shoulder, so I turned around and saw a couple of the elite runners racing past me. Don't forget they had set off three hours after me and I stopped and cheered them on, in awe of the pace that they were running.

I was exhausted. My shoulders were raw from carrying my backpack, my feet were killing me with multiple blisters and there was still 50km to go on the day. I was now on a huge salt flat that seemed to go on forever. It was white, so the sun reflected directly off it and there was no escape from the heat, I could even feel the heat coming up through the soles of my shoes, like walking barefoot on a beach in the sun, only I was not barefoot and there was no sea to cool off in. I had another ten hours of this torture ahead of me and it felt like it was never going to end. Mentally and physically, I was in a bad place. I was on my own, with the nearest runner 200 yards ahead of me and I was in pieces.

I stopped and burst into tears. If somebody had driven past and asked me if I wanted to drop out of the race, at that moment I think I would have been tempted. I was at breaking point and didn't know how I was going to carry on. I stood there sobbing and asked myself the question, 'Why the hell are you here, Kev?' It was then I remembered that I wanted to prove I could do this race and it was something I had wanted to do for 31 years. I wasn't going to drop out just because it was hard, and it hurt. I thought of all the people who had sponsored me and there was no way I was going to go back and tell them I had given up. I thought about everybody on the Prostate Cancer UK forum, who had helped me get to the race and I wanted to show them that I could get through the desert despite my cancer. And I wanted my medal, that bit of bling around my neck that would show everybody that no matter what you are struggling with you can still achieve your dreams. So, as you may have gathered, I gave myself a proper bollocking, shuffling along in the middle of the desert. I had reached my lowest point and the only way I could go was up. I stopped crying and continued along the salt flat, feeling positive and in a better frame of mind.

I made it to the next checkpoint had another quick 'splash and dash' and continued ploughing my way through the desert. The day wore on as I made my way past another enormous jebel, where the sand got softer, making each step very tough and, once again, I felt like I was wading through treacle. The light was fading and physically I was struggling when I reached the next checkpoint. I was just over halfway, 45km into the route for the day and I desperately needed a rest. I found a tent, sat down and mixed a powdered chocolate milkshake which I drank slowly. It was exactly what I needed, full of calories and gave me some energy. As I finished my shake, I looked up and noticed another runner watching me. I got up and said hello and she introduced herself. Her name was Victoria and she asked if she could join me for the remainder of the route, so we could help each other navigate the rest of the course in the dark. I totally understood where she was coming from and was happy to have the company, a real pick-me-up.

Victoria and I put on our headlamps and made our way into the night. The temperature had dropped, and every runner had a green glowstick on their backpack to light them up in the dark. We made our way across the desert and it was beautiful being under a night sky, full of bright stars which lit up the landscape. Victoria and I were happily making progress, chatting about all sorts of things and enjoying the race. I told her about my cancer, and it was great to have her company. The route was now flat, and we made our way through the night until we reached a checkpoint that can only be described as like no other on the MDS. It was 1am and we were exhausted, but we heard music and saw an enormous fire with deckchairs round it. It was a sight that I wasn't expecting, and I saw the Berber who had been at the finish each day serving his cups of sweet tea. We both got a cup, sat in a deckchair and stared silently into the fire. We were surrounded by other runners doing the same and nobody said a word. Even though it was tempting to stay there for a long time, we pulled ourselves out of the deckchairs and set off for the final 25km of the route.

We headed into some rocky terrain which was hard work, especially at night. Victoria suddenly tripped on a rock and fell flat on her face. I helped her to her feet and checked she was ok. She was shaken, but we kept going, making our way past another enormous jebel and somehow continuing to put one foot in front of the other. Eventually, we left the jebel behind and in the distance, we could see some bright lights. They were about 4km away and after looking at the roadbook we realised that was the next checkpoint. But 10km past that were some more lights and I realised those were at the finish. Mentally, being able to see how far we had left until this torture would end was brutal because we were completely exhausted.

We made our way to the final checkpoint and I noticed that some runners were getting into their sleeping bags and were obviously going to have a sleep before taking on the final 10km of the route. There was no way I was going to do that because Rory had told me to always try and finish the 'long day' in the dark. He said you can then sleep in the camp knowing you have the rest of day five off to recover. I couldn't imagine sleeping and then having to finish the route in the morning. We both thought sleeping now was madness, so we took on the final part of the route. The terrain was still flat, and we marched along at a good pace, knowing we were heading towards the finish. We didn't say anything to each other because we were shattered and were having to use all our concentration to put one foot in front of the other.

The lights at the finish slowly started getting brighter and I felt fantastic, knowing I was going to complete the legendary fourth day of the MDS. We could see the finish gantry and hear music and there were volunteers cheering us on. With 100 yards to go, I stumbled and fell flat on my face. I slowly got up, having cut my nose and grazed my hands and knees, but there was no lasting damage. Victoria and I fell over the finishing line and gave each other an enormous hug. I waved at the webcam that hung from the gantry, in case anybody at home was watching the live feed and I must have looked a state with my bloody nose. I said goodbye to Victoria and shuffled to Tent 105. It was 5am, I was in agony and every part of me hurt. I crept into the tent, trying not to disturb those who were back and already asleep, had a recovery shake and crawled into my sleeping bag.

I slept like a baby but woke up when the sun started streaming into our tent. I felt beaten up. I chatted to everyone in the tent apart from Jeff who was still out in the desert on his replacement knees. I made my breakfast and sat in the shade of the tent watching runners still coming across the finishing line. Each time a finisher walked past our tent we gave them a round of applause and the camaraderie was amazing. I rested during the morning, knowing I had the day off. I ate my luxury item for lunch, a tin of tuna which tasted like it had been sent from the running gods, and I saw Jeff making his way over the finish line. We gave him a standing ovation when he got back to the tent, which was beginning to look like a scene from *Casualty*. Phil was unable to keep any food down, Chris's feet were in a bad state and even Rory was not feeling well. But we were still a full house. I now had a massive blister on each foot and needed another trip to 'Doc Trotter's'. This time I got treated, which entailed a doctor slicing open each blister and then pouring iodine on each foot. It was agony and I hit the roof. I hobbled back to the tent, leaving behind a scene of carnage, runners lying everywhere, some of whom were in a bad way including Phil, who had been put on a drip.

I read some messages from home including one from Sarah, who explained she had been extremely worried about me and thought I might have dropped out of the race. Let me explain. When you run the MDS you are given a numbered tracker that goes on your shoulder and people can watch your progress on the race website. At the start of the fourth day, somebody mentioned that my tracker didn't seem to be working. I found a volunteer, who replaced the tracker with a new one and I set off blissfully unaware that Sarah was watching back at home. All she could see was my numbered 'dot' standing still at the start line, because she was still seeing my old tracker that had probably been thrown in a bin. By the time she got to work, my dot was still on the start line and she was understandably very worried. She sent numerous messages in every way she knew how to the MDS organisers, but no one could tell Sarah for sure that I was ok and still in the race. Poor Sarah was so worried, she was sent home from work, but thankfully my new tracker started working and by the evening she could see my dot moving across the desert. Panic over.

There is a tradition in the MDS that when the last person comes over the finish line on the 'longest day' everybody goes and supports them. Just before 3pm the tented village rose like Lazarus with people dragging themselves to the finish to cheer the last runners over the line. In the distance I could see the two dreaded camels, that must not overtake you and in front of them were two runners hobbling to the line. I suddenly realised one of them was Mark, my training partner from Richmond Park, who had overtaken me on the first day. We cheered him over the line just ahead of the camels and again I was overwhelmed by the camaraderie and generosity of spirit amongst the MDS family.

That evening there was a relaxed atmosphere in the camp. The long day was over and we had one more marathon stage to complete tomorrow. After that there was the final charity stage the following day, which we had to do, but in reality, the actual race finished tomorrow. We were called to a meeting by the organisers and given a can of iced Coke and never has Coca-Cola tasted so good. It is amazing how the simplest things can really lift your mood. We were also given a fresh set of race numbers to wear the next day, so they showed up clearly at the finish for the photographers and the sponsors.

The whole camp had an early night because we were all knackered and I had a 7am start in the morning. I slept ok, my normal routine was rushed because of the early alarm call and I made my way to the start line for the last proper stage of the MDS, with 42km standing between me and that medal round my neck. All around me were runners in pieces, including myself, but the atmosphere was like the last day of school. My final reserves of energy would be used today and even if I had to crawl across the finish line this was the day I was going to complete the MDS.

I set off feeling good and ran at my own pace. I had no fear of what the desert might throw at me. I was used to sand dunes, jebels, rocks, riverbeds and salt plains and nothing scared me anymore. Having said that, it was still a long slog and I was hurting. Between checkpoints two and three, I felt a tap on my shoulder and a Spanish runner called Sylvie introduced herself. She pointed to my Prostate Cancer UK flag and asked me why I was flying it over my backpack. I told her about my cancer, and she pointed to a flag on her backpack which had a picture of a gentleman on it. She explained that was her father who had died of prostate cancer just before the race. She told me that she had been wanting to chat to me because when she was struggling during the race, either her flag would get blown by the wind into her face, which she felt was her dad pushing her on, or she would see my flag in the distance and feel that was me pulling her on. Her story was so emotional and we both burst into tears and gave each other a hug. We ran together for a while, said a tearful goodbye and I continued to make my way through the desert.

It was hard work, but I got to the final checkpoint and knew there was only 10km to go. In my kit bag I had a GoPro camera which I got out, and for the final 5km I was an emotional wreck, chatting to the camera and thanking everybody who had helped me get this far. I was crying, knowing I was going to get to the finish and complete my dream of running the MDS. In my head I had the picture of Patrick Bauer hanging that medal round my neck, but as I stumbled across the finishing line, I remembered that the medals wouldn't be presented until after the charity stage the next day. I was an elated, proud, exhausted, emotional and physical wreck, but there was a feeling of anti-climax that I wasn't going to get my medal. However, nobody could take away from me that fact that I had finished and the bloke with terminal cancer had completed the MDS and fulfilled his bucket-list dream.

I got back to Tent 105, put my kit bag down and lay on my mat. There was no sign of Rory and I was shocked to be told he had been taken to the medical tent to be put on oxygen. Nick was struggling with his ankles and Chris's feet were even more of a mess. Selina had finished as the top female British runner, which was an incredible effort that had taken its toll. Everyone was buzzing, but concerned about Rory. I just sat there taking it all in. I had left my mobile phone in England, so I hobbled to the email tent and paid ten euros to use the satellite phone for three minutes. I rang Sarah and as soon as I heard her voice I completely broke down. I told her that I had finished the race and it was wonderful to hear her voice. I hobbled back to the tent a very happy and contented man.

That evening there was a prize-giving ceremony, but all I wanted was my medal. We were given a beer and the Berbers lit a fire, but I was feeling sad because my adventure was coming to an end. Back in the tent we were all delighted to see Rory, He seemed a little shell-shocked from having been put on oxygen, but he told us he would be finishing with us tomorrow. We discussed tomorrow's charity stage and agreed the only reason we were having to do it was to get us back to the coaches, that couldn't drive into the desert. Richard said he didn't want to sit on a coach for six hours back to the hotel and he suggested if we all contributed 20 euros we could pay for a minibus and travel back in comfort. We all agreed and somehow, he found a signal on his phone and rang his PA who booked the minibus to meet us at the finish. She also took our food and drink orders for the journey!

I fell asleep and had my normal night in the tent before waking up in the desert for the final time. I went through my morning routine and then said goodbye to Tent 105 as the Berbers took it away. We made our way to the start line and we had decided that all eight of us from the tent were going to do the final 17km together. Nick had been to 'Doc Trotter's' and been diagnosed with stress fractures in both ankles, so he was on crutches. Chris could hardly walk because of his feet and poor Phil was still very sick. But we were going to get through the day together. After listening to 'Highway to Hell' for the last time we set off. The route was flat, and we must have looked like the cast of a zombie film as we slowly made our way to the only checkpoint. We were one of the final groups to arrive because Nick was struggling on his crutches and after a short break we kept going. The day seemed to go on for ever and it was horrendous. The elation of finishing the 'proper' race had disappeared and it now felt like a pointless slog. Eventually after four hours of sheer torture we got to the finish. We crossed the line and Patrick Bauer was waiting with our medals. Finally, I had my 'piece of bling' round my neck, but I would much rather have had it the day before.

The Berber with the sweet tea was at the finish, so I had a cup and saw all the coaches lined up to take the runners back to their hotels. And there amongst them all was our state-of-the-art minibus. We all got in and there were crisps, cans of Coke and air conditioning. Richard's PA had done a brilliant job. I lay down on the back seats and felt fantastic as we left the Sahara. After a couple of hours somebody suggested to the driver that we stop at a Souk. The driver found one and we all hobbled off the minibus in our running kit. We ordered chips, beer, Coke and cheese and sat eating and drinking our banquet for 40 minutes. I found a toilet and it was amazing to use proper facilities and be able to wash my hands properly for the first time in a week. We clambered back into the minibus and four hours later arrived at our hotel in Ouzzazzate. I found my suitcase and went to my room and had the greatest shower of my life. I washed off the desert, put on some proper clothes and went and met everybody in the restaurant. There was an unlimited buffet and I filled my boots. I had five main courses and the same number of deserts, all washed down with quite a few beers. All the British runners were in the hotel and the atmosphere was fantastic as we celebrated finishing the MDS. I was knackered and crawled into a proper bed for a tremendous night's sleep, despite my cancer waking me up like clockwork.

The next morning, I was straight back to the breakfast buffet and once again I wasn't shy. Bacon rolls were consumed with unlimited cups of coffee and after stuffing myself I wandered to another hotel to pick up my 'MDS Finisher's' t-shirt and buy some race memorabilia. Later, on the advice of Richard who had been to Morocco before, I met Chris and we went for a Hamam massage which Richard said was the best way of getting the desert out of your skin. A huge gentleman dressed only in a loin cloth, covered me in hot water and used what felt like a wire brush to give me a proper scrub ostensibly to get the sand out of my pores although at the time it felt like torture. Afterwards we then had a more enjoyable massage and left feeling clean for the first time in a week. I felt incredibly relaxed and after lunch wandered to a market and bought some souvenirs to take home. That evening a gala dinner had been organised around the hotel swimming pool. I had a long chat with Steve, the UK organiser of the MDS, and Patrick Bauer gave a speech. I noticed the atmosphere was different and I think that was because everybody was starting to think about heading back to the real world the next day. One of my training partners from Richmond Park called Megan came and found me and gave me a little tube of sand from the Sahara with my name on it. I was really touched, and it meant and still means as much to me as my medal.

The following morning, I packed my bags and after another huge breakfast it was time to go home. I was sad when I got on the coach because it was all over. We arrived at the airport and I bumped into Steve, who I had spoken to the night before. When I had finished the race, I had sworn to myself that

I would never do it again. At that moment it had been too hard, and my body had hurt too much to consider running the MDS again. But now, after a couple of days of rest my attitude had changed. I wanted to do it again. I asked Steve if there were any places available for the following year and he said he would hold a place for me for the next couple of weeks. It was a gamble because I didn't even know if I would be alive in a year's time, but I was delighted with the news. Plus, two weeks gave me a chance to speak to Sarah about it!

I got on the plane and the atmosphere was very different to when we flew out. Everyone was tired and just wanted to get home. We landed at Gatwick and as I walked through arrivals, I saw Ollie and Sarah waiting for me. It was an emotional reunion and I was delighted to be back. We found the car and Sarah drove us home. As we turned into our road, I was greeted by 40 of my friends standing on a grass area near my house with banners and tambourines making a huge din. I got out of the car and hugged each and every one of them. I was exhausted and emotional, but I had done it. A man with terminal cancer had been to the desert and finished the 'toughest race on earth'. As I walked through the front door, I felt incredibly proud of myself. I had stuck two fingers up at cancer, raised loads of money for charity and proved that the seemingly impossible can happen with training and will power.

Chapter 7

Something to look forward to

PIE AND mash. That was my celebratory family dinner the evening I came home from the Marathon des Sables. It was fantastic to be back, telling Sarah and Ollie all about the race, but it started to dawn on me that my adventure was over. I was back in the real world and back to my normal cancer-dominated life. The MDS had been a form of escapism, pure fantasy for nine days. Even though it had been hard, every second of being in the desert was different from anything I had experienced before and now it was all over. Don't get me wrong. It was wonderful to be home, but now I was back to reality and back to facing terminal cancer. All that I had to look forward to was the stuff I had escaped from when I was training for and running in the MDS. I had lived and achieved my dream and the only thing on my bucket list was now ticked off.

I have always been somebody who needs something to look forward to. I am one of those people who books their next holiday while on their current holiday. I believe if you have something to look forward to you can get through the bad bits of life. But what was I going to do next? The day after coming back from the desert I felt completely flat. All I had in my diary was returning to work and going to the hospital for blood tests. I was worried how the MDS might have affected my PSA score and I sat with Sarah in the kitchen and explained how I was feeling. Sarah listened patiently and told me that I had to go back to the Sahara next year and run the MDS again. I didn't need to be told twice. I had been thinking the same thing, but thought I was being selfish with the time, money and effort it would take. Plus, I didn't know if I would be alive for the race next year. I had already dared to dream once; would I get away with it again? As soon as Sarah said those words, I was on the phone to book my place for the next Marathon des Sables. Sarah recognised the race gave me something to look forward to and a reason to keep living and to fight the cancer. I am a lucky man to have such an understanding and supportive wife.

I went back to work and received a fantastic welcome from everyone. They had been following my progress in the MDS via my daily emails and I could tell they were pleased for me. I had written an article for the bank's internal magazine about my illness and why I was going to the Sahara to do the MDS. The magazine was now published, and I was on the front cover. A few days after returning to work, my phone rang, and it was the chief executive of the bank. He told me he had read the article, congratulated me on my achievement and said he did not know how he would have coped if he had been given my prognosis. He asked me to think about my role at the bank and how I could use my time in the most constructive way for the company and myself. I couldn't believe it. A man who had far more important things to worry about had taken the time to ring and support me, I was so touched by his generosity of spirit and proud of the organisation I worked for, having someone like that at the top.

I went home and thought about the conversation with the chief executive. What could I do that would benefit the bank using the drive and determination I had to fight prostate cancer? I went back to my boss and told him I wanted to continue working for the bank and help show their human side through my story. I explained that I wanted to do more for Prostate Cancer UK because I was in a unique position. Lots of people when they are diagnosed with cancer might do something to support a charity but then be unable to do anything else because sadly, they become too ill or die. I felt ok and knew I could do more for the charity and encourage others to make the most of life. I am not a religious person, but I felt if I did more good things and helped other people, I might be allowed to live longer by whoever makes that decision. My boss went away, and the bank agreed to give me the time I needed for my treatment and hospital appointments, to allow me to work with Prostate Cancer UK and work for the bank on certain projects and be an ambassador for them. I will never be able to thank the bank enough because they were enabling me to continue working whilst also spreading the word on prostate cancer and pursuing my dreams that were, I believed and still believe, keeping me alive.

A couple of weeks after returning from the MDS, I had my first blood test since the race. My PSA score had gone down to 0.72, which was fantastic news because it showed that doing the race hadn't damaged me in terms of the cancer. I saw Professor Parker and he didn't seem surprised that I had finished the MDS. We chatted about the race and I told him I wanted to be a bloke with terminal cancer who was pushing the boundaries and hopefully inspiring people. Prostate Cancer UK got in touch to congratulate me on the MDS and asked me to write an article for them on my story and we chatted about me doing more for them. Sarah and I also decided to book a family holiday to Morocco in October and that gave me something else to look forward to. I had started running again about a week after getting back from the desert, my body felt ok and I was in a good place.

Shortly afterwards, I received some shocking news about Rory, who had been placed on oxygen during the MDS. He was in hospital and had been diagnosed with a rare illness called Guillain Barre Syndrome which is a condition where your immune system attacks your nerves and gradually paralyses you. Rory was unable to walk and I was devastated for him. To me he was an ultra-running legend and I couldn't believe he had gone from completing the MDS to lying in a hospital bed effectively paralysed in such a short space of time. I drew parallels with not knowing how my cancer could affect me and if it was all going to go wrong, it would all happen very quickly. The news really upset me and I immediately sent Rory a message of support and vowed to keep in touch with him.

Back at the office I got an email from the new head of my division, who I had never met, asking for a meeting. I had only been back for a few weeks and even though my role had been agreed with the bank, I was nervous. Had they changed their minds? I went to the meeting and it turned out that the new head, Rob, was an ultra-marathon runner and wanted to see how I was and see if there was anything he could do to help me. Plus, he wanted to hear all about the MDS. He said he was pleased with my role as an ambassador for the bank, showing their customers and staff they are indeed a bank that cares about wellbeing. Meeting Rob gave me a boost because I knew the bank trusted me to carry out my role and I felt I was an asset for them, giving me that all-important sense of worth.

Life carried on as normal. The good news was my PSA score kept dropping and by July it was down to 0.28. The abiraterone was still working. Prostate Cancer UK organised a video interview for me with *The Guardian* to discuss my cancer story. It was my first proper interview and I went to a recording studio, sat in front of a camera and told them my story. It was emotional, but I was glad I did it and the feedback was positive. The charity also asked me to speak at one of its conferences at Guy's Hospital. I hated standing up in front of people and talking, but I wanted to do it to help spread the word about prostate cancer. I put my presentation together and spoke about my cancer journey and the Marathon des Sables. I was nervous but when I finished my talk, I realised some of the audience were in tears. I had clearly got my message across to them and it was the first time I realised my story could have an emotional impact on people. My boss at the bank asked me to do similar presentations later in the year, which was another opportunity for me to show the work Prostate Cancer UK was doing and motivate my colleagues to make the most of life and do something themselves for the charity.

In June I had a date with a tattooist. Apart from the radiotherapy positioning dots, I had never had a proper tattoo, but when I ran the London Marathon in 2013, the year before my diagnosis, I saw a runner who had a tattoo of the Marathon des Sables symbol on her calf. I had never really wanted a tattoo, but I promised myself if I ever ran the race, I would have the same tattoo. Three years later I was in a tattoo parlour showing them the MDS symbol. After an hour of needlework, I had it proudly on my calf, a permanent reminder of what I had achieved.

When I was in Tent 105 during the MDS, I was lying next to Rich one evening and he mentioned a race called Fire and Ice that took place in Iceland. I told him I didn't fancy it because it would be too cold, but that conversation had sowed a seed in my mind. One afternoon I was sitting at my computer and decided to have a look at the official race website. The race was 250km across glaciers, lava fields and rocky terrain and it looked fantastic. It would take place in August 2017; it would be something else to look forward to, so I signed up for it. I was still training for the next MDS and in July ran the Race to the Stones again, which was enjoyable. It was great to see some familiar faces and be back with the ultra-marathon family.

The following week I had a meeting with the BBC. A lady called Sue Bourne was making a documentary called *A Time to Live*. It was about ten people with different terminal illnesses, and she wanted me to be in it. I was chuffed to be asked and Sue explained they would spend a couple of days filming me in October. In my head, I was still living on borrowed time and thought Sue's documentary would be something that would be there for people to watch when I died.

My knee was still bothering me when a friend called Stu, who had run the MDS in 2016, asked me to go to the Brecon Beacons and do some training with him. We spent a couple of days there and it was hard work. Cold and remote, it gave me some idea of what the Fire and Ice race might be like in Iceland the following year. On my way back from Brecon I stopped off to see Jeff from Tent 105. It was lovely to catch up with him and I got a wonderful surprise when there was a knock on the door, and it was Rory. I had been in constant touch with him since he was diagnosed with Guillain Barre Syndrome but I was shocked to see he was on a zimmer frame and could only manage to walk ten steps. Chatting to Rory was inspirational because he was determined to recover and was positive about the future. I took a huge amount away from seeing Rory and knew if anyone could recover it would be him.

I carried on working and training and the BBC came to film me for a couple of days for the documentary. It was great fun and they filmed me with Ollie and Sarah, training in the park and asked me lots of questions. They also came back to film a family Sunday dinner, including my dad, mother-in-law and Hayley and Ben. I was starting to get used to giving interviews and I knew how important it was to get my message across, so that others would think, 'If he can do that with cancer what's stopping me chasing my dreams.'

I was invited by Prostate Cancer UK to their annual conference at The Valley, the home of Charlton Athletic FC. I gave my presentation, which I was adapting for every speaking engagement. Again, my talk went down well with the audience and I was continuing to build my relationship with the charity. It was then time for our family holiday to Morocco. We went with our best friends, Jim, Jo and their family, and had a wonderful five days. I proudly showed everybody the conditions I had coped with on the Marathon des Sables. The holiday brought back some amazing memories and I went for a couple of runs in the heat to remind myself what I would be facing next year.

Back in England life carried on as normal. My PSA score was down to 0.17, so it was still going in the right direction which was great news. I gave a presentation to the Rainbow Trust Charity and I realised that standing in front of another charity and telling my story showed them how their efforts made such a difference. I spoke for the bank at a conference in Bishopsgate and there were lots of my colleagues in the audience and I really felt like I was giving something back to the bank through every presentation I gave. I made a trip to York for a two-day Fire and Ice Expo, which was a great weekend, meeting other people who had signed up for the race. The race was much smaller than the MDS, with only 80 runners competing and I was given a huge amount of information. Obviously, being in Iceland would be the complete opposite from being in the desert, and running in cold conditions would be a different discipline. I drove home knowing I had an enormous challenge on my hands, I was cautiously looking forward to it and had made some new running mates.

I headed to Birmingham and Manchester to give more presentations for the bank and I was starting to really enjoy my ambassadorial role. Training was going well; my knee was feeling better and at the end of November I entered a 50km event across Kent called the Gatlif Marathon. It was organised by the Long-Distance Walkers Association and at the start I was given instructions for the route that were like hieroglyphics. I had no idea what any of it meant or where I was meant to be going. I followed the crowd and bumped into a guy called Andy who was an old hand at these events and could decipher the instructions. We got chatting and he told me his wife had sadly died from cancer. We formed an immediate bond and stayed together for the rest of the day. Whilst we were plodding along, we were overtaken by Megan and Perry who did the MDS in 2016 too; the ultra-running community is a small but friendly world. By the time I crossed the finish line I was totally knackered, but I had made a new special friend. I tried to persuade him to do the MDS, but he was having none of it. Without Andy I would probably still be walking in circles somewhere in the Kent countryside; thanks, mate.

Next up I flew to Jersey to give my presentation to the Royal Bank of Scotland International annual conference. During my talk, a couple of people got up and walked out which threw me for a few moments. I found out afterwards that their lives had been touched by cancer and it was too raw for them to listen to my story, which I understood, but afterwards they were keen to speak with me in a less formal setting about the challenges they had faced. I felt I was getting the message about prostate cancer across to the right people and making a positive impact to most. I went for a run along the beach and the scenery was fantastic, but I was disappointed not to see Jim Bergerac! In early December I went to the Prostate Cancer UK Forum annual meeting at the Euston Flyer pub. I had first been to the meeting after my diagnosis in 2014 and it was lovely to see many of the same faces again and find out how their year had been. In all honesty it was reassuring to see so many from the forum who were still alive and had got through another year of living with the disease.

I managed to achieve a lifetime's ambition just before Christmas. My three favourite bands that are still performing are from America. They are called Yellowcard, Good Charlotte and Jimmy Eat World and I had never seen any of them live.

The rock planets aligned and all three of them toured the UK in October, November and December. I managed to get to each of their gigs, with the final one at Kentish Town. I jumped about like a lunatic and was the oldest person by years, but it was another opportunity that I had grabbed with both hands.

We enjoyed a happy family Christmas and I began the New Year with some more presentations for the bank. People were starting to get in touch with me after my talks and after reading my monthly blogs which I had been writing since my diagnosis. I was always honest in my blogs about my treatment and my cancer journey. I always wear my heart on my sleeve, and this made my story easy to tell since I never hide anything. My writing was positive because I wanted to help and inspire other people. I was also posting regularly on the Prostate Cancer UK forum and had gone from the 'reluctant newbie' to the bloke who was still alive and knew the highs and lows of living with cancer. I wanted to provide the right information to those at the start of their journey and show a diagnosis of cancer wasn't the end of your life. I had proved you could continue doing the things you love, despite having cancer, and through my talks, blogs and the responses I was getting on the forum, I could see I was having a positive impact on people.

There was a downside to the forum, however, as people who had got in touch with me when I was first diagnosed, some of whom I had met, had sadly died in the past couple of years. It made death a reality and my attitude had changed over the course of my journey. When I was first diagnosed, I felt sorry for myself for a couple of days. Then I felt sorry for my family and friends that were going to be affected. Then I felt sorry for anybody who had been diagnosed with prostate cancer. And now I feel sorry for anybody who is facing any sort of challenge in their lives. I understand that everybody is on a journey and some people are able to cope with problems better than others. Somebody who has lost their job or can't get their car started might think this is not as bad a problem as having terminal cancer, but it is their problem and just as important to them as what I am going through. Just because I am dying, doesn't make my problems any more important than theirs. I just might be better at dealing with them because of my cancer.

People were coming up to me after my presentations and saying my story had put their problems into perspective. It was kind of them to say that to me, but their problems were still there, and I wanted them to realise they were just as important as my terminal cancer and they should talk about them. I am not an expert, but I understand that you should never be afraid to share a problem. People were getting in touch with me asking for advice on issues ranging from how to fund-raise to how they could start enjoying life again. People who had been diagnosed with prostate cancer were reaching out to me, including colleagues at work. I would share my story and tell them there is life after diagnosis and you must grab every opportunity that comes your way. I wanted to help them and show that by continuing to do the things you love, you can get rid of the bad thoughts which take a massive mental and physical toll on people. I felt my story was having a positive impact and this was very important to me.

My training for the MDS was going well and my PSA scores were staying in the right place. At the start of February, I did the Pilgrims Challenge again, which was enjoyable, and it was great to catch up with so many familiar faces. I celebrated my 52nd birthday, an important milestone because after my diagnosis I didn't think I would reach it. I had felt like I was on borrowed time up until November 2016, when I was maybe meant to die. Now I felt like I was on bonus time and I was determined to make the most of every day. The world was my oyster because I was alive and cancer didn't rule my life. Until the day it all goes wrong, which I know it will, there is so much to look forward to. There are still days when I don't feel well, but that is just a feeling and the best way to deal with it is to go out and do something positive. As I mentioned, the dark thoughts still spring into my head but I have learnt to get rid of them as quickly as possible by thinking about something that makes me happy and this is still my philosophy today. If I can help people along the way, then that makes everything worthwhile.

After my birthday, my mate Graham called and asked me if I fancied going back to my old rugby club to watch a game. I hadn't been to Sutton and Epsom RFC for ten years and going back was wonderful. It was lovely to see so many old faces and be back in that environment. The club held a raffle with the proceeds going to Prostate Cancer UK and I was so glad I reconnected with the club, which had been a huge part of my life before cancer. I was now running ten miles four days a week and regularly going to Epsom Downs racecourse to use the sand track as part of my preparations for the MDS. The best piece of news was Rory had battled his way back from Guillain Barre Syndrome and was fit enough to compete in the race. His recovery was inspirational and he invited me to be in his tent, which I was delighted about, and I felt privileged to be given that opportunity again.

I surprised Sarah with a weekend in Iceland and we had a wonderful time being tourists in Reykjavik. Sarah had always wanted to go, and it gave me the opportunity to go for a couple of runs to see the conditions I would be facing at the Fire and Ice race in August. It was lovely to have a weekend with Sarah and be a normal couple. We were spending lots of our time together at hospital appointments and being in Iceland gave us the opportunity to get away from my cancer and create more happy memories.

I was still working four days a week and my PSA scores remained in the right place. I had been having monthly blood tests for a couple of years and I still had a fear of them. I always started worrying the week before the test because it was going to tell me whether the treatment was working or not. My blood tests were normally on a Thursday and then I had to wait until the Monday to get my PSA result. The four days of waiting were horrible, not knowing if it was good or bad news. I'm now much better and do not worry as much but my cancer is

PSA driven and I know one day the doctor will give me bad news. Every appointment is Russian roulette and one day the chamber will be loaded and the gun will go bang. Back in 2017 whenever I got my PSA result, I always spent a couple of days worrying about what would have happened if the result had gone the other way, like a near miss in the car, and the dark thoughts returned.

Before I knew where I was, it was time to head back to the desert for the 32nd Marathon des Sables. My training had gone well, and I boarded the plane to Morocco with the same excitement as the previous year. I had no fears about the race, but I wasn't complacent because I knew the desert could eat me up and spit me out. The fact I had already completed the race was no guarantee it would happen again, and I couldn't wait to take on the challenge.

The route was different in 2017 and the first day was better than the previous year. There was heat and sand dunes but no biblical sandstorm. That was no indication of what the rest of the race would be like, because it got harder and harder. I was in the tent with Rory again and the camaraderie was wonderful. I formed a strong bond with a guy called Craig, who had been meant to do the race the previous year, but during his training had suffered a massive heart attack whilst on a run and had actually died for a minute. He was lucky that 40 yards behind him there happened to be a doctor also on a run, who brought him back to life. Just like me he had been given a second chance and we spent most evenings together talking about our medical journeys and what the desert was doing to us. He was the top-placed finisher in our tent, and I was delighted for him.

I also spent time with a guy called Duncan Slater who is one of the most inspirational people I have ever met. Duncan was blown up by an IED during a tour of Afghanistan and lost both his legs. I had briefly spoken to him at the previous MDS, which he had to drop out of because he picked up an infection, but he was back to take on the desert again. He completed the race on his prosthetic legs and I was in awe of his courage and determination. We formed a strong relationship and celebrated hard together in the hotel bar at the end of the race. I was proud of myself when I crossed the finishing line and completed my second MDS. It was tough and everything I expected the race to be. Having that medal round my neck again was very special and unlike the previous year, I returned home with plenty to look forward to.

Chapter 8

Marching for Men

BEFORE LEAVING for the desert, I had a bone density scan and the results showed I had early-stage osteopenia. The drugs I was taking were making my bones weak and I was put on calcium tablets and had to have a drug called zoledronic acid, which I was to be given by infusion. I returned to the Royal Marsden hospital, nervous about having a canula put in my arm, as you already know how much I hate them. What I didn't realise was the infusion was being done in the chemotherapy room and I wasn't mentally ready to go back there. All the people sitting around me were having the bag of poison pumped into them and I knew how awful that was going to make them feel. I felt guilty that I was having a drug that would make my bones stronger and I left the room in shock, having been reminded of the dark places you go to when you are having chemotherapy.

I decided to head back to the Brecon Beacons and have a couple of days training with my mate Stu. He knew I would be doing the Fire and Ice race in August, but he kept mentioning another ultra-marathon called the 6633 Arctic Ultra. This is a nine-day, 383-mile race across the Arctic where you are totally self-sufficient and have to drag all your gear in a special sled called a pulk. The more Stu told me about it, the more I knew it was another challenge I wanted to take on. I did some more research when I got home and signed up for the race which would take place the following March. I entered the '120+' race where I would have three days to complete the first 120 miles and could then decide if I wanted to take on the remaining 260 miles. It is a non-stop race and even though I had no concept of what I was taking on, it was another challenge to look forward to and the training would fit perfectly with my trip to Iceland in August for Fire and Ice.

The documentary I had filmed with the BBC was broadcast and I was pleased with the final cut. *A Time to Live* was shown on BBC Two and I watched it with Sarah and I was happy with how my story was presented alongside other people suffering from terminal illnesses. I had made the right decision agreeing to be in it and it was something constructive that I could leave for my family, and that would inspire viewers not to give up, whatever the challenges they might be facing.

My next big event was another date with Jeff Stelling. In March, Prostate Cancer UK had asked me to join him on his latest challenge, in which he was doing 15 marathons in as many days. The March for Men would start at St James Park, Exeter City's ground, and finish at the other St James' Park, the home of Newcastle United. The charity wanted me to do all 15 days with Jeff and I was happy to agree because it was another way I could help them and it was a great challenge to take on. I think the charity wanted me to be involved because of my story and because I would be somebody other than Jeff who could speak to the media about the work the charity was doing and, of course, speak first-hand about having metastatic prostate cancer.

I mentioned the challenge in my monthly blog and some of my work colleagues asked me if any of the marathons were, in London because they wanted to join us. None of them were so I helped them organise a marathon around the capital before Jeff's challenge started, which I did with them. Our route took us past the headquarters of Prostate Cancer UK and collectively my colleagues raised £40,000. I realised my story was having an impact at work and people wanted to raise money for the charity because of me. The following week Dave, a friend of mine, organised a golf day at Surbiton Golf Club for Prostate Cancer UK, raising lots of money and, again, I felt my story was inspiring other people to organise events for the charity.

At the start of June, I travelled to Exeter and joined Jeff on his March for Men. It was a great experience, walking a marathon a day, stopping at different football grounds on the way and being joined by the likes of Matt Le Tissier, Charlie Nicholas and Robbie Fowler. I spent time with Jeff and did lots of interviews to promote the work of Prostate Cancer UK through my story. The support from the public was amazing, with people joining us each day and cheering us on. When we got to the Memorial Stadium, the home of Bristol Rovers, their physio had prepared an ice bath for Jeff. Jeff took one look at it and decided it was not for him, but I jumped straight in and sat in the home dressing room bath, freezing cold, getting acclimatised for Iceland later in the year.

At Stoke City I met the late, great Gordon Banks, which was a real thrill because he was one of my great footballing heroes. At the end of every day we were given a medal and at Manchester City another of my heroes, Denis Law was presenting them with Mike Summerbee. I was tired and there was a slightly shorter queue for Mike, so I chose his line. You know when you see people meet dignitaries and famous people on TV, they often say a few words? Well, I didn't really know what to say about his football as it was before my time, so I just told him he was great in the film *Escape to Victory*, although I'm not sure he knew how to take that, even though it was a genuine compliment!

On day nine, I got a phone call from my daughter telling me her grandad, my ex-wife's dad, had sadly died. She had returned to London from Swansea University, where she was studying and asked me if I could take her back to university the following day. I immediately jumped on the train at the end of the day and headed back home. My heart was still set on doing 15 marathons in 15 days for Jeff and the charity, so the following morning I ran 26.2 miles via some non-league football grounds and then drove my daughter back to Swansea. After a good night's sleep, I ran a marathon in Swansea and then drove my daughter home again because it was the end of her term at university. The next day I ran another marathon near home, got the train up to Harrogate and re-joined Jeff for the final three days of the March for Men.

The last day saw us starting from Durham's cricket ground and we were joined by my friend Lloyd Pinder, who I had met at Jeff's march the previous year. Lloyd had terminal cancer and I was shocked to see how much he had deteriorated in 12 months. It was lovely to see him, and we enjoyed our day together, catching up. Sarah also joined us, and it was a thrill to cross the finishing line with her at St James' Park, the home of Newcastle United. At the finish I was honoured to be asked to say a few words and I was proud to have been part of Jeff's fund-raising effort for the charity. The MDS had been a good warm-up for the challenge because my body felt good and it was a very enjoyable couple of weeks being on the road with Jeff.

Walking with Jeff had been the perfect start to my training programme for the 6633 Arctic Ultra. I would be walking across the Arctic and my training plan would build me up to the 45 miles a day I would have to do in March. Stu had recommended I got used to dragging my sled behind me by getting an old car tyre and pulling that on one of my training walks each week. Even though the race was eight months away I knew how important it was to do it properly because I was entering the unknown. It would also help me during the Fire and Ice race in Iceland that was only a couple of months away.

Two weeks after finishing the March for Men, I flew to Spain for a race called the Al Andalus Ultimate which I had signed up for at the start of the year. This was a five-day, 230km ultra-marathon and I felt fit and strong. Unlike the MDS, you run every day without a backpack which is good because you have less to carry but is bad in the fact the cut-off times for each day are shorter (no slow-moving camels in this race). It was as hot as the Sahara and the terrain was mountainous and rocky. I was in my own tent and there were only 80 runners competing and, much like the MDS, the camaraderie was amazing.

The first three days went well. I finished well inside the cut-off time and even though I was knackered, the body felt good. The fourth day was the 'long day': 67km of running from Jayena to Alhama de Granada and it destroyed me. It was the hottest day on record in Granada, with temperatures between 40 and 45 degrees centigrade. To beat the cut-off, I had to run the whole day and with 18km to go I was in pieces. I reached a checkpoint and decided to sit down for ten minutes to try to recover for the final push to the finish. I drank some Coke and slowly got back to my feet, only to be greeted by the race director who told me I had missed the cut-off time and was out of the race. I was devastated and angry with myself because I had gone too hard on the first three days and was now paying the price. Because I had done the MDS I thought I was invincible, and it was a real wake-up call. If I'm honest, I was complacent going into the race and that cost me my medal. I was allowed to run the final day but at the finish all I got was a handshake and no bling round my neck. Half the runners had either missed the cut-off or dropped out of the race and it had proved to be tougher than the MDS because of the cut-off times.

I came home with a feeling of unfinished business. I was gutted not to get a medal and complete the race properly. I didn't know if I would get the chance to do the race again next year because of my cancer. I might not be alive and I desperately wanted the chance to give the race another go. I went back to work for a couple of weeks before we had a family holiday to Canada and my two eldest children, Hayley and Ben, came with us. After our trip to America in 2014, I never thought we would all go away together again because the children would be too old to want to go away with Dad. But I think they really wanted to come because of my diagnosis (plus of course we were going to Canada and they had never been) and we had a wonderful holiday, staying with my brother-in-law in Toronto and creating more happy memories, like going to the Niagara Falls and watching baseball at the Rogers Stadium, home of the Blue Jays.

Shortly after getting home, it was time to head back to Iceland for the Fire and Ice ultra-marathon. My training and preparation had gone well for the 250km, six-day race. I would be carrying a 15kg backpack, which included all my dehydrated food, changes of running kit, sleeping bag and all my drugs. I was also allowed to take a 'drop bag' which had a spare set of kit and would only be given to us if the weather was extremely wet and cold and we needed dry, warmer kit. The previous year, 12 runners had been pulled out of the race in a short space of time due to hypothermia, which illustrated how tough the race was going to be. I had been told that the weather in Iceland could change dramatically in an hour. I was going to be cold and wet and wearing the right kit at the right time would be crucial in preventing me from getting hypothermia. It was going to be the complete opposite to running in the heat of the Sahara. One of my biggest concerns was how I was going to dry my running kit after each day. A side-effect of my cancer drugs is I sweat profusely when I run. I knew my kit would be soaking wet by the end of the day and, unlike the MDS, it wouldn't be drying in the baking sun. Being disciplined with my kit was going to be crucial to me completing the race.

Sarah dropped me at Gatwick Airport, and I met up with some of the runners I would be sharing a tent with. Martin, Mark, and Marcus (the three Ms as they were christened) had been at the Fire and Ice Expo the previous year and we had formed a bond. We had breakfast together at the airport and they were nervous because this was their first overseas multi-day race, whereas I was a little more relaxed. We got on the plane and flew to Reykjavik and were transported on a coach to an airfield where we got on another plane and flew the length of Iceland to Akureyi. The views were amazing, and the Icelandic landscape of glaciers, valleys and volcanoes didn't disappoint. We landed at Akureyi and were transported to a small ski resort. We stayed in chalets and after the obligatory kit check and a hot meal I went to bed. The next morning, we had breakfast, got on the coaches, and were driven to Vatnajokul National Park where the race would start the following day.

The journey was extremely uncomfortable because the road was covered in rocks and we were all bumped around in the coach, but we eventually reached our campsite and discovered the sort of tents we would be sleeping in for the next week. They were inflatable with eight runners in each one. In my tent, as well as Marcus, Martin, and Mark, there was Richard from the MDS, Mike from Canada, Tristan who had been in the United States Air Force and a gent called Georges Beaucoup. Georges was 70 years old and after we introduced ourselves we discovered he lived two miles up the road from me in Epsom and we bonded quickly.

Just like at the MDS, there was no spare space in the tent. We were like sardines in a can and the tent had to be sealed because of the plunging temperatures outside. We quickly discovered condensation was going to be a problem. There was no air flow, it was freezing cold and the condensation was causing everything to get wet. My worries about keeping my kit dry were justified, but there was a buzz of expectation about the race starting the following day. I lay in my sleeping bag, wearing my running kit, excited, nervous and freezing cold knowing it was going to be a tough six days of racing.

I slept ok and woke up to find it was still extremely cold and damp in the tent. We packed our kit and went outside to be greeted by a cold, grey day. It was raining and I got soaked queuing for my boiled water that I needed for my dehydrated breakfast. I stood in the rain eating my porridge and watched our tent disappear on to the back of a truck to be transported to the finish line. I was facing a 36km opening day and I stood at the start line nervous and excited. Only 80 runners were competing, so unlike the MDS there wasn't a massive queue to get going. An Icelandic runner suddenly started the 'Viking Thunderclap' that had become infamous at the European Football Championships the previous year (especially when Iceland beat England!). So, there I was, stood in the middle of Iceland's National Park, in the rain doing the 'Viking Thunderclap' and it was great. Like 'Highway to Hell' being played at the start of the MDS, it got the adrenaline pumping as I began the opening day of Fire and Ice.

The terrain was volcanic ash which was hard to run on and we had to make our way up the side of a huge rock, which meant lots of climbing. The climb was exhausting but we had been told we would get an amazing view of a glacier from the top. Eventually I got there, in the rain, and it was so cloudy you could only see 20ft in front of you and there was no sign of the glacier, which was disappointing. The weather was miserable, but the route was clearly marked so there was no danger of getting lost, which is always one of the fears when you are not navigating a race yourself. Despite the rain and cold, I was able to relax and get into my groove. Halfway through the day I heard one of the runners had tripped on a rock and smashed his face up so badly he had to be taken to hospital. This made me concentrate on where I was putting my feet and I was enjoying the opening day. I reached the final checkpoint and bumped into Victoria, who I had finished the 'long day' with at my first

MDS. It was the first time we had seen each other since then and we stayed together for the remainder of the opening day and crossed the finish line together.

I was tired, cold, wet, and delighted to get through the first day of the race. I realised I hadn't done enough training carrying my 15kg backpack and that had made it tougher than I expected. Back in the tent it was cold and damp. I changed out of my wet kit into my dry kit (which was in my backpack), went and got my boiling water and sat in the tent eating my dehydrated evening meal. It was too cold to go outside the tent, so we all discussed the opening day and agreed it had been hard work. I climbed into my sleeping bag, which was wet thanks to the condensation, knowing there were another five nights like this ahead of me. Tent life was not much fun because of the condensation, the cold, and the lack of space. As you know, I get woken up in the night at regular intervals for my 'prostate cancer wee'. This was no fun in Iceland because I had to get out of a warmish sleeping bag, creep across a freezing tent without stepping on any of my tent-mates, open the tent letting the freezing wind in, do my business whilst shivering outside and creep back to my sleeping bag, I was conscious of waking everybody up and I didn't relish my nightly trips to a bush, although at least there were no potential scorpions to deal with!

The next morning, I woke up freezing cold (it was a common theme of the week) and had to change from my dry kit back into my wet kit, which was horrible. There was no way

2014 The end of innocence, family holiday at Disney when symptoms started but little did I know what was to come

2015 Marathon training on chemo

2015 Brighton marathon, week 13 of chemo with Greg and Jim wearing the team colours (Peter Faris)

2016 On the pitch at Wembley for Liverpool v Manchester City. It was Ben's 16th birthday and I was guest of honour

2016 Tent 105 before starting my first MDS

2016 MDS. Sand, lots of sand, beautiful and brutal in equal measure

2017 Fire and Ice, somewhat colder than the Sahara but equally beautiful

2017 Finishing 15 marathons in 15 days on the March 4 Men with Prostate Cancer UK with Jeff and Lloyd in the Sunderland shirt (Jeremy Banks)

2017 MDS #2 The calm before the storm

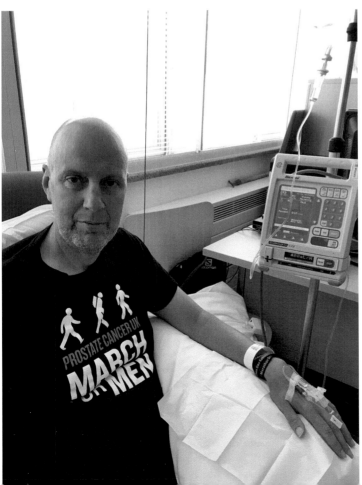

2017 Another infusion of something that will do me good but make me feel bad along the way

2018 With Dad the day before I set off to the Arctic, sadly the last time I would ever see him

2018 The beauty of the 6633 Arctic Ultra, a race of contrasts (Weronika Murray)

2018 Crossing the line second in the 6633 Arctic Ultra, never taken for granted even with only a few miles to go (Evan Davies)

2018 This time I managed to finish Al Andalus Ultimate in Spain after the previous year's disappointment

2018 Global Limits Albania finished more mountainous and hotter than expected but such an unspoilt country

2018 Family escape to New York, rare escapism as a family

of drying your kit overnight, so you had to take off your dry kit and squeeze back into your cold, wet kit for the day ahead. It was a tortuous routine and not the best way to start your day. It was still raining when I went to get my boiling water for breakfast and after our tent disappeared, I made my way to the start line for a 42km day of racing. After the 'Viking Thunderclap', we started running down a volcanic ash road and it stopped raining. I felt good as we arrived at the foot of a steep volcano known as The Queen. After a long climb, I arrived at the top and the sky was blue, the sun was out, and we were above the clouds. The view was spectacular, and my mood lifted. It was still cold, but the sun was shining, the landscape was amazing, and I could feel my kit beginning to dry out. I made my way down the other side of The Queen and continued to slog through the second day of the race. I reached the finish line with the sun shining and headed for our tent which had been put by a river. We were able to open the tent flaps and let some air in and the sun shining meant we were all able to relax outside even though it was still cold. Physically I was tired, and my shins were painful because the lava-field terrain we were running on was like uneven concrete. I wasn't the only person in the tent suffering from sore shins and we all knew they were going to get more painful the longer the race went on.

With no cloud cover, the temperature plummeted in the evening and it was freezing in the tent. We all decided to get into our emergency blankets (the foil ones you see at the end of most marathons), but after a couple of hours we were getting wetter wrapped up in them, because of the condensation, and our sleeping bags were soaking. Someone suggested lying the emergency blanket on top of the sleeping bag, but that kept everyone awake with the condensation dripping off the ceiling and landing on the foil blanket, making a constant noise that was like a form of torture. We tried moving around the tent to avoid the dripping water and eventually we gave up and 'enjoyed' another cold, wet night's sleep.

Day three was 42.8km of hard work. Unsurprisingly, it was cold again and my shins were starting to give me real problems. The terrain was like running on coal and much of the day was spent in these conditions. That evening we were treated to the Aurora Borealis, better known as the Northern Lights, which were spectacular and far more impressive than when I had tried to look at them through a telescope on my trip to Iceland with Sarah earlier in the year. It was a real pull to stay up and watch the swirling green lights for hours but I knew that I needed the sleep, so reluctantly I climbed into my cold, damp sleeping bag, satisfied with the knowledge that I had seen 'the Lights' properly, and knowing tomorrow was the dreaded 'long day'.

I woke up the next morning, cold as ever, facing 70km of Icelandic terrain and because of what happened to me during the 'long day' in Spain, I was going to treat the route with the respect it deserved. I ran most of the day with Victoria and it was tough. Volcanic ash and rocks made running hard work and my shins were very painful. We had to cross two rivers and that was horrific. I had to wade through ice-cold water, holding on to a rope, with my feet and legs getting soaked, trying not to trip over on rocks. I went into both rivers cold and wet and came out even colder and even wetter! We came to an area known as 'Little Sahara' which couldn't be more different from the actual desert. It was a long stretch of volcanic ash and there wasn't a sand dune or a camel to be seen. The highlight of the day was entering an area called 'The Hidden Valley'. It can only be described as an oasis with grass, flowers, insects, birds, and a river running through it. It was beautiful and a welcome contrast for a couple of miles to the volcanic ash.

I got through the day, but my shins were agony and I was concerned I might not finish the race. The final part of the route was at night, across a lava field and I crossed the finish line in 13 hours and immediately went straight to the doctor's because my shins were excruciatingly painful. They were bright red and I was extremely worried. The doctor said there wasn't much they could do, so I hobbled back to the tent and took some painkillers. I then stayed up to watch Georges come across the finish line. As we were waiting, the Northern Lights came out again and Georges came over the line around midnight, lit up by the green fluorescent night sky. For a man of his age, it was a hell of an effort and he was exhausted. I carried his bag to the tent for him and he produced a packet of Jaffa Cakes. He gave everybody one and it was the greatest biscuit I have ever tasted! We all respected Georges for running the race at his age and the Jaffa Cakes had elevated him to legendary status.

That night we were allowed our 'drop bags' because it was so cold, and the organisers were worried about hypothermia. A warm set of clothes meant I had a relatively good night's sleep and the next morning I set off on the 40km route. My shins were incredibly painful and I was unable to run. I got my head down, blocked out the pain with the help of some co-codamol tablets and slowly marched my way across more volcanic ash fields and lava plains. I was relieved to get to the finish because I was in real trouble with my shins. I took some more pain killers and rested in the tent. When all the runners had finished, the organisers drove us to some hot springs and it was amazing to have a proper wash and feel warm for the first time in days. Back at the tent, we were allowed our 'drop bags' again and everybody was in a good mood because tomorrow was the final day of the race – not because we wanted to get home but because everyone just wanted to be clean, warm and dry. I got into my cold, wet sleeping bag for the last time, excited about finishing tomorrow but also worried about the state of my shins.

The final day started with our last 'Viking Thunderclap' and mercifully it was a shorter day of just 20km. That was long enough though because my shins were screaming and I was in agony. It was very cold, and the terrain was rocky. It was hard work as we made our way past more lava fields and every step sent shooting pains up my shins. Eventually I saw a town in the distance and knew that was the finish. It was the first sign of civilisation during the race and thankfully it was downhill to the finish line. With 100 yards to go, all the flags of the world lined the route and I picked up the Union Jack and managed to jog across the finishing line. It was so painful, but I had completed the race and I was a proud man when they hung the medal round my neck. It's all about the bling, after all!

I was directed to a bar and was given a free beer and a bowl of lamb stew. I sat with everybody from the tent and it was a great atmosphere as we all celebrated finishing the race. One of the race volunteers came to find me and explained he had heard about my story and wanted to meet me because his grandfather had died of prostate cancer. It was lovely to meet him and he seemed to get lots off his chest chatting to me. After our lamb stew, we were driven back to the ski resort where we had started the week. After a hot shower, which was wonderful, I hobbled to the celebratory dinner at a restaurant the organisers had booked. It was an enjoyable evening and I had my first warm night's sleep in a week, back at the chalet.

The next day I had a six-hour coach trip back to Reykjavik. I had decided to book a couple of nights at a hotel and with my shins still killing me, I had a quiet meal and went straight to bed. The following morning, I filled my boots at the breakfast buffet and spent the rest of the day hobbling around Reykjavik. I enjoyed an evening meal with Mark and Marcus from the tent who were also staying an extra night and went to bed with extremely sore shins but some amazing memories of Iceland and the 'Fire and Ice' ultra-marathon. I also knew how much harder the 6633 Arctic Ultra was going to be next year. Would I be ready?

Chapter 9

Heading to the Arctic

I FLEW back from Iceland and I could hardly walk because of my shins. I was extremely worried and went to hospital for X-rays which showed I might have stress fractures. I was told to rest and do no running. That wasn't a problem because walking was agony, but it was frustrating. My biggest concern was I had done long-term damage and I had to stop training for the 6633 Arctic Ultra. I went back to work and life carried on. Prostate Cancer UK invited me to their gala dinner and asked my friend Lloyd Pinder (who also had a terminal diagnosis) and me to do a joint presentation. I met a cancer researcher at the dinner called Hayley. At the start of the year, the charity had asked me to write a letter to her explaining how important her work was to me and my family. She told me she had framed the letter and had it on her wall at work for inspiration, which made me feel extremely proud. Lloyd and I gave our presentation, which was emotional because it was in front of our family and friends who had joined us for the evening. After the dinner, we all sat in the hotel bar and it was lovely to be amongst the people who were most important to Lloyd and me, and understood what we were going through.

I returned to hospital to have my shins examined and was told to continue resting. My frustration was growing and there was a date in my diary coming up that was important to me. Rory, from the MDS, was running his 1,000th marathon at the end of September in Nottingham. He had intended to run it in 2016 but had been diagnosed with Guillain Barre Syndrome and had been unable to. Before heading to Iceland, I had signed up for the marathon without telling Rory, so I could surprise him on the day. My shins were so bad, there was no way I was going to be able to do the marathon with him and I had to make the gut-wrenching decision not to go. The night before the race, I went for a curry with Sarah and halfway through my chicken madras and with three pints of Cobra inside me, I said, 'I've got to go to Nottingham. It's Rory's 1,000th marathon and after everything he has been through, I have to be there.' I finished my curry, went home, grabbed some sleep, and left for Nottingham in the early hours of the morning.

I messaged Rory's wife to find out where they were meeting and when I arrived the first people I saw were Chris and Phil from Tent 105. It was the first time I had seen them since the Sahara and we all surprised Rory. I decided to try and run the first half of the race, and see how my shins held up. About five miles into the race, a guy tapped me on the shoulder and asked me if that was the Marathon des Sables tattoo on my calf and

I proudly told him it was, and it felt like a badge of honour. A little later I saw a girl running in a Prostate Cancer UK shirt and asked her why she was running for the charity. She told me her father had prostate cancer and I told her my story. She burst into tears, which I hadn't expected, and I realised again the impact my story could have on people.

The four members of Tent 105 were carrying injuries and we struggled round the course. With 400 yards to go, Rory's wife appeared with two of his children in a buggy and he pushed them over the finishing line with us. Nick from Tent 105 was waiting and he was on crutches due to a dodgy ankle. It was fantastic to run Rory's 1,000th marathon and I was so glad I made the late decision to go and do the race. It proved that I had to take every opportunity that came my way and I drove home knowing if I hadn't gone, I would have regretted it for ever.

My shins, however, were regretting me running the marathon. I had to knock running on the head again and rest because they were so painful. Prostate Cancer UK invited me to a conference of postgraduate students doing research into the early stages of the disease, part-funded by the charity. I gave my presentation and then heard presentations from the students about many projects they were working on to eradicate prostate cancer, which was fascinating to hear. Furthermore, I was pleased to see how the money I was raising was being used. Meeting a group of young, motivated, inspiring postgraduates was wonderful and I hoped that by meeting me they realised how important their work was. I had agreed to meet an independent film maker called Richard Alexander at the event. Richard had got in touch with me about the possibility of making a documentary on my cancer story. Richard filmed some of my presentation to the students and after chatting to him I was excited at the idea of being part of the documentary that might provide another potential legacy. We agreed to meet again and discuss the project in more detail and I was delighted he had an interest in filming my story.

In September I travelled to Bristol for a gala dinner, organised by my friend Nick Butter. Nick, as you might remember, had been in Tent 105 at my first MDS. We had got on very well and had spent lots of time together and one afternoon in the Sahara he had explained that he had a number of 'epic challenges' that he wanted to do, but I thought he might never do them because of his work and being stuck in the 'rat race'. After listening to him, I looked him in the eyes and said, 'Don't wait for a rubbish prognosis before you realise what you must do.' I could see he was young, fit, healthy and might not get the opportunities if normal life carried on for him like it does for most of us. I must admit I didn't really think about that conversation again until Nick rang me a few months later and told me our chat had inspired him to give up work and run 196 marathons, one marathon in every country of the world. He would be the first person ever to do this if he achieved it! Because of me he wanted to raise funds for Prostate Cancer UK. I was amazed and he asked me to talk at his gala dinner alongside Rory and Jeff from Tent 105. It was a terrific evening, which raised lots of money for the charity. I was proud my chat with Nick in the middle of the Sahara had inspired him to take on this monumental challenge and if he managed to complete it then, in a small way, I would be the inspiration for a world first.

Sarah, Ollie, and I went to Venice for the October halfterm and I organised a private taxi speedboat to take us to our hotel. It was my way of giving Sarah and Ollie a special memory because they were going through my journey with me and it was just as hard for them. My PSA scores were still heading in the right direction, but my shins were continuing to give me real problems. Even walking was hard work and painful and there was no sign of improvement. Even though the fracture clinic had signed me off I was worried I had caused permanent damage by running the Nottingham marathon. I took the decision to book an appointment with Dr Simon Kemp who was a specialist at the Parkside Hospital in Wimbledon. Simon was (and still is at the time of writing) the head of sports medicine at the Rugby Football Union and he was the team physician when England won the World Cup in 2003. He examined my shins and told me my left leg was 40 per cent stronger than my right and gave me a specific set of exercises to strengthen my right leg. He also told me to continue resting, so it was good and bad news. By doing the exercises my shins would get better, but I had to be patient because it would take time that I didn't feel I had with my cancer and the 6633 Arctic Ultra in March. I hobbled back to my car after the appointment and coming the other way was a guy called Colin who I had met during the Fire and Ice race. He had a similar problem with his shins and it confirmed Icelandic terrain may not be good for your lower legs!

I had been having acupuncture once a month since my first MDS and also taking Chinese herbal medicine twice a day (both of which I still do today) and I'm convinced this helped with my cancer, but I was also hoping it would help my shins. I started seeing a physiotherapist once a week and the combination of rest, the right strengthening exercises, acupuncture and physiotherapy started to work. By mid-November walking wasn't painful and I slowly started training again for the 6633 Arctic Ultra. I had been told by one of the organisers that the race was flat terrain and I didn't need to do any specific hill training. I got the car tyre out of the shed and started dragging that behind me once a week. I was feeling stronger and fitter and by the time I got to the race in March I wanted to be walking over 30 hours a week, so there was lots of training to be done. I knew fitting training around work was going to be difficult, but the bank were once again incredibly supportive. After explaining to them the training I needed to do for the 6633 Arctic Ultra, they agreed to be even more flexible to allow me to train properly (in fact it was the chief executive who signed it off!). I got back in touch with Andy, who I had walked the Gatlif Marathon with at the end of 2016, and we started meeting at weekends and walking between 15 and 30 miles.

I continued giving my presentations for the charity and the bank, including a return trip to Jersey, and I had another meeting with Richard, the filmmaker. When I told him what I was planning for the next year, he got quite excited and said that he wanted to come and film some of the races and spend more time with me. I was happy to have Richard with me because the documentary would be something else that I could leave for my family and that would hopefully inspire others.

At the start of December, I returned to the Royal Marsden Hospital, for my second infusion of zoledronic acid to help strengthen my bones which were weakened by my cancer. This time I knew the infusion would be in the chemotherapy room and decided I was going to share my story with the people receiving their chemotherapy treatment. I took my iPad with pictures of me on the MDS and Fire and Ice and whilst I was having my infusion, I chatted to the three people in the room and told them my story. I wanted them to believe their lives were not over and I left hoping I had made a positive impact on them.

I travelled back to the Brecon Beacons for the 6633 Arctic Ultra Expo and learnt more about what I would be taking on in March. It was a massive eye-opener as the organisers talked about frostbite, the hostile environment of the Arctic, the kit we would need to survive and how we had to be self-sufficient during the race. I met people who had done the race and got a better picture of what I was facing. I bought a tonne of kit and ordered the sled that I would be dragging behind me.

There were only 30 people doing the race and I was told that in some previous races nobody had completed it because of the conditions! I left the Expo feeling scared but excited about the challenge I was taking on and avoided telling Sarah about how much the kit I had bought cost me (us!).

Just before Christmas I was honoured to be invited to a lunch at the House of Lords. When I had done the March for Men with Jeff Stelling, I had met Michael Tattersall who was the chief executive of the National Football League. We got on extremely well and he kindly invited me to the lunch, which I was proud about because he thought I was making a difference and wanted people to hear my story.

We enjoyed a family Christmas and in early January I attended Nick Butter's farewell lunch before he set off on his challenge of running a marathon in every country of the world. It was mind-blowing what Nick was taking on and after meeting his parents I felt guilty that I had inspired him to leave them for over a year to run his marathons. I was so proud of Nick but worried he had taken on too big a challenge. I felt a strong personal responsibility for his safety and feared what his parents would say if something happened to Nick on his journey.

I continued training for the 6633 Arctic Ultra, including more trips to the Brecon Beacons, and my pulk sled that I would be pulling across the Arctic arrived. It was specially designed so wheels could be attached for the ice roads and I felt like a proper explorer once I had figured out how to put it all together! I was training hard and completed my largest hike in a day with Andy, over 30 miles across Surrey on The Fox Way. I got back to the car at the end of the day completely shattered, which worried me because in the Arctic I would be walking 45 miles a day, in freezing conditions, for hopefully nine consecutive days, with little sleep whilst pulling a sled. Driving home I was scared that the race was only two months away and I still had a huge amount of training to do. Richard had confirmed he was coming to the Arctic to film for the documentary because we agreed it was a terrific opportunity to record unique footage in hostile conditions. *Runner's World* magazine wrote an article about me, which was an honour and a thrill as it's a magazine in which I had read about so many inspirational runners over the years and now I was one of them!

At the start of February, I completed my third Pilgrims Challenge. I knew all the organisers and lots of the runners and it was great to be back with the grass-roots ultra-marathon family. I was asked to give a presentation after the first day, a huge honour to speak in front of other ultra-marathon runners. I spoke with Elizabet Barnes who had won the MDS twice and who I had listened to at my first Pilgrim Challenge. I walked both days of the race and my body and, more importantly, my legs felt good.

Sarah and I then went away for a few days to the Peak District, staying in Castleton, which is a special place for us because it is where I proposed to her. We did lots of walking, which was perfect for my training, and it was lovely to have some quality time together and create some more happy memories.

My focus was on the 6633 Arctic Ultra and I was walking 40 hours a week, including back-to-back days of 12 hours. I was doing my strengthening exercises and felt as ready as I was ever going to be to tackle the Arctic. Unfortunately, my dad was not well. He was 87 and had suffered from different cancers over the years. My mum had died in 2002 and he had lived on his own for 16 years. He was a stoic man and had always supported me, but his health had gradually deteriorated. He was admitted to hospital at the start of February and my brother and I took turns to visit him every day. One day Dad's doctor told us there was no more they could do for him in the hospital and we were going to be given a palliative care programme, so he could spend his last few months at home. The night before I left for the Arctic, I went to visit him in the hospital and he was in great spirits, telling everybody on the ward about the race and I could tell he was proud of me. I took our first and only selfie on my phone and left, feeling he was ok and looking forward to seeing him when I got back from the Arctic.

That evening I packed for the race. I filled two massive suitcases with enough dehydrated food to last nine days, because my intention was to do the long race. I had double sets of all my kit because I was allowed a 'drop bag' at the 120- and 240-mile checkpoints. I had base layers, top layers, two pairs of tights, a pair of overtrousers, a down jacket, two pairs of boots, a heavy-duty gas cooker, hats, sunglasses, goggles, headtorches, walking poles, medical kit including all my drugs and my all-important tent. I had practised putting my single-skinned tent up during my training and was able to assemble it in two minutes. Unlike the MDS, nobody would be taking my tent and putting it up for me. I had to be totally self-sufficient. My aim was to walk 45 miles a day, grab some sleep then get up and keep walking. I was taking a tonne of kit and I went to bed nervous and excited about what lay ahead.

The following morning Sarah and Ollie dropped me and my kit at Heathrow Airport. Unlike the MDS, I was on my own. There were only 26 competitors in the race, and everybody was flying in at different times from all over the world. Richard, who was making the documentary about me, was flying the following day, so I was travelling to Canada on my own. My brother-in-law, who lives in Toronto, had managed to use his air miles to get me upgraded to business class for the whole journey, which was amazing because I had never turned left on the plane before. After checking in my kit, including my sled, I went and relaxed in the Air Canada Business Class lounge. I was facing a long journey from London to Whitehorse, with changes at Toronto and Vancouver. I was worried about whether all my kit would make it to Whitehorse, but once I was on the plane and settled into my business class seat, all those worries disappeared. It was a strange feeling being waited on hand and foot, knowing in a few days' time I was going to be in the middle of the Arctic fending for myself, I did feel very privileged to be sitting there and so lucky to be going to the race when so many others in my situation were not able to, due to health reasons.

After a 21-hour journey, I eventually touched down in Whitehorse, Canada. There were some other competitors on the small plane for the final leg of the journey and in the small terminal Martin, the race director, was waiting for us. I then had the anxious wait to see if all my kit would appear on the baggage carrousel. Thankfully, it did and I walked out of the airport and was immediately hit by the cold. It was midnight and the temperature was -10 as we were driven to our hotel. I checked into my room that I would share with Richard when he arrived the following day and went straight to sleep.

The next morning, I woke up knowing we had a couple of days in Whitehorse before we were transported to the start of the race. I had breakfast and spent the rest of the day wandering around Whitehorse and meeting some of the other competitors. It was incredibly cold and felt like I was walking in a freezer. We were still 300 miles from the Arctic where, I kept getting told, it would be 'properly cold'! Whitehorse is a town built for cold weather and I enjoyed my day trying to acclimatise to the sort of conditions I would be facing. Richard arrived in the evening and we had dinner together and chatted about his plans to film me during the race.

At breakfast the following day, I checked my phone and there was a message from one of my dad's friends that said, 'I'm so sorry about your dad'. I phoned Sarah straight away and she confirmed the sad news that my dad had died the night before which, to be honest, I had already guessed from the previous sympathetic email. I then called my brother and he told me what had happened the night before with my dad passing. My brother and I had agreed that if anything happened to my dad he wouldn't let me know until I had finished the race because there was nothing I could have done from Canada. The kind message from my dad's friend, had made me find out the news about my dad unexpectedly and I was incredibly sad. I wasn't sure what to do, but after digesting the news I decided to stay and do the race because that is what I think my dad would have wanted. Plus, I would have plenty of time to focus on my dad during the race and think about everything he had achieved and done for me during his life.

I went to a race briefing where we were given our race number and a final presentation on what we might encounter in the Arctic. We were told about foxes, wolves, bears and moose, the latter being very aggressive and well capable of chasing us! The biggest warning we were given was about frostbite and we were advised to wear three pairs of gloves and never to take the bottom pair off. Frostbite was the biggest reason for people dropping out of the race in years gone by: I say dropping out, but in reality the competitor usually does not realise they have an issue and it takes a medic who routinely checks out the competitors every few hours to spot the symptoms of frostbite and pull out the disappointed competitor. Then we were warned about sweating too much because that could freeze and lead to frostbite. That made me really worried because, as I explained earlier, the drugs I am on make me sweat profusely when I exercise. I left the briefing knowing this was a race that could kill me if I didn't treat it with the respect it deserved.

In the afternoon, we had a practice walk wearing all our kit, pulling our sleds, and putting up our tents. This was so the organisers could check we at least had some idea of what we were doing in the icy conditions before letting us loose effectively on our own. We all gathered outside the hotel and walked for an hour, pulling our sleds through the snow. We stopped and had to put up our tents, boil some water and make a cup of tea. As I was putting up my tent, the end of one of the poles snapped, which meant it wouldn't erect as it was meant to do. I could still get in it, which was all that mattered, but I couldn't believe the pole had snapped at the first attempt and I wasn't even on the actual race in the Arctic yet. I made my cup of tea, packed the tent back into the sled and we all marched back to the hotel. Our sleds were put on a trailer to be transported to the start line and that evening we had a meal together and went to bed because we were facing a 300-mile drive tomorrow to the start of the race.

The 26 of us travelled in a convoy of cars on the eight-hour drive along frozen, snowy roads to the start line at Eagle Plains. The scenery was spectacular as we drove between mountains, through forests, past vast expanses of white virgin snow, under blue skies with the sun shining. Every time we stopped for a break, I got out of the car and the cold hit me and the reality of what I was facing continued to grow. We eventually reached Eagle Plains in the dark. Eagle Plains consists of a hotel that sits on a road called the Dempster Highway. I got my kit off the trailer and we were allocated our rooms in the hotel. Richard and I made our way to the bar to get some food. In the bar was a massive stuffed moose. All in, with antlers, it was about 12ft high and scared the bejesus out of me. I said a silent prayer that I would not be seeing one of those for real in the next nine days. After dinner I put my sled together, ready for the morning and I put a green sticker on the back, with 'Dad' written on it, so I would have him with me for the whole race. I climbed into bed knowing it would be my last night of any kind of proper sleep before I started my epic race into the Arctic.

Chapter 10

Crossing the Arctic Circle

PANIC. THAT'S all I felt waking up at the Eagle Plains hotel. I had three hours to eat, get packed, dressed, and ready for the start of the 6633 Arctic Ultra. After a large breakfast, my last proper meal for nine days, I filled my flasks with boiling water (which took a long time because all the competitors were doing the same thing) and packed all my kit into the sled. It was a rush, but finally I was ready to get my race started. I walked to the front of the hotel with the other 25 competitors and strapped my sled to my waist. The weather was cold, sunny and crisp and ten yards in front of us was the long ice road of the Dempster Highway. A banner with the race logo was fluttering in the breeze and a 'road closed' barrier had been opened for us. Spot trackers had been put on all our sleds so the organisers could locate us, because once we started, we were effectively on our own. I stood in the cold, excited, nervous and just wanting to get started. Suddenly, Eleanor, the lady who owned the hotel, came out with a shotgun, fired it into the air and we were away.

I started walking north, along the Dempster Highway and the first 10km were downhill. I felt good, pulling my 30kg sled towards the Arctic Circle although I had noticed some of the Romanian competitors had started the race by running along the ice road! I arrived at Eagle River, which was surrounded by the most beautiful scenery, crossed a bridge, and came to a steep assent up the ice road. I was with a guy called Ian, who had done the race before, and he had a sled which allowed you to pull the wheels into the side rather than having to physically take them off. When we came to the big downward slope, I couldn't believe it when he pulled his wheels up, lay face down in his sled and slid off down the ice road. He shot off, completely lost control, slid all over the road and crashed into a snowbank. He got up laughing and waved back at me. There was no way I was going to follow Ian's lead and I slowly made my way down the slope and got into a good rhythm.

I followed the ice road for another 15 kilometres and reached the foot of a hill. I was on my own and decided to have something to eat. I poured boiling water from my thermos flask into one of my dehydrated meals which I stuffed down my jacket and started walking up the hill. I was tired but enjoying myself and after ten minutes, my meal had cooked, and I ate it on the move.

I was wearing a backpack that had a bladder in it filled with drinking water. A pipe ran from the bladder, over my shoulder so when I need a drink all I had to do was suck on the pipe. I was thirsty after the meal but when I sucked on the pipe no water came out and I realised it must have frozen. This was a disaster because I needed to drink and stay hydrated, but I decided to wait and try and fix it at the first checkpoint. I kept walking along the ice road which for a mile also became an emergency airstrip where we had been warned to look out for planes landing. After 37km, I reached the checkpoint and the start of the Arctic Circle. There was a trailer which had benches and a heater inside it, and I tried to sort out the problem with my drinking pipe. I worked out if I put the bladder down my front and had the pipe coming straight up to my mouth, my body heat would stop it freezing. The only problem was it was awkward and uncomfortable having the bladder tucked into my trousers, but it was the only solution I could come up with.

I ate another meal, got some more boiling water for my thermos flasks and night was falling as I left the checkpoint. I put on my headtorch and followed the light of a couple of competitors ahead of me. I was still walking on a gravelly icy road with snowbanks on either side and as I made my way deeper into the Arctic, I started thinking about my dad. The euphoria of starting and being in the race had disappeared and this was the first opportunity for me to think about him properly in the total silence of the Arctic. As I walked along the ice road, the Northern Lights came out and lit up the night sky. This was not a small performance but a sky-filling exhibition of swirling purple, red and green light and it was an amazing sight. It felt like my dad was looking down at me and it was a peaceful and beautiful experience.

Physically I was feeling ok, but I was tired and eventually I reached an area known as Sheep Creek, which was just ahead of a steep descent known as the Big Dipper. I had walked 64km and I noticed some of my fellow competitors had stopped to sleep. I felt it was too early to stop, so I headed down the Big Dipper and arrived at a place called Rock River. I saw an old barn that the organisers had told us we could sleep in, but I was on my own, it was night and it looked very spooky. There was no way I was going to sleep there and even if I had wanted to, the snow was so deep it would be very difficult to reach it. I couldn't put my tent up on the frozen road because occasionally trucks would be driving along it and there was a danger of being run over too. I decided to keep going even though I was exhausted, but around an hour later I reached the Rock River campground and saw an official 6633 Arctic Ultra trailer. I clambered on board, sat by the heater and ate a hot meal. There were two people asleep in their sleeping bags, so I asked a race organiser if I could sleep in the trailer. He told me I couldn't and the two people asleep were competitors who had already dropped out of the race; that was a wake-up call for sure.

After getting warm, I left the trailer and noticed some tents in an area where the snow wasn't deep. I decided to put my tent up, because it was near the trailer and I needed to sleep. I unharnessed my sled, put up my tent and climbed into my sleeping bag at three in the morning. I slept badly, on and off for three hours, and heard everyone else leaving. I slowly got out of my tent and it was freezing. I ate a hot meal and started walking as the sun came up, with 77km of the race behind me. I reached the foot of the infamous Wright Pass which is a 22km uphill climb. It was hard work, pulling the sled in freezing conditions, in biting winds, and I was totally exposed. I kept climbing and started to notice the ice road disappearing into a white haze a mile or so ahead. The strong wind was blowing the snow around me and I was struggling to pull my sled through the snow drifts that had formed. It was so cold I knew I was never going to be able to remove the wheels off my sled and it kept getting stuck. Suddenly out of the white haze a car appeared with Martin, the race director in it. He told me that further ahead the snow was horrendous, and he had just pulled two competitors out of the race who were stuck in the blizzard. He asked me if I wanted to continue, which of course I did, and he told me I would have to start doing loops back down Wright Pass to Rock River until the blizzard had stopped. I turned around and headed back down to Rock River and then started climbing back up Wright Pass. I was gradually joined by six other competitors and after a few hours, Martin arrived in the car and told us the blizzard had stopped and he was going to drive us over Wright Pass to the next checkpoint at a place called James Creek. We got in the car and were driven to James Creek where the checkpoint was in a depot for all the snow ploughs that cleared the ice roads.

My plans had been messed up because I had intended to walk to James Creek, have a quick stop and keep going. It was four in the afternoon, later than I thought, and I decided to sleep in the depot and then walk through the night. I put my sleeping bag down amongst the snow ploughs, but everywhere stank of oil and every half an hour there was an announcement on the loudspeakers requesting a plough to head out and clear the snow off the roads. I slept off and on and after four hours decided to get going again. I ate a hot meal, put on my headtorch, and walked into the night. I wasn't sure how many kilometres I had done because of the loops on Wright Pass and it was bitterly cold. The ice road seemed to go up one hill, followed by another and it was relentless, false summit after false summit. I had no idea where I was and felt shattered.

Mentally I was in pieces, having had little sleep at the depot and I started hallucinating. I looked to my left and saw Dover dockyard in the snow. To my right there was a filing cabinet and I thought to myself, 'what sort of person fly-tips a filing cabinet inside the Arctic Circle?' I was in serious trouble and every shadow I saw was scaring the life out of me. I started falling asleep as I was walking, drifting across the road, and waking up when I bumped into the snowbanks on either side of the road. I needed to find somewhere to put my tent up and get some rest. I couldn't sleep on the road as I knew a competitor called Didier had been pulled out of the race after having to move his tent off the road, getting wet then suffering the early onset of hypothermia with no way of drying out or warming up. I was panicking and each time I saw a patch of snow where I thought I could put the tent up, there were paw prints, which scared me even more. I didn't know what to do but I suddenly saw a lay-by where the snow wasn't too deep and most importantly there weren't any paw prints. I staggered over to it, put my tent up, climbed into my icy sleeping bag and tried to go to sleep. It was so cold out there that you had to sleep with your water and boots in your sleeping bag so that they didn't freeze and I was paranoid about the water leaking into my bag but it just had to be done that way if I wanted to not get my cooker out and melt snow for water, which really is a last resort.

Every time I drifted off I thought I could hear other competitors' footsteps going past the tent which made me anxious about stopping, but I knew I needed sleep. For three hours I lay in my tent, and after probably sleeping for 30 minutes in total, I decided to start walking again. I poured boiling water into a dehydrated meal, stuck that down my front and got out of the tent. I immediately saw paw prints surrounding where I had been trying to sleep. The footsteps I had heard in the snow would have been those of my fellow competitors but also some sort of animal that had been walking around the tent. It might have been a squirrel, but it could have been a wolf and my brain was so tired it gave me a proper fright. I quickly packed up my tent, strapped on my sled and started walking along the icy road. We had been taught to leave our sled in the direction we were travelling because people had been known to get up and go back the wrong way, and that was a godsend because at that moment I just went the way my sled was facing without thinking.

The sun was coming up and I was shattered. I ate my meal on the move, got my head down and plodded on. The gravelly, icy, snowy road went on for miles and it was high up so you could see it going off into the distance, which was mentally tough because there seemed to be no end in sight. My hot meal decided to come back and haunt me and the snow on either side of the road was too deep to go into so I was left with no choice but to squat down in the road and do my business there and then. I was about to clear it up when I saw a police car coming down the road towards me. I started panicking, thinking I was going to be arrested for 'defecating in the Arctic' as the police car's flashing lights came on. I felt guilty but kept on walking and the car pulled up beside me. The driver stuck his head out of the window, asked me how I was doing and wished me good luck for the rest of the race. Visions of Sarah visiting me in a Canadian jail disappeared and I continued walking, not having the energy, physically or mentally, to go back and clear up what I had left.

Eventually I came to a steep descent that was difficult to walk down, but I slowly made my way to the bottom and arrived at Peel River Ice Crossing. This was the 174km mark of the race, but I couldn't remember how much farther it was to the Fort McPherson checkpoint and the 120-mile point. I slowly made my way across the river and a car pulled up alongside me, driven by a competitor who had dropped out of the race. I asked how far it was to the checkpoint and she said it was only a couple of kilometres away. It was fantastic news because I was hungry, tired, and cold but there wasn't too far to go until I could have a rest and something to eat and, at that point, I thought I could manage another 2km. Even though I was knackered, I was still going to continue the race after the checkpoint because my intention had always been to do nine days even though I had entered the '120+' race.

I kept walking but there was no sign of the checkpoint. I walked and walked, desperately looking for some sign of Fort McPherson and eventually after ten kilometres I saw a race flag with a race official standing next to it. I walked to the flag and the official looked at me and said, 'You owe us 8.2km because of the lift we gave you to James Creek. I need you to walk up this hill to the cone with your name on it and them come back here.' I couldn't believe it. I was hungry, tired, mentally in pieces and now I had to do at least another hour of walking. I slowly started moving up the hill, feeling completely deflated. My intention of doing all nine days went out of the window at that point because I can only describe having to do the extra kilometres as the massive steel girder that broke the camel's back. In the blink of an eye, I had gone from getting to the checkpoint, having a rest, and continuing the race to wanting to stop and go no further. My spirit was broken, but I managed to get to the cone and back to the flag, where Stuart my mate from the Brecon Beacons was waiting for me. Physically and mentally I was wrecked as Stuart walked me into Fort McPherson. As we were getting to the school hall where the checkpoint was, Martin the race organiser stopped me and asked if I was finishing or carrying on. At that moment I was done, and I told him I was finishing. I was cheered over the finishing line when I arrived at the sports hall and Martin told me I had come second in the '120' race. The elation of finishing and coming second filled me with a euphoric sense of pride.

I dumped my kit, saw the doctor who checked me for frostbite, ate a hot meal and went to sleep. I woke up the following morning, had breakfast and chatted to the other competitors who had finished or dropped out of the race. I realised my body felt ok and all I had needed was some sleep and part of me regretted not continuing the race. But deep down I knew I would never have completed the whole race because it was so tough. The next day we were driven 95 miles to the tiny village of Aklavic, which was the fifth checkpoint on the race. I wanted to support the competitors that were still doing the race and not spend the next few days hanging around waiting for my flight home. Aklavic was a desolate place, a small village with spread out buildings covered in heavy snow. The village was on top of a hill, meaning it was exposed and even colder.

We got out of the cars and went into a building that surprisingly had a games room, complete with pool table, a small kitchen and bizarrely an empty swimming pool. This was our home for the next couple of days whilst we waited for the competitors still in the race to come through the checkpoint. I helped tidy the room and sorted out a space for my kit.

The atmosphere was strange because our group was made up of competitors who had dropped out of the race or had finished the '120' like me (in fact I was one of only two people to finish the '120', along with a guy called Rob who came first). There was a mixture of disappointment and wanting to go home, so I spoke to one of the race organisers and asked if they had any problems with me walking out to meet the competitors and giving them some company on their way to the checkpoint. They had no problem with me doing that, so I spent the next couple of days meeting competitors between 5 and 10km from Aklavic and walking them back to the checkpoint. I was in awe of their efforts and I think they enjoyed having the company and support. Once we were in the games room I would make meals for them, put boiling water in their thermos flasks and try and help them in any way I could. I enjoyed being constructive and I still had plenty of miles in my legs, so it was good to be back out there, walking in the Arctic on a frozen river ice road.

Some of the competitors were struggling when they got to the checkpoint and sadly had to be pulled out of the race, including a lovely guy called Patrick who had suffered frostbite and Ian who had skated down the hill on his sled on the first morning of the race. I caught up with Richard who was making the documentary about me. It was the first time I had seen him properly since the start of the race because he had been based with the support team and had been filming the leaders from the car. We went for a walk around Aklavik, watched the locals play ice hockey and on the second evening we were invited by the locals to a presentation where they treated us to some traditional 'drum dancing'. They told us the history of the village, which was fascinating, and not for the first time I felt privileged to be part of something amazing in an incredible part of the world.

The final competitor to leave the checkpoint was called Tony, who was told in no uncertain terms he had to get on with it because he was in real danger of missing the cut-off time at the finish. Once Tony had left, we packed up and drove 70 miles from Aklavik to a town called Inuvik. The journey was on ice roads as we went further into the Arctic Circle. Just before we reached Inuvik, we were treated to the bizarre sight of huge tanker ships that were frozen by the side of the ice road, as we were driving along a mile-wide frozen estuary. It reminded me how vast the Arctic was and I felt very small. We were taken to some huts known as the 'Arctic Chalets' and these formed the sixth checkpoint of the race. I was put in a chalet with two competitors who had dropped out of the race, Jerome and Didier. I let them have the beds and I slept on the floor; this was our home for two nights. We were a day ahead of the competitors still doing the race and the good news was Inuvik was not a dry town like Aklavik. We found a local bar and spent the afternoon having a few beers and letting our hair down. On the first night, I walked back to the frozen ships and supported a couple of competitors on their walk to the checkpoint, including a lady called Jen who was in the Canadian police force.

With only a handful of competitors left in the race there were fewer people to walk in with so, along with another couple from the race, I took the once in a lifetime opportunity to go dog sledging. I have always been a bit wary of dogs, but it was impossible not to fall in love with the huskies and my team of five pulling me along the frozen wastes is an experience I will never forget.

The next morning, we drove to a town called Tuktoyaktuk, which was the official finishing point of the 6633 Arctic Ultra. Tuk, as it's commonly known, is in a hilly region on the shores of the Arctic Ocean and on the 90-mile journey there we drove past the competitors still walking along the ice roads. Arriving in Tuk, we were taken to the local school where we would be staying for a couple of days. The kids treated us like visiting dignitaries as were shown to the sports hall, where we put crash mats down and sorted out individual spaces for everyone. After a good night's sleep, Richard and I did some recording for the documentary, including footage of me walking in the snow on the frozen Arctic Ocean and talking about my feelings about the race. On our way back to the school we passed the local headquarters of the Canadian Mounted Police. A policeman saw us and invited us in for a coffee and a look round. We were treated to a conducted tour of the tiny police station and I was amazed to find out that there were only eight mounted police covering an area the size of England. We were also shown the police cells and I had a flashback fear of being put in one after squatting in the middle of the ice road and depositing my dinner during the race.

Later, I also went for a walk across the Arctic Ocean on my own, which was spectacular. There was nothing but a white expanse as far as the eye could see and, as I was marching along, a local man turned up on his skidoo and offered me a lift back to town. He ended up giving me a tour of the area and for half an hour I rode the Arctic Ocean on the back of a skidoo, another happy memory to keep forever.

Richard had done some filming at the school and they asked me to talk to the children about my story. I explained why I was there and how important it was to chase your dreams and it was a privilege to talk to the kids at a school on the edge of the Arctic Ocean. Richard filmed my talk and got some footage of me meeting the kids and it was a special afternoon. Afterwards they took great pride in showing me a video of the day that the polar bears came to town. Various web cams had caught a couple of polar bears behaving like unruly teenagers bashing into things before being chased away by the locals in pick-ups.

Every time we heard a competitor was near the finish, we jumped in the cars, drove from the school to the edge of the Arctic Ocean and set up the finishing line. Several times, I walked out to meet them but always left them to walk the last kilometre and cross the line on their own, because that was their moment. The first across the finishing line was a Romanian called Tibi who won the race by over half a day. He was awesome and had won the race the previous year as well. Second over the line was Tony, who had left Aklavik in last place and had somehow managed to overtake everybody, apart from Tibi. I loved cheering everybody over the line and helping to make them feel special. Over three days all the remaining competitors finished the race including an ex-SAS soldier called Pete. He had been forced to drop out of the previous year's race, with only a few miles to go to the finish. He had stopped to help somebody whose sled had collapsed, took his gloves off and got frostbite. I was delighted for him that he had come back and managed to finish the race.

When the final competitor came over the line we went back to the sports hall, packed the kit, said goodbye to Tuk and started the 383-mile drive back to Eagle Plains where the race had started nine days ago. The nine-hour journey gave me plenty of time to think about the size of what I had achieved. I was proud that a man with terminal cancer had managed to come second in the '120' race but I was disappointed to have stopped at Fort McPherson. I wasn't sure if I would do the race again and give myself the opportunity to go farther because it was a huge commitment and extremely expensive. I pay for every race I enter, so each penny I raise goes to the charity and the 6633 Arctic Ultra understandably cost an awful lot to compete in. As we drove to Eagle Plains, I thought if somehow the chance ever presented itself to come back and do the race again, I would be better prepared from the lessons I had learnt.

We eventually arrived at the Eagle Plains hotel and went straight to the bar and celebrated the end of the race, long into the night. The next morning, we drove back to Whitehorse and I was sad my adventure was coming to an end (the hangover might have had something to do with how I was feeling!). We arrived at Whitehorse late in the afternoon and I still had two days ahead of me before my journey home. That evening there was a prize-giving ceremony in the hotel and I was presented with a statue for being one of only eight competitors to finish the race distance they had entered. I had prepared little bottles of stones from the ice road, that I gave to the competitors I had got close to including Patrick, who had been forced to pull out of the race because of frostbite. I think it cheered him up because by not finishing the race he felt he had let his family down. I subsequently found out that, to this day, he still has the bottle, so he must have been pleased with it.

I spent the following day wandering around Whitehorse, saying goodbye to the competitors who were leaving (including film maker Richard who was heading home) and having a session with a physiotherapist I found. My knees and ankles were painful, and my body was still sore as I made my way to the airport to start my journey home. I was one of the last to leave and when I arrived in Vancouver I was on my own. Thanks to my brother-in-law my flight home was in business class, but it was strange to have left the Arctic and everyone I had shared the experience with. I was now facing the reality of losing my dad and only having two weeks until I headed back to the Sahara for my third Marathon des Sables.

Chapter 11

Saying goodbye to Dad

COMING HOME from any race is lovely but returning from the Arctic was different because of the passing of my dad. My brother Ian and Sarah had been dealing with everything whilst I had been away and the day after I got home my brother came with me to Dad's house to start organising his possessions. The reality of losing him hit me hard and I think my brother was pleased to have me home and we supported each other. We spent a couple of weeks organising the funeral and starting the paperwork that needed to be completed and I found myself thinking about Sarah having to do the same when I die. The bleakness of my cancer hit me all over again, but I was pleased that my dad wouldn't have to see me die. When I first told him my diagnosis, the hardest part was thinking of him having to bury one of his children. At least I knew he would never have to go through that, which was a personal comfort. Losing Dad had reminded me how quickly everything could change and it made me think about my situation, which I suppose I had escaped from when I was in the Arctic. Dad had gone from being an independent man to dying in just a couple of months.

I returned to work and my first blood test after getting home showed my PSA level was still low, which was great news. It is always nice to see the doctors and nurses, including Professor Parker, after a race and thank them for their support, without which I would never have been able to compete. My body was battered, bruised and tired as we enjoyed a family Easter and then it was time to head out to the Sahara for my third MDS. In the fortnight between coming back from the Arctic and flying to the desert, I had done a couple of 10km walks but had mainly given my body time to rest. It was exciting travelling back to Morocco and I felt like an experienced campaigner. On the flight and coach journey, I noticed first-time competitors were asking me lots of questions, just like I had done two years before.

Rory had asked me to be in his tent again, and I was honoured because this was going to be his final Marathon des Sables. Tent 103 turned out to be a multinational home of middle-aged men who should have known better. We had Matheus from Germany, Jon from Holland, Drummond from South Africa and, from England, myself, Lloyd, another John, Rory and Craig (who had been in the tent the previous year). We immediately hit it off and the banter in the tent was exceptional, often near and occasionally over the mark. We supported each other throughout the race as ever and really enjoyed ourselves.

Unusually, the MDS route was identical to the previous year and, just like the two other years, I loved every minute of it. The fact that I had done the course before gave me an extra confidence as I knew what was coming up each day. My body held together somehow and it was lovely to be back in the heat after the cold of the Arctic. The third day of the race was amazing because it included a massive ridge run, high up along a jebel. I was climbing when I came across Lloyd from my tent effectively hugging a rock. This was his first MDS and although he was much fitter than me, he explained that he suffered from vertigo and he couldn't let go because he was terrified he would fall. I persuaded him to hold my hand and guided him along the ridge and down the other side of the jebel. We split up at the base and after running for an hour I came to the infamous Jebel el Oftal with its steep climb taking you 3,000 feet above the desert floor. I thought of Lloyd, who was behind me, and decided to wait for him because there was no way he would be able to do the climb on his own. This was steeper, had a narrower path, required scrambling, using ropes and there was farther to fall if you slipped. Drummond from the tent was just behind me, so I asked him to wait and together we guided our buddy up and over the Jebel el Oftal. We stayed together and over the final 12km of the route put together a synchronised 'dad dance' for the web camera at the finish line. Our choreography was perfect, good enough for 'Britain's Got Talent'! I was so proud of Lloyd, who had overcome his fears to get through the day and I hope he was proud too, as facing your demons head-on and winning takes real guts.

I of course reacquainted myself with 'Doc Trotter's' over the week because of two bad blisters on my feet but I am delighted to say that everybody in Tent 103 finished the 33rd MDS. This 100 per cent completion rate reflected well again on Rory and the training plans he puts together for those that go to him. The fact he also chooses a great blend of characters to be together in his tent is testimony to what a great coach and judge of character he is. I was delighted to have another medal to add to my collection and my third MDS had been a wonderful experience.

Arriving home from the desert, I went straight to the dentist because my jaw and teeth were painful. The dentist explained that my zoledronic acid infusions had probably caused the tooth bed in my jaw to slightly change and, in a worst-case scenario, I could lose all my teeth. This had sadly happened to a man I knew with prostate cancer who had spent the last few months of his life in agony because of sores in his mouth from tooth issues. I decided there and then to ask Professor Parker if I could stop having the infusions as I didn't want that kind of misery added to what was already likely to be a long list of unpleasantness in time to come.

The Friday after returning from the desert was my dad's funeral. I had done my grieving in the Arctic and had my dad's spirit with me during that race and the MDS. The funeral was at the church he had attended and lots of people came to the service, which was a comfort. Afterwards we had a small family gathering at the crematorium and held the wake at Dad's local pub, which was a lovely occasion. We gave Dad a proper send-off. During the funeral, though, I was looking at Dad's coffin and could not help think about the inevitable day when it would be me in the box. Sadly, I had been to several funerals of friends from the Prostate Cancer UK forum and it always made me realise the finality of death. We only have one life and when it's gone, it's gone. You will never get the chance to do the things you talked about doing and that is why I grab every opportunity that comes my way. After Dad's funeral, life carried on as normal. I returned to work and my PSA scores continued to stay at the right level. My body was tired because of the Arctic and the Sahara, but after a period of rest, I started running again.

I sometimes wonder if people see me as a macho, tough guy, who is able to take on so many races despite what's going on inside his body. If that is somebody's opinion of me, they could not be further from the truth. Before I was ill, I was never tough, just full of confidence which generally helped me get away with it and I suppose I always talked a good game. But once I started my prostate cancer treatment, my body changed.

Initially, prostate cancer is usually fed by testosterone and the first drugs they put you on effectively destroy your male-inducing hormones. In cases of advanced prostate cancer, these drugs are prescribed for the lifetime of the patient; the treatment is effectively chemical castration.

For me this translates into the loss of any sexual or 'manly' feelings and with that goes the ability to 'be a man' too. As a 49-year-old bloke, I found that very hard to accept, plus there was an onrush of mood changes and high emotion, which, coupled with my situation at that time, just seemed to magnify the tears and sadness. As time has gone on, I have managed to accept those changes and so has my amazing wife (although she hasn't had a headache at bedtime for six years now!), but I still occasionally look back at what life used to be like with a tinge of sadness, knowing it will never be like that again.

Throughout my cancer journey, other changes to my body have happened. My ability to build and retain muscle with no testosterone has diminished, which isn't great for somebody that runs ultra-marathons. Every day I have regular hot flushes that disturb my sleep and I sweat lots, as I have mentioned before, which makes me feel extremely self-conscious on occasions. The hot flushes are worse if my body is under any kind of mental or physical stress. I guess what I am experiencing is the male equivalent of the female menopause.

On top of all of this, I think the biggest noticeable change has been my appearance. The drugs I am on have stopped my body hair growing which doesn't bother me, but the drugs have also shrunk some important 'parts' of my body, which is hard to take. In complete contrast, I now have gynaecomastia which for those of you not of a medical persuasion, means expanding 'man boobs', aka moobs. It's quite a tough gig to see myself in the mirror because it's a harsh, visual reminder of the changes to my body that will be there forever. My man boobs cause issues when I run, so I often use tape and running backpacks to stop soreness and chafing. But I can't bring myself to wear a sports bra.

All the changes to my body have in some bizarre way just added to the challenges I take on. I always want to finish races despite all these things and I never want to be seen as a victim. Whenever I have success, I want to celebrate it and I will never use my physical changes as an excuse if a race or challenge goes wrong.

In May of 2018, Sarah and I were shown an unbelievable act of kindness. Many years ago, we both worked in the same office with a lady called Julia. She had called us out of the blue to say that she had entered a competition to win a long weekend break at The Tree Hotel in Sweden. There had been thousands of entries, but Julia had won because she said that she wanted to win the prize for Sarah and me because of my situation. The experience was amazing, staying in our private UFO-shaped tree house in beautiful scenery far away from it all. It also ticked a box for Sarah, who had always wanted to go to Sweden. Thank you, Julia, for the most amazing act of kindness and the memories that act created for Sarah and me.

On the running front, my focus was the Al Andalus Ultimate in July. I had entered again because I felt I had unfinished business with the race after missing the cut-off time the previous year. I was determined to be fitter and in better condition this time,, so I could get the medal round my neck. My training schedule had me running 10km two days a week, and 20km one day a week combined with a 30km run once a week. Prostate Cancer UK had been in touch and told me that, due to other commitments, Jeff Stelling was sadly unable to do the March for Men fundraiser this year. That got me thinking and I spoke to a colleague of mine at the bank called Liam about us putting a challenge together. He was director of the northern region of the bank and had walked the Liverpool leg of Jeff's march with me in 2017. He put me in touch with Monty from his team and after a couple of discussions we came up with the idea of doing seven marathons in seven days, with Liam and Monty encouraging each of the offices in the north of England to take part. I mentioned the idea to Richard who was making the documentary and he said he would take me to each marathon in his camper van, enabling him to do some filming and allowing me to walk all seven marathons. Monty's organisation of the challenge was brilliant and each of his offices agreed to do one marathon in the week. Joining me to do all seven were Michael Tattersall, the CEO of the National Football League, Monty and a lady called Georgie, who worked at the bank and whose father had been diagnosed with prostate cancer. In early June, Richard and I drove to Newcastle in his campervan and did the first day of our March for Men with some colleagues from work. During the first marathon, I stopped at a hospice and met a guy with prostate cancer. He was so enthusiastic about the journey I had been on since my diagnosis and he told me that he felt he was doing the march with me, which gave me a lift.

After Newcastle, we did marathons in Leeds, Sheffield, Manchester, Preston and Liverpool, a total of 120 people from the bank took part and together we raised £90,000, including a generous donation from the bank, for Prostate Cancer UK. I was delighted that colleagues from the bank had come together to organise and take part in the March for Men and it made me feel my role as an ambassador was continuing to make an impact. For most of those walking, it was the first time they had ever covered a marathon distance on foot in their lives and they were justifiably proud of what they had achieved. It added weight to my efforts and I felt I had a worth for the bank, justifying their unquestioning support of me. Under their internal 'Do Good, Feel Good' campaign, the bank had supported the march and the feedback was excellent. We had raised a large sum of money for the charity and Richard made three short videos for the bank to inspire and encourage other members of staff to do something for others. As a bonus we had also got some excellent footage for the documentary. It proved to be a very successful week and showed the power of people coming together.

I have been a Wimbledon football fan since the age of 13, so I was honoured when a couple of weeks after the march, AFC Wimbledon asked me to give a presentation to their development squad ahead of the start of their season. I was nervous because I didn't think a group of 18-year-old footballers would have any interest in listening to my story. They were fantastic though and after my talk I was presented with a signed shirt. A few of those lads have gone on to play for the first team and I feel so proud to have spoken to them.

Two days later I was flying to Spain for the Al Andalus Ultimate. This was all about unfinished business. After missing the cut-off time the previous year, I had trained harder and better, including some Bikram hot yoga sessions to get ready for the heat. I was ready for the race and visualised having the medal hung around my neck on the finish line. The course was the same, so I knew what to expect and I was excited about taking on the challenge again. Richard came with me to get some more footage for the documentary and we arrived in Loja and had a relaxing afternoon at a local pool. I met a few of the other runners, including a friend of mine called Duncan, who lived locally and had come to support me the previous year. He had decided to enter the race this year and it was great to catch up with him. The following day the organisers did a kit check and gave the race briefing and I listened intently to the cut-off times after my previous experience.

After an early night, I woke up nervous and excited for the opening day of the race from Loja to Alhama de Granada. There were only 50 of us competing and the opening day went well. I was fitter and better prepared and it wasn't as hot as the previous year. At the end of the opening 39km, I felt good and not as tired as I had after the first day the previous year, which was a good sign. I paced myself through days two and three, felt comfortable and was enjoying the race. I felt relaxed and made sure I rested in the evenings and hydrated properly. The 'long day' arrived and I was extremely nervous on the start line. This was when it had gone wrong last year, and I didn't want to make the same mistakes again. It was roasting hot but probably ten degrees cooler than the previous year and that made a hell of a difference. I ran at a steady pace, walked up the hills and worked my way through the day. After 40km I joined forces with a runner called Maggie who, like me, had not finished the previous year. We stuck together and eventually I reached the dreaded checkpoint where it had all gone wrong 12 months before. This time, however, I was about an hour inside the cut-off time and even though I was tired, I was going to complete the race without fail and get my medal. We left the checkpoint and I kept running with Maggie. It was a wonderful feeling when the finishing line came into view. Richard was there and filmed me coming over the line in ten hours and 59 minutes; I was ecstatic. I had set myself the goal of finishing the 'long day' in 11 hours, so I had beaten that time and that night I slept extremely well in my humid and sticky tent.

The final day of the race was the shortest (19km) and generally downhill. I was tired, sore, happy and satisfied. I ran the last few kilometres with a German runner called Sascha who I had got on well with all week. The finishing line was at the top of a steep hill and with 200 yards to go I told Sasha to go ahead of me. I followed him towards the finish and standing there were the same two race officials as last year, with their clipboards checking the cut-off times. This time they nodded at me because I was well inside the time and it was a fantastic feeling crossing the line and being given my medal. The satisfaction I felt coming back and completing the race was indescribable and I celebrated my achievement at the dinner that evening. I was humbled to receive an extra award for being 'a great inspiration' and the next day I flew home, having put a big tick in the unfinished business box.

Back at home, I started worrying again about how much longer I was going to live. The abiraterone had been working for 18 months, but I had no idea how long it would continue to keep me alive because I knew the average time the drug worked for was probably up. I was approaching the four-year anniversary of my diagnosis when the doctor told me I would be lucky if I lived for another three or four years. I honestly did not know if I would be alive next year and that made planning ahead very difficult. I was worried about my family and from a running perspective I wanted to enter the race in Spain again, but didn't know if I would be well enough to do it or even be here to run it. Before doing the March for Men with my bank colleagues in June, I had verbally committed to the MDS and the 6633 Arctic Ultra. I did not have to pay for either race until later in the year, which gave me time to see how I was feeling before fully committing. Both races gave me something to look forward to, especially the 6633 Arctic Ultra, where I wanted to try and complete the longer race. In my heart I didn't know if I would be well enough to do them, but I still had some breathing space before I had to make a final decision.

We had a family holiday in South Carolina, staying with my brother-in-law and I was able to relax and put my worries about the following year to the back of my mind for a couple of weeks. Back home, an old scouting mate of mine, Julian, had let us use a holiday home in Somerset for a few days. What I didn't know was that he had also arranged for an experienced pilot friend of his to take me up in a Chipmunk aeroplane. I was somewhat nervous when I got into the tiny cockpit of the old aeroplane but was taken on the trip of a lifetime as we looped, barrel-rolled and stall-turned our way over the skies and I managed to keep the contents of my stomach in the right place. More unbelievable kindness from generous people.

Back in the office, work was going well, and at home I had started training again. My legs had been painful since the race in Spain, so I was doing three 10km runs a week and lots of walking. One afternoon I was looking at a running website and saw a race in Albania being advertised. The Hidden Treasure was a six-day, 220km event, in September, and the more I read about the race, the more I wanted to do it. Even though I was worrying about next year, I knew I would still be here in September, unless something went disastrously wrong, so I signed up. I bought a book called *The Accursed Mountains* and read up on the history of Albania, because the only thing I knew about the country was that Norman Wisdom films were popular there! Only 60 people had entered the race and they were from all over the globe. I got in touch with the race organiser, a great guy called Stefan, who sent me a list of entrants because I wanted to see if I knew anybody who was also running the race. The name Mark Roe jumped out at me because he had written a book called 'Running from Shadows'. I had read the book because it was about Mark's experience of running the MDS a few years before. I contacted Mark and we agreed to meet at Gatwick Airport as we were booked on the same flight to Albania. We immediately got on very well and over a coffee at the airport we agreed to share a tent during the race.

We flew to Tirana and after we had checked into our hotel, I made a trip to a local supermarket. Mark had told me it was his birthday on the third day of the race and had also mentioned his love of crisps! I bought him a large packet of crisps to give him as a treat, so he could celebrate his big day during the race. Little did I know just how welcome they would be. Wandering around Tirana I felt an undercurrent of tension and it had been suggested we should be careful if we decided to leave the hotel at night. It was also much hotter than I had expected, which was a concern. Back at the hotel there was the customary kit check and I chatted to some of the other runners. I went to bed feeling excited and pleased that I had decided to do the race.

The following day we were driven to the start point at the World Heritage Site of the ruined castle of Berat. It must be one of the most spectacular starting points for any race in the world and our tented race village nestled in the shadows of the castle. We had a race briefing and Mark and I settled into our very small and very hot tent. After dinner, we had an early night and I woke up refreshed for the opening day. Like every race I have done, the final preparations were chaotic but after an hour of panic, Mark and I made our way down from the castle to the start line.

We were facing 38km on the opening day and it was already very hot. The race opened with flat terrain, but after crossing a bridge, the road turned into a gravel path and we started climbing a steep hill. My legs were hurting and the race was already tougher than I expected. The heat made it feel like I was running in a furnace. It felt like the whole of the first day was uphill and it was horrible because I hadn't done much hill work during my training. I managed to get through the opening day, and we spent the night in a local school, sleeping on the classroom floors. I was knackered, my knee was hurting and I knew it was going to be an extremely hard week. The good news was that there were no cut-off times, unlike in Spain, so that took some of the pressure off.

The following day was more of the same: 31km in the heat, up and down hills, with a final long descent into the village of Peshtan. Again, I managed to get through the day and when we had all completed the stage, we were allocated local homes to stay in for the night. Six of us made our way up another steep hill, carrying our bags and arrived at a house that looked like it might collapse at any moment. The couple who owned the house met us, but they spoke no English and after several hand signals it became clear they were moving out for the night and staying in a small shed. Mark and I were given the couple's bedroom, including the marital bed to sleep on together! After settling in we made our way to a small café in the village. The owner showed us a collection of guns and bullets she had collected from the mountains surrounding the village. These were from the various historic troubles that the country had been through in the not too distant past and it was a real eye opener.

After a couple of drinks, we all went back to the house and the home owners cooked us dinner. To thank them for their hospitality I gave our lovely hosts a tin of biscuits with a picture of the Queen on the front that I had brought from England. We also had a collection amongst us to supplement what they had been paid by the race organiser, which made them quite happy. The husband brought out some beers and we had a great evening sitting outside the house, in the middle of the Balkan Mountains smiling, making hand gestures and enjoying life.

I felt the race was a proper adventure and after a good night's sleep we woke up to find a cooked breakfast waiting for us. We said an emotional goodbye to our hosts and set off on the 55km 'long day' of the race. It was incredibly hot and 15km in we faced a brutal climb up a mountain. It was horrendous and almost broke me because it was so hot and my knee was giving me real trouble. I wished I had done more hill work because this was turning out to be a mountain race.

To make matters worse, the soles of my nearly-new running shoes had started coming off because of the heat and the rocks, something that had never happened to me before even in the Sahara. I managed to get to the top of the climb and thought my heart was going to jump out of my chest. I was shattered, but thankfully the next 20km were on a flat path through the mountains and the views were spectacular. I bumped into Mark and he was in a bad way because he had gone too fast on the opening couple of days. I kept plodding along and eventually finished in ten hours and I was exhausted. Mark collapsed over the line a while after me and was immediately seen to by the medics because he was almost delirious. I suddenly remembered it was his birthday and went and got the packet of crisps I had bought him. I found him with the medics and amazingly the salty crisps seemed to help. After rest and crisps, Mark perked up and we were able to go back to our tent, which was in an enormous dried-up lakebed.

The following morning, I helped Mark get ready for the 38km day that was in front of us. My knee was agony and running was extremely painful. Thankfully, the start of the stage was flat, and I stayed with Mark, who was struggling. After 10km we came to the town of Lazarat, which had become famous in 2014 when Albanian police besieged it, as it then produced 900 tonnes of cannabis annually with a value of £3.6 billion. There was a four-day gun fight between the locals and the police, until the police eventually seized control and destroyed the cannabis plants. It was extraordinary to run through a town, which had in places the characteristics of a war zone with some buildings covered in bullet holes or destroyed by grenades.

After Lazarat, I faced another steep 5km climb up a mountain. There was no path and I had to scramble over the rocks. I was struggling but somehow kept going despite my knees and ankles which were screaming in pain. Eventually, I got to the top of the mountain and there was a road down the other side which I managed to run on without too much pain. The rest of the day was spent going up and down hills and I walked much of it because of my knee. The heat was unbearable, but I managed to get to a stone bridge that crossed a river, and on the other side was the finish line, next to a cultural monument of Albania, the ancient monastery of Mesopatam. Unfortunately, I arrived at the bridge at the same time as a crowd of local sheep and got stuck in a 'sheep jam'. I finally made it to the other side and was able to cross the finish line. Our tents were on a patch of grass outside the monastery and I waited for Mark to finish. He was still in a bad state and after a refreshing and cleansing plunge in the icy waters of the river we spent a quiet evening by the monastery trying to get as much rest as we could.

Day five of the race was 43km of hills, including another horrific climb up the side of a mountain. The first 29km were tough, but the climb almost destroyed me. My knee and ankles were agony and I was so hot I thought my head was going to explode. I crawled the last part of the climb and mercifully the descent down the other side was more gradual, so I could slowly jog. I had drunk all my water and had stopped eating because it was too hot, and I had no energy. Somehow, I kept putting one foot in front of the other and got myself to the bottom where I found a small concrete trough full of icy cold mountain water. I climbed into the trough and sat for ten minutes trying to cool down. I clambered out and slowly ran the last 5km to the finish line, which was in the middle of a small town. My body was in pieces and our tent had been pitched on a school field, directly in the sun, so it was too hot to sit in. I found some shade, drank lots of water and after an hour started feeling human again. Mark had also got through the day and a local couple were selling hamburgers, so we sat together, eating burgers, knowing we only had the short day to do tomorrow. In the evening, the village put on a show for us, which included food and traditional Albanian dancing. Everybody had a great time and I went to sleep looking forward to the final day of the race.

The last day was 15km and thankfully flat. We left the village early in the morning which was a blessing because it wasn't too hot. Even though my body was hurting I was enjoying running, all the time feeling remarkably good. With 4km to go until the finish I suddenly tripped over on a rock on the road and fell flat on my face. It was a heavy fall and I lay on the ground, dazed and unable to move. I had cut my head open and blood was pouring down my face and I had grazed my knees and elbows. I was on my own and after a few minutes I slowly sat up. Two runners came past and asked if I was ok. I gave them the thumbs up, but I wasn't sure. I got back to my feet, a complete mess and slowly started jogging. The race ends at the Roman amphitheatre at the World Heritage Site of Butrint and before you get there you first cross a small river on a ferry. I sat on the ferry and cleaned my cuts with some wet wipes. In my backpack I had a Union Jack flag with 'Prostate Cancer UK' written on it, which I carried as I jogged the last 2km. I ran into the amphitheatre and crossed the finish line feeling like Russell Crowe in *Gladiator*. It was a spectacular place to finish the race. I sat down amongst the tourists, looking a real state, and soaked up the surroundings. Mark came over the line and his wife was there to meet him, which was lovely because I knew what he had been through to complete the race.

Once all the runners had finished, we were driven to a hotel in the town of Saranada. We arrived at lunchtime, and after I had had a shower and cleaned my wounds, we wandered into the town and had a few beers to celebrate the end of the race. In the evening there was an official race dinner and awards ceremony at the hotel where I was presented with a beautiful stone carving of the roman amphitheatre for completing the race. After dinner there was a raffle and the top prize was a discounted entry fee to Global Limits' (the company that organised the Albania race) next race, which was in Cambodia. The first name out of the hat could not do the race and this happened seven or eight times, with each person unable to do the race in November. The race organiser, Stefan, said he would pull one more name out of the hat and it was mine. I asked him if I could ring Sarah, just to check she was happy for me to enter the race at such short notice. Sarah gave me the go-ahead, so I told Stefan I would take the prize. I had a trip to Cambodia to look forward to in less than three months. I had a few more drinks with Mark and his wife at the hotel bar and the following day, after a seven-hour drive to Tirana, flew home shattered but proud that I had completed another ultra-marathon, raised a few more quid for charity and made more people aware of prostate cancer.

Chapter 12

Jungle adventure

THE RACE in Cambodia really excited me. It was a country I had always wanted to go to and because the opportunity had suddenly been presented to me, I wanted to grab it with both hands. It was under three months away and unless something went horribly wrong with my cancer, it was a race that I would be able to do. The race in Albania was very well organised by Stefan from Global Limits and the atmosphere amongst the runners had been terrific, so I felt sure Cambodia would be the same.

In early October, I travelled to London for the Marathon des Sables Expo. I had been before, but this time it was different. Steve Diedrich, the British organiser of the MDS, had asked me to be a guest speaker. Don't forget, this was the race that had been the one thing on my bucket list and now I was being asked to speak about my experiences of doing the race to an audience of people I had the utmost respect for. I had listened to speakers at previous Expos and had been in awe of their achievements and how they had handled the race. One of those speakers had been James Cracknell, whose documentary on the MDS had convinced me to do the race, and it was a proud moment for an ordinary bloke to follow in the footsteps of an Olympic champion.

Richard had made a short film about me, called *Bad Day*, in which I explained how much the MDS meant to me and included footage of me in the Sahara. The film was played to the audience and at the end there was a huge round of applause. I came on stage and gave my talk in which I spoke about why you should always run for a charity. I explained that once you are sponsored by somebody it makes you do the training because you are committed to that person. When you are doing the race, you don't give up because you would be letting down your sponsors and the charity you are running for. Finally, when you finish the race, you get your medal, but you haven't just run it for yourself, you have run for other people as well. My message was that you should always run a race for a charity because it is an opportunity to make a difference to somebody else's life.

After I finished my talk, a young guy in the audience came to find me and told me that after they had shown my video, he thought Steve was going to tell everybody that I had sadly died. He confessed that he had burst into tears when I walked on to stage and I was very touched. I also met a guy called Michael who told me he was running the race for the first time and we immediately formed a bond and promised to keep in touch with each other. I was proud to have told my story at the Expo and seeing so many familiar faces made me excited about running the race again the next year, which I had paid for and committed to doing. Even though I was still worried what the state of my health would be by then, I had to have the race to look forward to.

I left the Expo early because I was heading to Doncaster to meet up with Richard and his mobile home. I was heading north as I had organised a solo March for Men fundraiser, inspired by Michael Tattersall, the then CEO of the National Football League. The league was sponsored by Vanarama and for that week, in conjunction with Prostate Cancer UK, they had changed their name to 'Manarama'. I was going to walk seven marathons in seven days, via National League clubs, finishing at Halifax's televised home game against Chesterfield on the Saturday. I started at Blyth Spartans and before I left, the chairman presented me with the club's shirt, which was the plan for every club I visited. I wore the shirt as I walked from Blyth to Gateshead, and when I arrived at the Gateshead International Stadium, a small boy was waiting for me. He had read about my walk on the club website and asked if he could interview me for his blog. I was delighted and gave him a specially made Prostate Cancer UK armband that all the captains in the National League were going to wear on Saturday to raise awareness about prostate cancer. That young fan made me feel proud about what I was doing, and I was humbled that he would come out on a cold, damp Sunday night to meet me (although I am not sure his dad was so pleased that he had to drive him there!).

Richard and I slept in the campervan in the car park of the Gateshead stadium and the next day I walked to Hartlepool along the coast. The sun was shining, and it was a lovely walk. I never realised just how beautiful the north-east coast is, but amongst the beauty were many towns now past their former industrial glory. It reaffirmed my belief that nothing is forever, and you must make hay whilst the sun shines.

I arrived at Victoria Park, Hartlepool's ground, and made a personal video for Jeff Stelling, the inspiration behind the March for Men campaign, because Jeff is a massive Hartlepool fan. I was early for my scheduled meeting with the chairman of the club, so I went to a local pub for a pint. I was wearing my Hartlepool shirt and I got chatting to some of the locals, told them what I was doing and they immediately had a whip-round and gave me £100 for the charity. One of the gentlemen at the bar suddenly said, 'I've got prostate cancer,' and all his friends were surprised because that was the first time, he had told them all. It proved how important it is for men to talk about prostate cancer because a few of the guys over 45 in the pub said they would go and have a test after our chat. I went back to the ground and met the chairman who took me on to the pitch and introduced me to Hartlepool's first-team captain and I was given a warm welcome.

We spent another night in a club car park and the next day I walked to Darlington, stopping at Spennymoor where the local mayor came to meet me. I also met a guy called Mark Solan, who had lost family members to cancer and had started his own charity to financially support people in the local area who were suffering from the disease. They did things like fixing a broken boiler, which may not sound much, but when you have no money and you are knocked out by cancer the thought of no hot water is hard to contemplate. What he did made me realise just how lucky I am; despite having cancer. Mark raised money in all sorts of different ways, including fighting in a charity boxing match despite never having been in the ring before. Mark walked a couple of miles with me when I left Spennymoor and meeting him was inspirational and left me with a head full of ideas of what could be achieved for others with effort.

When I arrived at Darlington's ground, Blackwell Meadows, I was taken to the training ground to watch the first team and meet the players. From Darlington, I was aiming to walk 43 miles to York and spent most of the day walking up the busy A19. I had planned the whole route trying to avoid main roads; but this was the only road to York, so with no hard shoulder or footpath it was a scary experience. A couple of times I had to dive into a bush to avoid the oncoming traffic! About 30 miles into the walk, it got dark and Richard found a campsite where the owner let us stay for free and gave £20 to the charity. I was able to have a shower and we spent a comfortable night in the van.

I had to be up early the next morning to do an interview with BBC York and after chatting on the radio, I walked the remaining 13 miles to York. I arrived at Bootham Crescent and the players were there to meet me which was a lovely surprise. I did another interview with BBC York and set off to Harrogate Town which was 19 miles away. I arrived in Harrogate as it was getting dark and as I walked to the club's ground, I noticed the floodlights were on. There was a kid's training session running and a club representative took me to watch. As I was walking along the side of the pitch, I was greeted by my mate Lloyd Pinder, who was still battling terminal cancer. Lloyd had come to surprise me, and I gave him a massive hug and burst into tears because after our last conversation about his health, I thought I might never see him again. But there he was, having made the effort to come and support me, which meant everything at that moment. I think he was embarrassed by my reaction, but I was just so pleased to see my 'cancer twin' that all my emotions came out. He was with his mate Colin, who had walked with me on previous Jeff Stelling marches and it was great to see them both. Phil Priestley, the club's goalkeeping coach, asked me to make a presentation to the club's walking football team and a couple of the men told me they had prostate cancer. I had my photo taken with some of the kids that were training, and Phil asked me if I would come back in the morning and talk to the first team.

I was honoured to talk to the Harrogate Town first team and tell them my story and I encouraged them to live for today because you only have one life. After leaving Harrogate, I walked to Guiseley with some of my mates who had come to support me, including Perry and Michael who I had met at the MDS Expo. To make it a marathon distance we walked to Guiseley via the scenic route and it was great to have some company because I had been on my own for most of the week. We arrived at Guiseley and I was met by the first-team coach who gave me a tour of Nethermoor Park. That evening I had dinner with my mate Mark Roe who I had shared a tent with in Albania as he had turned up to say 'hi'. After a good night's sleep, I set off on my last marathon from Guiseley to Halifax. Michael Tattersall and a couple of colleagues from the bank joined me and there were ten of us walking via Bradford Park Avenue's home game against Kidderminster Harriers. After a brief stop, we kept walking and arrived at Halifax a couple of hours before kick-off for their game against Chesterfield, which was being televised live on BT Sport.

We were taken to a hospitality suite at the Shay Stadium where 150 people were having lunch. I was asked to give a talk about the march, and I was given £500 for the charity that had been collected from everybody in the room. Representatives from Vanarama and Prostate Cancer UK were there, and before the match I had a long chat with the Chesterfield manager, Martin Allen. He was clearly touched by my story and wasn't the 'Mad Dog' I had heard so much about. Just before kick-off, I was given the honour of taking the match ball on to the pitch and as I waited in the tunnel, they showed the film of the march that Richard had made on the big screen. As I walked on to the pitch, both teams formed a guard of honour for me and the crowd gave me a huge reception. Remember all of this was being broadcast live on BT Sport and I was presented with a £150,000 cheque for Prostate Cancer UK from Vanarama to celebrate 'Prostate Cancer UK Non-League day'. It was an amazing experience and after watching the game, I was introduced to a Halifax fan, who was in a wheelchair, I gave him one of the Prostate Cancer UK armbands that captains all over the country had worn during matches that day. It was so humbling to see how much the armband meant to that young man and, despite being severely disabled, you could see he was a true fighter.

Richard and I celebrated the end of the march with a curry in Halifax and it gave me a chance to reflect on the generosity and welcome of all those clubs and fans. In these days where the elite seem to be solely focused on money, I do hope that people continue to support these clubs that are genuinely part of the community.

The next day I drove home and straight back to reality. I had to have all my vaccinations for the trip to Cambodia. My body felt ok and the week of walking had done my knee good because it didn't hurt as much as it had done when I came back from Albania. I then got a fateful phone call from BBC Surrey telling me about a sports journalist called Mark Church, who was running 20 miles a day between the Oval cricket ground and Lords, for 50 days, to raise money for the Pancreatic Cancer Research Fund. Mark was a cricket commentator and had lost his dad to pancreatic cancer, so I went up to London and spent the morning running with him. Mark took me up to the commentary box and we did an interview with BBC Surrey. It blew me away that Mark was running 1,000 miles and we got on well and promised to stay in touch with each other. Little did I know that morning was the catalyst to getting this book written.

On 6 November, it was the four-year anniversary of my diagnosis. Sarah and Ollie gave me a cake with four candles on the top and we celebrated the fact that I was still alive and still the same dad and husband. The doctor had told me I would be lucky to live for four years, so every day was now even more of a bonus. To mark the anniversary, I paid my entry fee for the 6633 Arctic Ultra and finally ran the Druid's Challenge after missing the previous two years for various injury reasons. The 135km, three-day race along the Ridgeway was hard work and when I finished, my right leg was in agony. My ankle, calf and knee were all in a bad way, but I was really pleased to have done the race and caught up with so many familiar faces. I met a guy called Rob Brown, who was a diabetic and had collapsed in his hotel room one evening during the race. I was in awe of how Rob coped with his diabetes and managed to get through the race. He was a truly inspiring man, doing his best and not giving up. Like so many other great people I have met along my journey, Rob and I are now great mates and regularly run together.

My brother and I had been spending a lot of time together since my dad died and he mentioned that he would love to do a challenge with me. I had always wanted to take on the

Camino de Santiago Pilgrimage across Spain and we chatted about the logistics of doing it together. We estimated that we would be away for about a month and that's a long time away from our families and to be off work. We had been left some money by our dad and we both thought that spending some of it on this would be a fitting tribute to him. He was a keen walker himself and we knew he would have been be proud of us doing this together. My leg was still painful, but my brother and I started training together, which was also helping me get ready for Cambodia at the end of November.

On 20 November, which is my son Ollie's birthday, we all travelled to London for the Just Giving Awards. I had been nominated for the Endurance Fundraiser of the Year award and on our table were a couple of representatives from Prostate Cancer UK and Jeff Stelling. It was lovely to see Jeff, who told me he was there to present an award. After the meal, the presentations began. They got to my category and showed a short film about me that Richard had made, alongside films about the other two nominees. I wasn't concentrating, however. I noticed Jeff was no longer at the table but on the stage. Jeff said he was proud to present the award to somebody he regarded as a friend and announced my name! I couldn't believe it! My table erupted as Ollie and Sarah gave me a big hug. I went up to receive my award and got everybody to sing happy birthday to Ollie, which he still hasn't forgiven me for. I felt I had won the award for Prostate Cancer UK and I was touched that Jeff had made the effort to travel to London to present it to me.

My next appointment was in Brecon for my second 6633 Arctic Ultra Expo, where I met lots of runners who had entered the race for the following year. Being at the Expo confirmed that I had made the right decision to enter the race. I felt excited about the prospect of taking on the Arctic again. First though, it was time to head to Cambodia for the Ancient Khmer Path Ultra-Marathon. I would only be carrying water and snacks on each day of the six-day, 220km race, but I was becoming an expert at packing for ultra-marathons as my drop bag was restricted to just 12kg. My right knee and ankle were still giving me problems, but I had trained well, and my core fitness was good thanks to the race in Albania and the walking I was doing with my brother. Cambodia was going to be hot and extremely humid and I had been going regularly to the steam room at my local gym to try and acclimatise. The race wasn't taking place in a high-risk malaria area of Cambodia, but mosquitos would still be a problem. There's a whole range of mosquito repellents on the market and I decided to buy some long running socks that were effectively pre-soaked in mosquito repellent. Wearing long socks in the jungles of Cambodia may sound like madness, but they worked well and stopped my ankles and calves getting eaten by the 'mossies'. I also packed Avon dry oil spray, after reading an article that said it was the choice of the special forces to keep mosquitos at bay. It also kept my skin smooth!

Richard was coming to Cambodia with me, to film the race, so we flew together. The flight over wasn't crowded and we were able to spread out on the plane. After a change at Bangkok, we flew into Phnom Penh. I have always been fascinated by Cambodia since watching a report on *John Craven's Newsround* when I was a kid. The report had been on Pol Pot and the horrific regime of the Khmer Rouge. I was excited to arrive in the country and we were met by a lady called Harri, who I knew from the race in Albania. Harri and her boyfriend Olly live in Cambodia, working for NGOs and were helping crew the race. They drove Richard and me to our hotel and after checking in we decided to visit the Tuol Sleng Genocide Museum in Phnom Penh. The museum was situated at the security prison known as S21, where the Khmer Rouge had imprisoned, interrogated, and carried out genocide on 20,000 people. Richard and I got a tuk tuk from outside the hotel and the journey to the museum was quite an experience. I was scared when we first set off because the roads were jam-packed and there didn't seem to be any rules about how to drive. Once we got into the journey and I realised our driver knew what he was doing, I enjoyed the hustle and bustle of Phnom Penh.

S21 was an old secondary school and it was a heartbreaking, tear-inducing experience visiting the torture chambers and seeing the pictures of the people who had been murdered there. It was a horrendous place but one I felt I had to visit. It made me realise how lucky we are in the UK. The atrocities of WW2 should have been lesson enough to the world, but sadly it seems there will always be more to do.

We returned to the hotel and went to the pre-race dinner that was on the roof terrace with amazing views of Phnom Penh. There were 60 people running the race and I recognised quite a few faces from Albania. It was exciting to be in the heat and humidity of Cambodia preparing to start my next ultra-marathon. The following morning, we were taken on a walking tour of Phnom Penh, which I really enjoyed. After just 24 hours, I had fallen in love with Cambodia because it was everything I had hoped it would be.

We checked out of the hotel and started a four-hour coach drive to the starting point of the race. Halfway through the journey we stopped at a 'bug market', but I wasn't tempted to eat the caterpillars, locusts or centipedes that were on offer and invested in the safe option of a can of Coke instead.

After a 180km drive we arrived at a Buddhist temple which was our home for the night and where the race would start the next day. The monks had moved out of the temple for us and we were going to sleep on the floor, where the race organisers had hung mosquito nets. I was blown away by the beauty of where we were and as I got used to my surroundings it dawned on me that I was standing in a Buddhist Temple in the middle of Cambodia getting ready to run my next ultra-marathon. These unique experiences were all about creating memories. This one got better when lots of excited children arrived at the temple and one of the runners, called Stan, handed them all cuddly toys that he had brought with him. It was lovely to watch. You could see how much it meant to the children and I promised myself that I would do the same thing if I ever came back to run the race again.

That evening, I had my first dehydrated meal of the week and Stefan, the race director, gave a briefing on the steps of the temple. One topic of conversation was the danger of landmines. The race route had obviously been cleared of them, but there was a general understanding that if you needed the toilet during the race, you stayed on the official route even if there wasn't much privacy. There was still a risk that not all the landmines had been found and any deviation from the path could spell real danger. I didn't want to be the 'lucky' person to discover the last one in the area! The atmosphere amongst the runners was tremendous as it always is the night before a race starts, with a general mix of excitement and nerves about what was to come over the next six days.

After a night on the temple floor, I had my breakfast sitting on the steps and chatted to a couple of American runners called Becky and Brandon who were doing their first ultra-marathon together. I was amazed to see they had completely covered their bodies with long-sleeve shirts and running pants to protect themselves from the mosquitos, even though it was already hot and extremely humid. I had my long socks on and had covered myself in the Avon dry oil and I was roasting, so Becky and Brandon must have been cooking in their kit. I made my way to the start line, facing an opening day of 32km. Before we got going, the monks came out of the temple and said a prayer for us and then we were off.

I was with a Danish guy called Soren and we ran through the temple entrance and on to a dusty trail. I was already sweating buckets due to the humidity and I combined running and walking on the first day because I wanted to protect my leg and knew there were no cut-off times. Soon after the start I was on my own as I ended up being for most of the day, going at my own pace and enjoying my first experience of racing in Cambodia. I went through several villages and noticed there were orange boxes outside many of the houses. Stefan had told us these were 'cool boxes' filled with ice, bottles of water and cans of Coke. The water we were given disappeared quickly due to the heat and humidity and we had been encouraged to stop and buy a drink from the villagers because it was a source of income for them and a source of hydration for us. The village houses were all on stilts and consisted of one room with only a thin sleeping mat covering the floor. The race was the biggest thing to come through the village every year and the local children were amazing, coming out to support us and always smiling and waving. I stopped a couple of times on the first day to buy cans of Coke; running through the villages was very much part of the Cambodian experience.

The first day's finishing line was at the far end of a village. We had to run through light local traffic to get there and I was passed by vehicles that looked like a cross between lawnmowers and the Chopper bikes of my youth! Children rode in the trailers on the back shouting and waving at me as they overtook, always with big smiles. I crossed the line and it had been a tough opening day because of the heat and humidity, but an enjoyable one.

That night I and 20 others were billeted in a house that the owners had vacated for the night. There wasn't much space, but I found a spot and set up my sleeping bag and mat inside a mosquito net. It was still hot and got even more uncomfortably humid as the sun went down. I was so tired, though, that after my dehydrated meal I had no energy left for anything other than crawling on top of my sleeping bag for a sticky sleep.

The next day was 36km and once again it was hot and sweaty. Even though the route was straight and not a huge distance, it seemed to go on forever as I ran through paddy fields and bamboo forests. The end of the route was through the jungle, where the humidity was more intense and my right foot was hurting, having got worse throughout the day. I knew the finishing line was at a temple and I kept walking through the jungle, when I suddenly came to a wall. I followed the line of the wall for a kilometre and came to the entrance of the Preah Kham temple and saw the finishing line. I hobbled over the line, found some shade, and tried to cool down. My foot was worrying me, but Richard and I decided to have a look round the temple and we saw a sign saying 14,000 landmines had been cleared from the area. The temple was enormous and you could see where the Khmer Rouge had tried to knock it down, failed and hacked off the faces on the Buddha statues instead.

I hobbled back to the campsite and was greeted by a policeman selling cans of Coke out of the back of his car. I bought a couple and sat in our tent, resting my foot which was extremely sore, and I knew I would have to walk the rest of the race. I settled down for the night knowing I would wake to the long day with 62km of Cambodian heat, humidity and terrain waiting for me. I was sharing my tent with Keishaku from Japan who spoke as little English as I speak Japanese, but we got on very well through hand signals and smiles. It was a memorable night and meeting characters like him is another reason why I love being involved in ultra-marathons.

We started early on day three and despite telling myself I was going to walk the rest of the race, I decided to run the first kilometre out of the temple, back up the slope and into the jungle. That was a mistake because my foot was killing me, and I sensibly went back to my decision of the previous evening to walk the rest of the route. I got my walking poles out of my backpack and the long day had just got longer! I marched through the jungle for 20km until I reached the first checkpoint, grabbed some water, and kept going. After another 15km, I reached the second checkpoint which was in a village that mercifully had a café with shade. Inside the café was like a warzone with several runners in a bad state and being looked after by the race officials. I sat in the shade, drank a can of Coke and gave my foot a rest. As I left, a competitor called Lisenka, who had started an hour after me as she was a faster runner, sped past me and said hello, but I wasn't tempted to run with her.

I kept plodding along at my own pace, regularly buying cans of Coke from the orange boxes in the villages I walked through. It was incredibly hot and humid and after ten hours of walking I arrived at another café. Inside was Lisenka who had said hello to me earlier in the day and she was in a very bad state. She was dehydrated and agitated and one of the race officials was trying to calm her down. There was nothing I could do to help, so I started walking the final 10km of the route. About a kilometre later, Lisenka suddenly came up beside me, having made a dramatic recovery of sorts. She asked if she could stay with me because it was starting to get dark and she felt it would be more sensible to walk at my pace rather than be tempted to run again after her collapse earlier. We walked the rest of the route together until we came to the Prasat Beong Mealea temple which had a long stone path in front of it. We climbed the final steps, which was hard work at the end of a very long day, and crossed the finish line.

I immediately sat down, I was shattered and needed to find some energy, as the heat and humidity had taken their toll. After 20 minutes I began to feel better and walked back down the steps of the temple to a house in a nearby village, where I would be spending the night. I found Soren, Becky and Brandon in the house and they told me they had all dropped out of the race at the first checkpoint. It showed how brutal the long day had been. After a dehydrated meal, I got into my sleeping bag on the floor, for some much-needed sleep. A few people had gone to a bar in the village and much as I would have loved a beer and some non-dehydrated food, I couldn't walk another step that night.

The following morning, I packed up my kit, made my way back to the temple and started the 30km fourth day of the race. There is almost nothing worse than having to walk the best part of a kilometre just to get to the start of a race when you are battered and shattered, but that's where the start was so I had to effectively add another kilometre to the route that day. My foot was agony and I had taken some painkillers to try and help me get through the day. The first 15km were thankfully flat, but the route then took me into the thickest jungle I had encountered on the race. Instead of a path, the organisers had cut a route through the jungle using a machete and it was hard to follow. I came to a steep slope that I had to scramble up, which was hard enough in itself, but it was now the hottest time of the day. A couple of times I had to stop because I thought my heart was going to come out of my chest as it was beating so fast. I kept going and eventually reached the top of the slope to find two enormous carvings of elephants and standing next to them were Harri and Olly. It was fantastic to see them and their support gave me a welcome boost. This was the checkpoint and after some much-needed water, I continued making my way through the jungle and, even though the route was short in terms of distance, it seemed to go on forever.

I left the jungle and started walking on a straight long road which eventually led to a village next to the Phnom Kulen waterfalls. My foot was extremely painful, but thankfully the waterfalls were the finishing point of the day and I hobbled across the line. After a rest and some lunch, we went swimming underneath the waterfalls which was amazing. It was fantastic to sit in the ice-cold water and feel clean rather than hot and sweaty. My foot was swollen and extremely painful, so I went to the race doctor, but she couldn't work out what was causing the pain and inflammation and gave me some more painkillers. That evening we went to a restaurant in the local village and after we had eaten, the owners cleared away the tables and chairs and we spent the night in our sleeping bags on the floor. You certainly don't get that type of service in London!

After another good night's sleep, I set off on the penultimate day of the race. The start of the 44km route was uphill and from the top there were the most amazing views of the Cambodian landscape. My foot was painful as I walked through more paddy fields and villages, but mercifully it was mainly on a flat, well-maintained trail. After 30km, I came to a checkpoint and could see a mountain in the distance which I slowly began to realise I was going to have to walk up. I got to the foot of the Ta Aek mountain and started climbing the steep slope. It was a proper scramble with jungle surrounding me and the trail was marked by coloured plastic ribbons, tied around trees, that I kept failing to spot. The slope was slippery, it was dark because of the jungle canopy and every time I put my hand down, it got covered in ants. The climb was horrendous but eventually I got to the top and was greeted by the sight of the Ta Aek Temple and another policeman selling cans of cola out of the boot of his car! After a ten-minute breather, I slowly made my way down the other side of the mountain, but every step was now agony. The remainder of the route consisted of more villages and paddy fields and it was tough. The final couple of kilometres was a straight trail and some kids from a nearby village joined me and we jogged to the finish line together, which was a great experience. I was completely exhausted and my foot was screaming. The tents were all by a school, but all the ones in the shade had already been taken by runners who finished ahead of me. Richard eventually found a shady tent in an area covered by a tin roof at the back of the school.

After a rest we all got on a coach and were driven to a building near the Angkor Wat temple, where the race would finish the next day. This was so that we could each buy a ticket to gain admission to the temple where the race would finish. Bizarrely, Cambodian regulations wouldn't allow the organisers to buy the tickets for us, so I queued up with my identification and bought my ticket. We were driven back to the campsite and after a dehydrated meal and a couple of painkillers, I settled down for the night, with only the short, final day ahead of me.

The last day of the race was, fortunately for my foot, just 16km and it opened with a long, flat trek along a trail with trees on either side. The trail turned into a proper road, the first one of the week, which went past several temples and took me into an area known as Angkor. I walked for 3km alongside a wall that housed the Angkor Thom Temple and through the Bayan Temple with tourists everywhere. It was a surreal experience having been on my own for most of the week, to be surrounded by people with cameras, taking photographs of everything, including me! In the distance I could see three large towers, which I knew marked the entrance to the Angkor Wat Temple and the finish of the race. I crossed a bridge, and entered the temple, remembering to show my pre-purchased ticket. I held my Union Jack flag with the Prostate Cancer UK logo on it and managed to run the last few yards over the finishing line. My whole body hurt, but I felt fantastic as I found a tree, sat in the shade, and cheered all the remaining runners over the line. We were given a couple of hours to have a drink, relax and explore the temple. I bought a couple of cans of Coke and hobbled round the temple in all my sweaty, dirty kit but I didn't care. I felt on top of the world; despite being tired, I was buzzing.

We were driven to a town called Siem Reap and checked into a hotel that can only be described as five-star. It was pure luxury and this was my home with Richard for the next couple of days because we had booked to stay two extra nights. After I had washed the Cambodian jungle off me in the shower and had a couple of relaxing beers in the hotel bar, Richard and I went to the end-of-race dinner. Stefan presented me with a stone carving of a Buddhist Temple for finishing the race. After dinner some of us went into Siem Reap to visit some of the bars on the aptly named 'pub street'. The next morning, I enjoyed the buffet breakfast and spent the morning with

Richard looking at the temples in the town. We paid a lovely guy to drive us around on his tuk tuk and after lunch back at the hotel, we spent the afternoon relaxing by the pool. We went back into Siem Reap in the evening and had dinner with Harri and Olly. We came across a bar serving five-litre towers of beer with an ice core to keep it chilled: it turned into a very long night! Extending my Cambodian adventure by two days was definitely the right decision and left me with more amazing memories to treasure.

The following day I visited the war museum in Siem Reap which was fascinating. Whilst there, I met a man called Sinarth who had been a 'boy soldier' for the Vietnamese army despite being Cambodian, because when the Vietnamese slowly ousted Pol Pot the children in the liberated areas seemed to have little choice if they wanted to eat. He was an amazing man. He had lost a leg after stepping on a landmine and showed me three bullet wounds all received as a teenager. He had written a book called *A Dedication to Life*, which I bought and asked him to sign. Meeting Sinarth was a humbling experience and illustrated what the people of this beautiful country had been through.

After a relaxing evening at the hotel, the following morning Richard and I had to take a taxi back to Phnom Penh for our flight home. It was a terrifying seven-hour drive as our driver hurtled along narrow roads, overtaking slow-moving water buffalo, people and vehicles. We arrived at the airport in one piece and luckily our return flight wasn't crowded, so we were able to spread out. After a changeover in Bangkok, we eventually touched down in England. I was tired, my foot was painful, but I was elated to have been to Cambodia: a country I never thought I would visit and one that I had fallen in love with. I had made some more memories and the bloke with terminal cancer had successfully completed another ultra-marathon.

Chapter 13

Walking across Spain with my brother

MY PSA scores were staying where they should be. As I enjoyed a family Christmas, my score was 0.06 and at the start of January it was the lowest it had ever been at 0.05. I was calm and relaxed about the scores with my diet, exercise regime and drugs all seemingly working well together. I felt in a good place and had lots to look forward to in 2019. My training at the start of the year consisted mainly of walking with my brother. My next three big events, the 6633 Arctic Ultra, the MDS and the Camino de Santiago, would all involve plenty of walking, combined with some running and even though my foot was still painful, it was manageable. I was getting out four or five times a week and walking 25km each time.

In January, I surprised a mate of mine called Chris, who I had shared a tent with on my first MDS in 2016. Chris had been running a marathon a week for a year and his final one was the Cakeathon in Kent (there was cake at every checkpoint and a cake-shaped medal!). Without telling him, I turned up to run his last marathon with him. I think he was blown away to see me, and we slowly ran together. It was a fantastic day and an unbelievable achievement from Chris. It was not a great idea for my foot recovery, but just like running with Rory on his 1,000th marathon, I would have regretted it forever if I had not made the effort to join Chris.

At work, I had been permanently seconded to the sustainable banking team, which fitted my role much better. It covered the bank's charitable side and they wanted me to be the ambassador for their 'Do Good, Feel Good' initiative for staff. It was a new challenge and one I relished because I felt I could be more of an asset to that team. I was pleased about my new role, although I was sad to leave the team I had worked with for many years as we had been through a lot together both in terms of work challenges and my personal situation, where they had been so amazingly supportive.

My first ultra-marathon race of the year was the Pilgrims Challenge at the start of February and I walked the opening day with cricket commentator Mark Church. It was interesting to hear his plans about setting up a foundation in his father's memory to help people suffering from pancreatic cancer. We enjoyed each other's company and shared so many similar ideas. The weather was lovely, blue skies and snow underfoot. As we marched across the Surrey Downs, Mark mentioned to me that it seemed as if I knew everybody and it was obvious the respect the other runners had for me, which was nice to hear. My friend Alastair met us with 10km of the route remaining and walked to the finish with us. Alastair has always come to support me at the Pilgrims Challenge, and he showed what a good man he is by driving Mark 30 miles back to the station where he had left his car. I walked the second day of the race on my own, which gave me time to reflect. I knew I was lucky, I felt good and realised again how special the ultra-marathon family is.

I am conscious that I spend lots of our family money on entering races and I come back to Sarah and Ollie with amazing stories of the countries I have visited and the people I have met. I also spend quite a bit of time away from them both and I feel they deserve to be treated to amazing experiences because of the support they give me. Sarah had always wanted to go to Stockholm, so that is where we headed for the February school halfterm for a wonderful family holiday. I also got to celebrate my 54th birthday while we were there, although I think our visit to the Abba museum was the highlight for Sarah! I also managed to sneak in a couple of runs in sub-zero temperatures, which was great preparation for the 6633 Arctic Ultra which was less than a month away.

Once home, I headed to Cardiff with some mates to watch Wales play England in the Six Nations at the Principality Stadium. We were fortunate to be in a hospitality area and before the game, former England prop Gareth Chilcott and World Cup-winner Matt Dawson came to speak to us. I gave them both a Prostate Cancer UK 'Men United' badge and it was a proud moment for me when the two of them put their badges on. I was helping to spread the message again.

At the start of March, I was on a plane heading back to Canada for the 6633 Arctic Ultra. This year, I had entered the full race, with no option of finishing after 120 miles. I thought my training had gone well, walking between ten and 15 miles every other day with my brother and I knew how the race worked. I had a new tent, new shoes that I had been training in and lots more kit that I knew would work for the race. Part of my training had been walking a 10km loop on the streets around my house, coming back, putting up the tent in my living room, sleeping for an hour and a half and then heading out again. I did this eight times, covering 84 kilometres over 24 hours to practise getting the tent up quickly, grabbing some sleep and walking back-to-back distances.

My brother-in-law had managed to get me upgraded again for the flights to Canada and I sat in my business class seat, feeling confident about the race and ready for the 383 miles ahead of me. Richard was also returning to film me again and I was to meet him in Whitehorse. It felt great to be back and catch up with familiar, friendly faces.

The practice walk out of the town went better than the previous year, when my tent pole broke, although I did notice my feet were very cold when we got back to the hotel. I realised my new shoes did not have enough insulation and after speaking to the race director, he suggested putting tin foil in them which seemed to work and that put my mind at rest. I thought about my dad a lot when I was in Whitehorse because it was the first anniversary of his passing. I think he would have been pleased that I had come back to the Arctic. I remembered him proudly telling everybody on his ward that I was doing the race before I set off the previous year. That was the last time I saw him, but I knew he was with me again for this year's race.

We made the long drive to the Eagle Plains hotel, where the race would start and I met a Zimbabwean guy called Kirk, who had also been in the race the year before. We got on well and decided to do the race together. I liked the idea of being with someone, having some company and being able to look out for each other during the low points of the course. I was delighted to see a lady called Hayley at the hotel, who was doing the race for the first time. I had met Hayley on my first MDS as I had taken a photo of her race badge with her name on it, as she shares her name with my daughter. She was with a guy called Mark Whittle, a triathlete, and they ended up teaming up to do the race together. We started outside the hotel again, but for some reason this year there was no shotgun start, just a 'three, two, one, go!'

It was a glorious day, with blue skies and a temperature of -10 centigrade, which was warmer than the previous year. Kirk and I set off and the opening 36km towards the Arctic Circle and the first checkpoint were great fun as we plodded along enjoying each other's company. Kirk was wearing ice spikes on his shoes to help with grip and I was looking forward to getting to the opening checkpoint. The previous year there had been a big trailer with a heater in it, so you could warm up and get fresh boiling water. This year was the complete opposite and a shock. We arrived to find a cold, damp empty trailer, with no boiling water and it was a miserable place. The water was lukewarm, which meant my dehydrated meal didn't cook properly and I wasn't able to refill my thermos flasks with boiling water. This was a problem because my meal tasted foul, wasn't hot and I realised why the race director, Martin, had said they were going 'back to basics' at the race briefing. I knew at some stage before the next checkpoint, which was 86km away, I would have to do something about my boiling water supply. I should have spent more time trying to heat up the lukewarm water, but Kirk and I wanted to leave, and we set off again.

I started to realise that Kirk had a completely different race strategy to me. He would stop frequently to have a handful of nuts and dried fruit, whereas I wanted to walk for three hours and then stop and have a hot meal, although I was going to struggle to do that without boiling water. Every time Kirk stopped for a snack, I would wait with him, but understandably when I stopped for a hot meal at the first checkpoint he didn't want to hang around for too long, waiting for my meal to heat up. I allowed myself to get sucked into Kirk's tactics, which meant I missed out on a couple of hot meals, substituting them with a handful of snacks.

We walked into the night and after 62km reached the Big Dipper, which is a steep uphill climb. Halfway up, I was exhausted and was convinced the slope was steeper than the previous year. We came down the other side and discovered there wasn't a trailer at Rock River, where I had warmed up in my tent and got some sleep the year before. I was tired, not feeling well and my feet were frozen (the tin foil wasn't working in my shoes). Kirk decided to sleep in the large shed at Rock River, but I decided to sleep outside as the path to the shed appeared to be deep snow and I didn't fancy that.

I put up my tent, had a snack because I had no boiling water for a hot meal and tried to get some sleep. I lay in my sleeping bag for three hours, but I was freezing and couldn't stop shivering nor could I feel my toes at all. As we agreed, Kirk came and got me after three hours and we continued walking. I felt terrible as we walked past the Rock River campground and came to the start of the long slog up Wright Pass. This was where I had been stopped the year before and had to walk loops back to Rock River because of a blizzard. We started climbing the 25km to the top of Wright Pass and I was starting to feel better. I needed a poo but there was nowhere to hide, so I had to squat down and go in the snow. I had flashbacks of the police car turning up last year, but I was able to do my business without feeling guilty and carry on walking. The sun was out, which helped me get warm and my feet no longer felt like blocks of ice. About halfway up Wright Pass, I realised I hadn't heard anything from Kirk for a while because we had both been in our own worlds, concentrating on getting over the pass. I stopped and looked behind me. Kirk was 200 yards away, sitting on his sled. I walked back to check he was ok and when I reached him, he told me he had pulled out of the race because his feet were killing him. I couldn't believe it. His ice spikes had caused his feet to blister and I was devastated for him. I sat with him for a few minutes, but with the organisers of the race on their way to pick him up, there wasn't much I could do for him. We said goodbye and I carried on walking up Wright Pass.

I was on my own for the first time in the race and felt sad that I had lost my companion. The slope got steeper and steeper and I eventually got to the top a couple of hours after leaving Kirk. I was shattered and couldn't remember how much further it was until the next checkpoint at James Creek. I was convinced it wasn't that far, but after another steep climb I realised the checkpoint was farther than I thought, and I needed to stop and have something to eat. I met a photographer and asked her how far it was to the checkpoint and she told me it was, 'just around the corner'. I was tired, hungry, cold, and feeling awful but decided to continue walking and found there was no checkpoint 'just around the corner'. It was getting dark and I kept walking, but there was no sign of the checkpoint. I knew I was looking for the Highways Depot, where I had slept the previous year, but it was nowhere to be seen. I was in big trouble because I was exhausted, frozen, feeling sick and extremely worried about frostbite. Eventually, I did go 'just around the corner' and there was the Highways Depot. I staggered to the checkpoint and a couple of the race crew came to meet me because they could see I was in a bad way. They took me into the depot, which was warm and sat me down.

One of the medics made me a hot meal, but after a mouthful I thought I was going to be sick. Somebody laid my sleeping bag on the floor and I crawled into it shivering uncontrollably and feeling terrible. I asked one of the officials to wake me up in three hours and I immediately went to sleep.

Three hours later, I was woken up and told I had to leave straight away if I wanted to continue in the race. I was half asleep, felt terrible and had no energy, so I made the horrible decision to drop out of the race without really thinking it through. I like to think I would have continued if it had been a couple of hours later, but at that moment I was cooked. I went straight back to sleep and woke up four hours later feeling dreadful and the first person I saw was Richard. I felt guilty that he had come all this way to film me and I had dropped out miles from where I had finished the year before. I felt a complete failure and there was nothing anybody could say to cheer me up as I packed up my kit and got in a car that drove me to the town of Fort McPherson. This year, the checkpoint was in a church hall where I had a hot meal and started to feel better physically. Mentally I was devastated to drop out of the race, but I had already decided that I was going to support the runners still in the race as I had done the previous year.

Mark and Hayley arrived at the checkpoint and I made them a hot meal, so they could concentrate on getting some rest and I went out and walked with some of the runners back to the church hall. I spent time with Kirk, and he explained a bit more about why he had dropped out of the race and it was good to be back with him. I still felt like I had let everyone down but hoped I was being some use to the other runners rather than just sitting around feeling sorry for myself.

Supporting the runners still in the race gave me a purpose and I had a memorable night in Anuvik, helping the race crew. We got an emergency call in the middle of the night about one of the runners called Didier and drove out to find him. We knew his location because he had pressed the bleeper on his tracker, but when we got there all we found was a couple of abandoned sleds and one was on fire. We had no idea what was happening, but after a couple of calls found out that Didier had been suffering from hypothermia and had become delirious. He was trying to walk back to the previous checkpoint when he was found by two other competitors, Patrick (who had been pulled out with frostbite the previous year) and David. David decided to set fire to his sled to try and warm Didier up and when we arrived it was still burning. Didier had been taken to hospital and Patrick and David had continued with the race, but it was a surreal and dramatic night. Thankfully, Didier was fine after a day in hospital.

The race finished in the town of Tuktoyaktuk once again and the atmosphere was great as I went out and walked into town with everyone still in the race, including Mark and Hayley. The 380-mile drive back to Whitehorse gave me plenty of time to think about where the race had gone wrong for me. I felt like a failure on every level and as I assessed the race, I realised I had made four key mistakes. Firstly, I had worn shoes without proper insulation which froze my feet, causing me problems for my entire race. Secondly, I didn't take enough boiling water with me at the start of the race because I assumed it would be available at the first checkpoint and, even then, I should have boiled my lukewarm water because I had a stove. My third mistake was my food strategy, which had been a disaster. In no way do I blame Kirk because I never told him what my strategy was, but I should have stuck to my plan of eating hot meals every three hours because just eating snacks destroyed me. Finally, I just wasn't fit enough. I hadn't done as much training as the previous year and paid the price. Any one of these reasons would have been a problem, but all of them together had been a disaster. In the back of my mind, there was a concern that my cancer had caused me to have no energy during the race, but when you have a terminal illness you accept there are going to be days when you don't feel well. You just have to get on with it. I did also wonder if my drugs might have had an effect on me during the race.

I enjoyed the end of race dinner at Whitehorse but I just wanted to get home. I couldn't shake the feeling of letting everybody down as I sat on the plane heading back to England. When I got home, Sarah and Ollie immediately lifted my spirits and I didn't want to be miserable around them even though I was still gutted at how my Arctic race had turned out.

A couple of days after getting home I had a blood test and the results showed my PSA score was 0.14. It had trebled since my last test, but the doctor reassured me it was nothing to worry about because the machine that gave the result had been recalibrated. He told me the 0.14 score was the same as the 0.05 score before the recalibration, but I was worried. Even though I knew the score hadn't really gone up, it reminded me of the time a couple of years before when my PSA score had been regularly doubling. I was scared the same thing was happening even though the doctor had reassured me everything was ok. The fact the number had increased sowed a seed of doubt in my mind and made me worry.

I couldn't dwell on the PSA result, though, because two weeks after returning from the Arctic I was off to the Sahara for my fourth Marathon des Sables. My foot was painful and I had not done as many miles as I wanted to in the Arctic, but I was looking forward to getting back to the desert. The big difference this year was there was no Rory in my tent because he had run his last MDS the previous year. My tentmates this year were Trevor, Chris, Paul, Gavin, Ben, Matt and Carly, and we all got on very well from the moment we got together. I enjoyed the race, but realised on the first day I would have to walk the whole thing because my foot was too painful to run on. I did manage to jog the final two miles of the race, but if I had tried to do any more running, I wouldn't have finished. I came home with another MDS medal for the trophy cabinet and received the great news that my latest PSA had remained at 0.14, which was a huge relief.

A couple of weeks after the MDS, I spent a day in London with my mate Nick Butter, who was running the London marathon as part of his extraordinary challenge of running a marathon in every country of the world. It was over a year since Nick had set off and we had stayed in regular contact. It was great to see him and we did an interview together with Adrian Chiles at the BBC on Radio 5 Live. Listening to Nick, I was amazed by his energy and the enormousness of his challenge. He mentioned his last marathon was going to be in Athens in November and asked me to join him, which gave me something else to look forward to. I didn't have a place in the London Marathon but spent the day with Sarah at the Prostate Cancer UK stand cheering on the runners. We had a fantastic day and I saw lots of people I knew from other races and managed a brief man-hug with Nick as he ran by.

A couple of days after the London Marathon, my brother Ian and I were heading to France to start the Camino de Santiago. The ancient pilgrimage is a 780km walk from St Jean Pied de Port to Santiago and we had given ourselves a month to complete it. I was looking forward to spending time with Ian and our training had gone well. It would be a different experience to running an ultra-marathon and the pilgrimage was something I had always wanted to do. Ian is a fit bloke who had cycled from John O'Groats to Land's End and is a practical guy who is focused when he puts his mind to something. I think he was a bit nervous about the distance we would be walking every day, but we were both excited about the challenge we faced as we said goodbye to our families and headed to the airport. We were well prepared and knew the route was well marked by signposts, yellow arrows and the traditional yellow seashells. We also had our guidebooks, so were not worried about getting lost and we would be staying in a mixture of hostels ('Albergue') and hotels. An expression often used by pilgrims is: 'the Camino will provide.' And we hoped this was true.

After a night at an airport hotel we took an early-morning flight to Biarritz. We met three other lads doing the pilgrimage as we got off the plane: Owen, a prison chaplain, Phil, who had recovered from bowel cancer and Miles, an ex-paratrooper. We all shared a cab from Biarritz to St Jean Pied de Port and on the journey I told the lads my story and they kindly gave me 40 euros for the charity and I gave each of them a Prostate Cancer UK badge to wear. After lunch we got our 'passports' for the pilgrimage – a piece of card that would be stamped at various points on the journey to prove we had done the route once we got to Santiago. Ian and I bought scallop seashells to put on our rucksacks because these are the symbol of the pilgrimage. The first pilgrims used them to eat and drink out of. Ian, Miles, Phil and I decided to start our pilgrimage (Owen wanted an afternoon resting in St Jean) and we walked five miles steeply up the Pyrenees to the Refuge Orisson, where we had planned to stay the night. It was hot and the air was clear, but when we got to our accommodation, we were told it was full, which was not a great start to the journey. The owners told us they had somewhere else we could stay and kindly drove us there. Sadly, it was a mile outside St Jean, so we ended up back where we started but had a comfortable night in a refuge, sleeping on bunks.

The next morning the owners drove us back up to the Refuge Orisson and on the way we passed Owen who had started his pilgrimage from St Jean. We climbed to the top of the Pyrenees, which were covered in snow and came down the other side into Spain. It was raining as we marched along, stopping at a monastery to have our passport stamped, and after 26 miles we arrived in the town of Zubiri. We decided to stop there and spend the night. We then discovered, however, that the two main hostels were closed for redevelopment and it was like Bethlehem on Christmas Eve with no room at the inn anywhere in the village. The proverb of 'the Camino will provide' came true when the sports hall was opened, and we were told we could spend the night there with 40 other pilgrims, free of charge. Sleeping on the floor wasn't a comfortable experience and we left early the next morning and walked another marathon in the rain. We stopped for lunch in Pamplona and I was enjoying being with Ian, Miles and Phil. After another steep climb we arrived in the town of Zaraquiegui and stayed in a hostel that was more comfortable than the sports hall floor of the previous evening.

We left Miles and Phil the following morning and set off on our own. The day started with a steep mountain walk and it was worth the effort for the views at the top and the magnificent iron sculpture of silhouettes of pilgrims that stretched for 40ft. Coming down the other side of the mountain, we met an American lady who was in her 70s and told us she was walking 12km a day and would be on the road for three months, which was amazing. The weather was perfect, and a hard day of walking was made easier when we passed through a village that had a drinking fountain where you could fill up your bottles with water or free wine! Sadly, it was too early in the morning to take advantage of more than a mouthful of the free wine, which felt like a missed opportunity. After 20 miles we reached a country inn where we decided to spend the night. Ian was tired and my ankles were hurting and at dinner we met a mum and her son who told us they had seen a man have a heart attack and die on the route earlier in the day. The experience had obviously affected them and it was a stark reminder of how challenging the pilgrimage was.

The next couple of days were uneventful with lots of hard walking through vineyards and cornfields with the sun beating down and we met some more interesting characters doing the pilgrimage. My knee was sore and Ian didn't seem to be enjoying the experience as much as I had hoped he would. The route was extremely challenging plus he had a bout of food poisoning which was making it even harder for him. He never complained and got his head down and kept going, but he was obviously in discomfort.

We had a couple of nice evening meals with other pilgrims and spent one night in what felt like a glorified caravan although it had a washing machine, which was a bonus. We continued our journey through northern Spain and Ian's spirits lifted, which made me happy because I wanted him to look back on this adventure with fond memories. We were covering an average of 20 miles a day and in the village of Tardajos we shared a double bed together, which wasn't ideal but showed how well we were getting on!

We had got into the routine of grabbing breakfast in the villages we walked through as on most days we left before any breakfast was served at the hostels. A café we stopped at one morning had a wall with messages written by pilgrims from all over the world and I stuck a Prostate Cancer UK badge to the wall and the owner of the café gave us both a gold pendant of a saint to wear, telling us it would bring luck for the rest of our journey.

We started the second week of the Camino with a 35km walk that ended in one of the maddest places I have ever been to. Our hostel was like a hippy community with the smell of marijuana everywhere (it certainly made my knee feel better!). There were donkeys in the garden and concrete tubes that you could sleep in. We decided to sleep on bunks in the hostel and we shared a fantastic dinner with some very laid-back pilgrims. It was exactly the type of experience I had wanted to get from the pilgrimage and an evening I will never forget. After saying goodbye to the donkeys, we spent three days walking along old Roman roads in the sun and recovering in hostels at night.

I got a Facebook message from a friend called Pete, telling me his dad had been diagnosed with prostate cancer and was starting treatment at the Royal Marsden. It made me appreciate how lucky I was to be doing the pilgrimage and how important it was that I kept telling my story and making people, especially men, aware of the disease. Physically, the Camino was hard work and both of us had niggles, but we kept going and eventually reached Leon. We visited the cathedral, got our passports stamped and the next day after a wet afternoon we stayed in a hotel which had the most bizarre check-in process. We arrived to find all the room keys spread over an empty reception desk and a phone with a number written next to it. I rang the number and the owner told us which keys to take, which seemed a strange way to welcome your guests.

For the next couple of days, we kept plodding along in the heat until we reached the highest point of the Camino, which is 1,500 metres higher than Ben Nevis. At the summit, there is a cross surrounded by rocks and I laid a stone I had brought from our garden in memory of my dad, my mum and my father-in-law.

We kept seeing statues of pilgrims on the route, some realistic and some bizarre but we took our photographs with many of them just for the memory. In the town of Ponferrada, I even managed to find a physio who did some much-needed work on my shoulder which had been causing me issues for a while. She explained that it was because I was not doing up my chest strap on my backpack, so the straps were compressing my collar bones: lesson learnt!

Most days we saw other pilgrims that we recognised and we continued to meet some lovely people on our journey, most with a story to tell. Three weeks into our Camino, we reached O' Cebreiro and were kept up most of the night by a German couple having a blazing row, which didn't add to the ambience of the otherwise traditionally peaceful village. We met a preacher from Minnesota called Gary, whose church had paid for him to do the pilgrimage and he was walking it wearing a Southampton football shirt, something you don't see every day on the Camino!

Twenty-five days into our journey, we came to a signpost telling us it was 100km to Santiago. There were many more pilgrims on the route from now on because many had started at the town of Sarria, 108km from Santiago, which is the shortest distance that was recognised as being a pilgrimage. We had a tough 33km day, walking through a eucalyptus forest and stopping at a bar where we had a bottle of 'Pilgrim's beer'. The owner gave us a white pen and I wrote the names of my family and the charity on my bottle, which was placed on a nail amongst thousands of other bottles that had been signed by pilgrims. Three days later, after a steep climb, Ian and I came to the top of a hill and in front of us was Santiago. It was an emotional moment, being with my brother and knowing we were going to complete our pilgrimage together. We walked to the town square and took our passports to the pilgrims' office where we were told our 'Compostela' would be ready for collection in an hour. We went and had a couple of beers and picked up our official document saying we had completed the Camino de Santiago, which was a proud moment for us both.

We had booked a house in Santiago and the following day Sarah and Ollie arrived with Ian's wife Helen and his daughter Becs to spend a couple of days with us to celebrate our achievement. It was lovely to see them all after a month on the road and we spent that day looking around the town. I had decided to add another couple of days of walking to Finisterre, where the 'spiritual' pilgrimage finished. Ian very sensibly had decided not to do the extra couple of days, because his ankle was giving him problems, but I was so proud of him walking the 780km 'religious' pilgrimage to Santiago. We decided to hire a car, so Ian could pick me up at the end of each day and bring me back to a flat we had booked which was just over halfway to Finisterre.

After waving goodbye to our families, I set off alone towards Finisterre and walked the final 80km in three days, enjoying the views and spending the lunchtimes and evenings with my brother. I bumped into a lad called Andreas from Argentina, who we had met on the third day of our pilgrimage and spent an enjoyable afternoon walking with him. Ian joined me for the final 2km to the Finisterre lighthouse and I was so pleased to have him with me as I completed both the religious and spiritual pilgrimages.

Ian and I had a final day in Santiago and celebrated finishing the Camino in style. We did end up having our one and only argument of the entire month, which was alcohol-fuelled but everything was fine the next day when we flew back to England. The Camino de Santiago had been tough and it was an experience I will never forget. Being with Ian was very special and we spent lots of time chatting about Dad. I think he would have been proud of his boys. We had met some extraordinary people and made some wonderful forever memories. Arriving home, I was proud that I could officially call myself a 'pilgrim' and I would recommend the experience to anyone who ever fancies having a go.

Chapter 14

Following in the footsteps of Lawrence of Arabia

THE CAMINO de Santiago had taken a month and it was lovely to come home and be with my family again. There genuinely is 'no place like home' and when you are away it makes you appreciate everything you have that little bit more. The Camino had given me the freedom to just think about myself, which sounds selfish, but I was able to switch off and go wherever I wanted with my thoughts. Even though I was delighted to be home, I missed having the time to think about everything in my life which the Camino had given me. It always takes a couple of days for me to come down from the buzz of doing a race, but coming back to my family and friends is always special and the Camino had given me some wonderful memories.

A couple of days after getting back from Spain, Sarah and I went to the Celtic Manor in Wales, where I was involved in giving out an award, as ever representing Prostate Cancer

UK, at the National Football League Awards Night. I felt my story was continuing to make an impact on people and I was proud to be representing the charity, speaking to many people involved in football in order to encourage them to spread more awareness about prostate cancer.

Back at work, I was enjoying being part of the sustainable banking team, working mainly on different projects for their 'Do Good, Feel Good' campaign. If you remember, the previous year I had helped the director of the northern region of the bank organise a challenge that involved walking seven marathons in seven days, which had been a huge success for the bank and raised lots more money for Prostate Cancer UK. This year, that team wanted to do something different and came up with the idea of doing three ultra-marathons in three days covering Sheffield, Manchester and Liverpool. We did the challenge in June and I walked each ultra-marathon with staff from the bank and it was once again a great success. The desire of my colleagues to finish each ultra-marathon was inspiring as many of them had never walked 50km before. I was proud of the effort everybody made and we raised around £50,000 which was spilt between Prostate Cancer UK and MIND. The challenge was not all about the fundraising though. Along the way, I spoke to many colleagues who also discovered the magic of distance challenges. Like me, they found the time to free their mind for a day enabled them to focus and speak freely about some of their own personal challenges. It helped remind me that under the surface of someone there is sadly all too often a tragic memory or thought that still needs exorcising. I hope those walks did that for some.

On the way home, I stopped to see a friend of mine called Si, a prostate cancer mentor and legend in my eyes. It was he who took me under his wing when I was first diagnosed and posted on the Prostate Cancer UK forum. Si gave me hope mixed with realism. Sadly, like me, he had advanced prostate cancer and when I saw him he was struggling with the disease, having battled so well for many years before. I could tell he knew the cancer was going to get him, but that didn't stop us having a lovely couple of hours together watching the cricket on the telly and catching up.

As you will have gathered by now, spending time with my family and making special memories is very important to me. I have always loved baseball and I managed to get tickets for the MLB game between the Boston Red Sox and the New York Yankees at the Olympic Stadium in Stratford. I went with Ollie and we had a fantastic day, just the two of us, father, and son, spending some quality time together. Two days later, I went with my mate Jim to Centre Court at Wimbledon and it was a perfect few days, watching sport with my son and my best mate. Two days I will never forget and the opportunity to create memories that will last forever.

But when it came to the running, my foot was becoming a major concern. It was still extremely painful after the three ultra-marathons in three days and I started seeing a physiotherapist to try and solve the problem. My next race was due to be the Al Andalus Ultimate in a month but my foot wasn't improving and my physio eventually told me I needed a proper rest. After much soul searching, I reluctantly decided not to do the race in Spain because I was never going to be fit enough and I didn't want to go there and not have a chance of finishing the race. It was a hard decision to make because this was the first time since I had finished my initial cancer treatment I had been unable to do a race of my choosing and I started to worry again about whether I would still be around next year to give this race another go. My cancer forces me to only plan short-term and there was a part of me thinking, 'Go and do the race, if you fail at least you went, because you might not be alive next year.' But I had to be sensible and knew deep down that my foot needed rest. My injuries are always down to general wear and tear but also the drugs that I take, have, I think, a big effect. I was worried that my foot wasn't going to get better because it flared up whenever I did any exercise. I was scared I might not be able to run again, but I did have the comfort of already having achieved so much at this point. But there was still so much I wanted to do and I had no idea how much time I may have. I knew if I wanted to run again, though, I had to do what the physio was telling me and be sensible with my body. I started seeing the physio every week, rested the foot and slowly it began to improve.

My eldest daughter Hayley was graduating from Swansea University, so we travelled to Wales to see her receive her 2:1 in history. From the age of 15, Hayley had talked about wanting to be a history teacher and after doing her GCSEs and A-Levels, she became the first person from our family to go to university. When I was diagnosed with cancer, she was 16 and I didn't think I would see her get her A-Levels, so to be there, watching her collect her degree, was an extremely proud and emotional day for me. The whole family were there, including Hayley's mum and grandmother and we had a lovely day all together, creating some more special memories. Hayley is now a history teacher and my eldest son Ben works for one of the largest insurance companies in the world. Ben was like me at school, not really into the academic side of things but after getting his GCSEs he went to college and got himself an apprenticeship at the local council in their insurance department. He got his head down, studied hard and passed all his insurance exams with distinction. Ben was headhunted and offered a job at a major city insurer where he is now thriving. I am so proud of Hayley, Ben and my youngest son Ollie, who is still at school. I am so grateful still to be alive and able to see how well their lives are going. Every day I spend with each of them is a special day.

We took a family holiday to Spain with my mate Jim and his family, and Hayley and her boyfriend Ieuan joined us for part of the holiday to celebrate her graduation. We had a relaxing couple of weeks, and I decided to test the foot with some 5km runs in the heat and it felt ok, which gave me a real lift. After coming back from Spain, Ollie went to scout camp for a week and Sarah and I went to the Lake District and stayed in Keswick. We did lots of walking, which was another good test for my foot and enjoyed a lovely time together, forgetting all our worries because the lakes are such a beautiful place to unwind.

After the Lake District I gave my foot its first proper test when I ran the Hangman Ultra-Marathon in Hampshire. I had run the first ever Hangman three years before and had done it every year since, one of only two people to have run every year. The Hangman is organised by Andy Nuttall who is passionate about all things ultra-running as well as being a thoroughly nice guy. It's a one-day, 34-mile race out and back to the massive Coombe Gibbet high on a hill in Berkshire. My foot held up, but I walked most of the race with just a bit of running on the flats to be on the safe side. I saw lots of familiar faces, including my mate Perry and a few other friends I had met at the MDS, who had come to do the race with me. I am always proud when people put themselves out to support me at races. It was my slowest Hangman Ultra, but I got through it and that did my confidence the world of good. It proved the work I was doing with the physio was working and if I was sensible my foot was going to get better.

I celebrated by coming home and entering a race in October called the Ultra X Jordan, which had previously been known as the Wadi Run Ultra. It was a race I had always wanted to do and I was fascinated by Jordan because as a kid I had loved the film *Lawrence of Arabia* and much of the race took place where it had been filmed. It was the only race I had lined up for the rest of the year, which would give my foot and me plenty of time to prepare properly and I was looking forward to doing a different desert race to the MDS.

At the start of September, I joined Jeff Stelling for his latest March for Men, raising money for Prostate Cancer UK. Jeff was walking four marathons in four days in four different nations and I joined him for the whole event. We walked marathons in Glasgow, Belfast, Cardiff and London, and 60 people from the bank joined us and hundreds of others on different days. It was a great challenge and a miracle of logistics, getting us to the next city via planes, trains and automobiles.

A sign of both the importance of prostate cancer and the draw that Jeff has was the number of celebrities who took part. In Scotland, we were joined by ex-Arsenal footballer Charlie Nicholas, current (at the time of writing) West Ham manager David Moyes and *Trainspotting* author Irvine Welsh. Ex-Southampton footballer Iain Dowie, boxer Carl Frampton and broadcaster Colin Murray joined us in Belfast. Former England footballer Matt Le Tissier joined us in Cardiff and in London ex-footballers Trevor Brooking, Chris Kamara, Francis Benali, Mark Bright, and David Seaman, to name a few, met us at various clubs along the route.

We finished at the Tottenham Hotspur Stadium and I was honoured to be presented with my medal by the late, great England goalkeeper Ray Clemence, who sadly died of prostate cancer a year later in 2020. Sarah joined us for the final marathon and, as a complete surprise, my 'cancer twin' Lloyd

Pinder turned up to support us at the finish, as he was sadly too ill to walk with us this time. The charity asked me to make a speech to the 500 people at the ground and I explained why the money Jeff had raised was so important. I told everybody that I hoped the effort we had made with Jeff would mean prostate cancer wasn't a killer by the time my kids were 40. And if that was the case, what bigger gift can you give a father than potentially saving his children's lives? The charity then announced that Jeff's three marches had raised over £1 million which was greeted with great applause. That last day was quite emotional for me on so many levels and I was proud to have played a small part in raising those funds with friends and colleagues over the years.

Sadly, a week later the reality of what advanced prostate cancer really means came home to me when I received the awful news that my friend Si had died from the illness. As I have already explained, he was the person who took me under his wing when I first went on the Prostate Cancer UK forum after my diagnosis and he was a legend to me. I had texted Si after finishing the march with Jeff Stelling and below are a couple of lines from that text, because they sum up how much Si meant to me.

'Si. I have just finished marching four marathons in four days with Jeff Stelling. I made a speech to 500 people and I was thinking about you and how you kept me going at the start when I didn't believe I had a day's future. Take care. Remember the good times. I'll be thinking about you, always.'

Si was so important to me; we had been brought together by something horrible and had helped each other along the way. I still think about him often and remember what a great bloke he was.

A week later, I spent an enjoyable afternoon with Mark Church in the BBC commentary box at the Oval watching a Surrey cricket match. Mark interviewed me live during his commentary and I was grateful for the opportunity to tell my story. It was a great way to watch the cricket too!

Inspired by Jeff, I then set off on another solo walk from Bromley Football Club to Dover Athletic FC to help launch Prostate Cancer UK's 'Non-League Week' supported by the National Football League and raise more money and awareness for the charity. I left on a Tuesday night after Bromley's home game and Vanarama kindly lent me a camper van for the week. Vinnie Jones presented me with the keys, which was tremendous because I am a massive AFC Wimbledon fan (my eldest son's middle name is Vincent, after Mr Jones) and he kindly signed his autobiography to Ben for me.

I walked for four days and got a lovely reception from all the clubs I visited. I arrived at Dover Athletic for their televised home game on BT Sport and I was interviewed on the pitch by Matt Smith from BT Sport. Once again, I was blown away by the support I received from the footballing community and enjoyed helping launch 'Non-League Week'.

As September ended, two friends at work called Mark and Geoff did a charity gig (aptly called Kevstock) for Prostate

Cancer UK for a second time. They both play in bands and hired a pub in London, raising £2,000 for the charity, which was a brilliant effort. It was a fantastic night and I even got up on stage with them as they played the Proclaimers song, 'I'm Gonna Be (500 miles)'. They put the gig on under the bank's 'Do Good, Feel Good' campaign and it was another event that made me feel I was making a positive impact on people and influencing them to help the charity.

It was time to get on a plane and head out to the Ultra X Jordan ultra-marathon. My foot felt ok with rest, physiotherapy and the right training having done the trick and I was excited to be going to a country that had always held a fascination for me. The five-day race took place in the desert, including an area known as the Valley of the Moon and covered 250km in total, so each day would be a marathon distance or more. It was going to be extremely hot, but I was used to desert conditions thanks to my MDS experiences, and I was looking forward to the challenge. On the flight to Jordan, by sheer luck I was sat next to one of the doctors for the race and we clicked straight away. She was able to give some more details about what was coming my way in the desert and I told her my story and why I was doing the race. When we arrived at Queen Alia International Airport, getting a taxi to our hotel in Amman was chaos, with our bags being strapped to the roofs of various cars that proceeded to hurtle down the motorway. It was a miracle when we arrived at our hotel to find our bags still on the roof.

Even though we arrived late at night, it was still hot and sticky and I checked into the room that I was sharing with a German runner called Rob who I had never met. We introduced ourselves, unpacked our kit and went to sleep. The next morning, I went for a walk in Amman, which was beautiful, with many temples and a busy market. I enjoyed my first proper taste of Jordan and spent the afternoon back at the hotel where the race briefing would be that evening, enabling me to meet some of the other runners. There were 73 of us competing and it was good to get to know some other people because, unusually, I didn't know anybody doing this race.

The following morning three coaches drove us to the Wadi Rum desert where the race would start. I enjoyed the journey and at one stage we drove parallel to a steam train that was pulling a flatbed truck carrying a machine gun and two men dressed in World War One military uniforms. It was obviously a tourist train, but I did feel like I was on the set of *Lawrence of Arabia*. I kept seeing signs for Aqaba and fully expected to see Peter O'Toole and Omar Sharif riding across the desert on camels.

After a couple of hours, we arrived at a small village and were greeted by a line of battered old pickup trucks. I threw my bag on a truck, climbed aboard and was driven into the desert. After five miles we arrived at our campsite and unlike the MDS, I didn't know who I was going to be sharing a tent with. I found a tent, introduced myself to the other nine occupants and found some space to lay my kit down. It was cramped, so

I had my first dehydrated meal sitting outside, soaking up the desert. It was different from the Sahara with more rocks and I could see why it was described as the Valley of the Moon, because it did feel like we were on another planet.

After my first night in the tent, I made my way to the start line, facing an opening 46km day. We knew the first two days were looped marathons to the campsite and standing at the start, in the heat of the desert, my adrenaline was pumping. I had decided to run the first day and see how my foot felt, but what I hadn't expected was the volume and softness of the sand. Most of the first day was spent in sand and it was extremely tough because it was so unforgiving on your legs. The field spread out very quickly, meaning I spent most of the day on my own. Because of the distance, I was running long into the afternoon, the hottest time of the day, which was different to the MDS and extremely tiring. I felt ok when I came over the finishing line after seven hours and I was happy being back in a race environment. My foot had managed to survive a day of running and I continued to run on the second day, which was 50km.

At the halfway point I came to a rocky area and as I put my foot down to climb, I slipped and fell heavily on my knee. I knew straight away I had done some damage because my knee was bleeding and when I tried to run again the pain made it impossible. My ankle was also in trouble and, after cleaning the wound, I resigned myself to the fact that I was going to have to walk the remaining 25km that day. The heat was relentless and because I was walking slowly, I was out in the sun longer and was basically getting cooked. Walking was painful, but I managed to get to the finish and spent the evening trying to rest my knee, foot and ankle; thank heavens for the walking poles that I always carry!

Day three was the 68km 'long day' and at the start I tried to run about 20 steps and had to stop because my leg was too painful. I got my walking poles out of my backpack, got my head down and started making my way across the desert. I slowly got into my rhythm and even with the pain in my leg, I was overtaking other runners who had gone out too hard at the start. I kept marching at a good pace and refilled my water bottles at the various checkpoints on the route. The distances between each checkpoint were long and the organisers sent out jeeps with freshwater bottles for us because it was so hot.

I was on a long stretch of sand, heading towards the final checkpoint of the day and I had run out of water. My leg was hurting and it felt like I was in an oven as the temperature continued to rise. There was still a long way to go until the checkpoint and I was struggling. Suddenly, I saw a jeep, which drove up next to me and the driver gave me a frozen bottle of water. I couldn't thank him enough: it was a godsend and water has never tasted so good. I continued walking and the landscape never changed. All I could see were rocks, sand and valleys and eventually I reached the final checkpoint. I thanked the organisers for sending the jeep out with water and they told me it was nothing to do with them. It turned out the 'water angel' was a Jordanian who had decided to drive through the desert handing out water to the competitors. I would like to meet that gentleman one day and shake his hand.

Whilst at the checkpoint, I asked how much further it was to the finish and was told there was only 8km of the route left. I was hot, tired and my tank was nearly empty, but I knew I could get through another 8km. I left the checkpoint and was met by an uphill climb which was hard work but made easier by the fact I could see a Landover in the distance which I assumed was the finish. As I got closer, I realised I couldn't see any tents. My fuel tank was just about empty when I reached the Landover only to be told there was another 5km to go before the finish. Physically I was shattered, I had eaten all my snacks and my mind had switched off, thinking it was the end of the day. Somehow, I pulled myself together and continued climbing up the slope as it started to get dark. I was angry that I was still walking, but I was just trying to find someone to blame because I was exhausted. I should have learnt my lesson in previous races never to trust anyone's opinion of how far it is to go but clearly hadn't! I plodded along, but there didn't seem to be any sign of the finish and I started to worry I was lost, which didn't improve my mood as by now I was having a massive sense of humour failure.

Eventually, in the distance, I could see a light so I headed towards it and started making out the silhouettes of people stood on top of a huge rock. I reached the light and thankfully it was the finishing line because I was shattered and don't think

I could have gone much further. I looked for the campsite, but there didn't seem to be any tents, but I started to notice runners lying in their sleeping bags on the rock. It dawned on me there were to be no tents tonight and I would be sleeping al fresco under the stars. My leg was hurting, I felt awful and if I am honest, I wasn't in the right frame of mind for sleeping on a rock. I had a dehydrated meal and reluctantly climbed into my sleeping bag and fell straight to sleep.

Ironically, I slept well on the rock and woke up to a spectacular view of the desert which immediately lifted my mood. I ate breakfast, packed my kit and set off on the 46km fourth day of the race. The good news was my knee, foot and ankle were not hurting as much, so I was able to do some gentle running on the flat stretches. The landscape changed as I went through ravines and followed twisting trails through the rocks. I really enjoyed the day because I felt better, and the scenery was interesting and gave me something to look at other than rocks and sand. At one point, I came across a random camel sitting in the middle of a trail and pickup trucks full of tourists drove past me at regular intervals, going to different landmarks in the desert. At the campsite that evening, I took advantage of the excellent team of race physiotherapists who worked on my leg and I went to sleep knowing there was only 40km of the race remaining.

My leg felt good as I started the final day and I ran the flat stretches and walked the hills. At the final checkpoint, I caught up with Dave, who had been in my tent all week.

He was much faster than me but today he was struggling, having probably gone out too hard on the first four days of the race. He asked if he could stick with me to the finish and I was delighted to have the company. Together, we marched and occasionally jogged through the final miles of the desert and eventually reached the finish line. The atmosphere was terrific, with the race organisers cheering us over the line. I was ecstatic to have completed another ultra-marathon in foreign conditions and to be given my medal. After a complimentary can of Coke, which was very welcome, I managed to have a shower, via a hose pipe off the back of a lorry and in the evening we had the awards ceremony at the campsite and a barbecue. I was asked to say a few words and told everybody about my prostate cancer, which I think made an impact because I hadn't mentioned it to many people during the race. We celebrated into the night and the next morning, I packed my kit and was driven back to the coaches in a pickup truck, driven by a boy who could not have been any older than 12. His feet could only just reach the pedals and he thought he was Lewis Hamilton as he took us on a white-knuckle ride across the desert. Back on the coaches the pace was more sedate, and we stopped at Petra and spent a couple of hours walking around the Lost City and had some lunch. The coaches drove us back to Amman and after checking into the hotel, I went for a Turkish bath and a massage which was wonderful after a week in the desert.

Back at the hotel I went to the bar and had a beer with some of the runners and organisers, but I started to feel unwell and went up to my room. I had to dash to the toilet and was there for the next six hours with the most awful diarrhoea. It was the middle of the night and I felt terrible. I was due to be flying home the next day, but I needed to be seen by a doctor. I managed to find a hospital that was only 100 yards from the hotel and two hours before I was meant to be leaving for the airport, I was being seen by a doctor. I told him that I didn't think I would be able to fly, but he gave me a prescription for some anti-nausea pills and told me I should be ok. I got the pills, went back to the hotel and immediately had a spectacular vomiting session in the reception toilet. I was in serious trouble, feeling delirious and dehydrated and one of the race doctors saw me and I was immediately taken back to the hospital and put on a stretcher. This time I was admitted by the doctors, taken to a room, and put on a drip. I was scared, being on my own, but also relieved to have the right medical attention because I was very ill. The owner of the hotel was brilliant and came and found me because everybody from the race had flown home that day. He translated everything for me and even got in touch with my travel insurers to tell them what was happening. I was completely out of it on the first day, delirious, being sick, suffering from awful diarrhoea and I ended up spending four days in the hospital with severe food poisoning. I was just blown away by the kindness the hotel staff afforded me.

I managed to book another flight home and everyone at the hospital was brilliant. One of my biggest worries was that I had run out of the abiraterone drug for my cancer, but after emailing Professor Parker, he assured me that missing four days was not a problem, which was a huge relief. After I was discharged from the hospital, the owner of the hotel met me and said I could have a room for the night free of charge. I was amazed by his generosity but insisted on paying and that evening I risked a bowl of pasta in the hotel restaurant and thankfully managed to keep it down. Just before I left, I thanked the owner and he said, 'You are in my country, you stayed in my hotel, you are my family.' Just amazing.

The following day, I finally caught my flight home, still feeling awful. I managed to get through the flight without any repeat performances from either end and seeing Sarah and Ollie at Heathrow was wonderful. It took me a few days to start feeling human again, but slowly I started getting back to my old self. I went back on the abiraterone and had a nervous wait to see whether my bout of food poisoning had had any adverse effect on my PSA score, but thankfully it had stayed the same.

I couldn't do any exercise as I recovered which was good news for my foot, ankle and knee. They all continued to improve with a period of rest and I was focusing on making sure I was fit enough to join my mate Nick Butter for the final race of his amazing challenge of running a marathon in every country in the world. As I have already mentioned, his final marathon was in Athens, and I had been in touch with him after getting back from Jordan and he told me he was on target to finish in Greece. In the second week of November, just after celebrating my fifth year surviving prostate cancer, Sarah and I flew to Athens a couple of days before the marathon and stayed in a lovely hotel near the finish line. We went to the Expo, so I could pick up my race number and had an evening meal at a rooftop bar overlooking the Acropolis.

The following day we went to meet Nick and it was amazing to see him as he neared the end of his incredible journey. Chris and Jeff from Tent 105 of my first MDS were also there and around 50 people had come to support Nick on his final marathon. We all had dinner together and the following morning we met early at Nick's hotel and took one of the official coaches to the start line in the town of Marathon. One of Nick's friends had the great idea of holding a red balloon, so we would always know where our group was during the race and we managed to stick together for the full 26.2 miles. Along the way Vassos Alexander from Virgin Radio joined us as he too had been touched by Nick's achievement and I enjoyed a few miles chatting to him. Vassos has accomplished so much in the running world and was good company. It was a wonderful day. Seren and Seb from Prostate Cancer UK had come out to maximise the media exposure for Nick and the charity, and had brought charity running shirts with them which we all wore. The whole event was great publicity for the charity and we created quite an impact when we went by as a group.

Finishing in the Panathenaic Stadium and crossing the line with Nick was a moment I will never forget. There were thousands of people inside the stadium cheering all the runners and the atmosphere was electric. I was in awe of Nick's achievement and I was proud our chat in the Sahara Desert had inspired him to 'run around the world' and raise well over £100,000 for Prostate Cancer UK. My wife Sarah rarely comes along to see me race as it's just not practical, but she was there for this one and it was an added bonus to have a hug with her just after I finished.

Coming back from Athens, it wasn't long before I was back on a plane with my mate Perry to run the Ultra Trail Ibiza. We had decided to enter the race when we did the Hangman challenge together earlier in the year. We enjoy each other's company and Ibiza made sense because of the Harry Enfield film *Kevin and Perry Go Large in Ibiza*, so we set off, wearing bucket hats so we would be in character!

The race consisted of a 10km run on Friday evening through San Antonio, a mountain marathon on the Saturday and a 10km run in Ibiza Town very early on the Sunday. We arrived on Thursday and spent a disappointingly quiet night in San Antonio because everywhere was shut as it was out of season. On Friday evening we ran 10km through the town, which was fun with a party atmosphere, and on Saturday morning we got a coach to the start of the marathon. Even though it was late November, it was still hot, and it was a mountainous route involving some steep climbs. The scenery was spectacular, the course was tough, and we had an enjoyable day running through the mountains of Ibiza. My leg felt good, but I knew we had made the right decision not to attempt the alternative double marathon because I don't think I would have finished.

The following morning, we ran 10km up and down a steep slope to Ibiza Town around the fabulous historic citadel and at the finish we were both knackered but delighted to get our medals. We spent the afternoon in the town, had a few beers in the evening and flew home the next day. I'd had a great time with my mate and raised a few more quid for Prostate Cancer UK in the process.

Back home, as ever, we enjoyed a family Christmas and I ended the year with plenty to look forward to in 2020. I was planning to run the MDS for a fifth time plus races in Sao Tome, Bhutan, Spain, Mexico, and Cambodia, continuing to raise money and awareness for Prostate Cancer UK. But none of us knew that something was happening thousands of miles away that would drastically change everybody's plans for the foreseeable future.

Chapter 15

Running the MDS in the back garden

THE NEW year was one of hope for me. I had plenty of races to look forward to and my PSA scores were staying where they needed to be, which meant my drugs were still working. The first thing I do every morning is take my pills and there are always 20 seconds when I wonder, 'is today the day they stop working?', but I always push that thought to the back of my mind and get on with my day.

For me, 2020 was looking action-packed. I had the Marathon des Sables and races in Africa, Bhutan and Spain all lined up for the first six months of the year, plus other plans formulating in my head to raise more money and publicity for Prostate Cancer UK. I had made the decision not to enter the 6633 Arctic Ultra because the training and the race itself involved so much walking and I wanted to concentrate on running in 2020. I was already running every day as part of a challenge I had set myself to run a minimum of 2km every day for the year. This had started back in December, when I had completed a virtual race with Ultra X (the company behind the race in Jordan), running 100km in ten days. After completing that I decided to keep running every day. Somebody had told me about RED January (Run Every Day) and that fitted perfectly with my personal challenge, so I just kept going. Part of my inspiration was a legendary runner called Ron Hill, who lays claim to holding the longest streak of consecutive days of running, an incredible 52 years and 39 days from 1964 to 2017. I found running every day tough at the start of the year, but as January went on, I found myself quite happily doing two longer runs a week (between 10km and 20km) and shorter runs on the other days. I will happily admit I was becoming obsessed with my running streak!

My first race of the year was the Pilgrims Challenge in early February, which, as you now know, is one of my favourites. I impressed myself by running a personal best in the two-day race, plus my body felt great. I was also asked to present to the runners at the overnight lay-over. This always gives me a sense of pride as I like to think that people walk away from hearing me knowing more about prostate cancer and understanding more about doing good whilst living in the now.

Unusually, I had no injuries and my confidence was sky high. I felt fit and strong as I got on a plane to head to Africa for a six-day ultra-marathon known as The Hemisphere Crossing. The 250km race took place on the tiny island country of Sao Tome and was organised by Global Limits, the company behind the fantastic races in Albania and Cambodia that I had run.

Back in the middle of 2019, Stefan, the head of Global Limits, had announced they were organising the race in Sao Tome, which was to be a one-off event and only open to competitors who had already run Global Limits' other races in Cambodia, Albania and Bhutan. I had only done two of the races, but I was desperate to go to Sao Tome because it was a pure jungle race and the finish was on the line of the equator. I emailed Stefan and begged him to let me enter because I had already entered the Bhutan race for later in the year. Stefan told me he would put me on the waiting list and, thankfully, I got a call from him in November telling me I had a place.

On the long flight to Sao Tome I was excited because I knew this was going to be a unique experience. My journey involved an overnight stay in Lisbon, which included runs in the city and round the airport hotel to keep my streak going. I had never been to that beautiful city before and when I left I vowed to go back with Sarah as I think she would love it there too. I always feel bad about Sarah not having the opportunity to see some of the amazing places I get to when running, although I don't think she would miss back-to-back marathon days followed by humid nights in a small tent being bitten by mosquitos!

From Lisbon, I flew to Sao Tome via Accra and the journey was really enjoyable because I knew so many of the runners from the previous races in Cambodia and Albania. Once we were airborne, I spent most of the time chatting and catching up with them all.

We landed at the tiny Sao Tome International Airport and as we queued to enter the terminal, the reality of Covid struck me for the first time. Before I had left, Coronavirus was being mentioned in the news and now we were greeted at Arrivals in Sao Tome by doctors wearing face masks and full PPE clothing, who took our temperature before letting us through. It was a shock and not something I was expecting.

After getting through passport control and collecting our bags, we left the airport and entered a scene of chaos. There were people everywhere, despite it being late at night and everybody was offering us a lift in their taxi. Stefan had organised minibuses, which we found and they took us to our hotel. It was past midnight and my first impression of Sao Tome was one of decaying splendour. It was obviously a beautiful country but very run down and after a comfortable night, sharing a room with an English runner called Simon, I got up and went for a 2km run to continue my streak. The roads were full of potholes and my impression of the previous night proved correct. The town certainly looked like it had seen better days. I enjoyed the run but found it difficult to comprehend what I was seeing. There was poverty everywhere amongst buildings that had once been magnificent but were now in a state of disrepair.

After breakfast, we all went for a walk in the heat and humidity to explore the town and I started to warm to the place and people before heading back to the hotel for the customary kit check. Even though I have completed many races and therefore had many kit checks, I couldn't help worrying that I had forgotten something that would stop me for being able to run. Fortunately, all was in order but to be fair, even if I was missing something I know the organisers would do all they could in that situation to help sort out the issue.

The following morning, after our final relaxing evening of relative luxury, Stefan had organised for us to run a 5km parade run with some local runners through the town. The ultra-marathon was the first international race ever to be held in Sao Tome, so we were big news! A local television crew came to film us running with lots of local athletes, including the two best runners from the island. It was a wonderful experience running through the town with them and we finished at a beautiful historic fort next to the sea. After lunch we were driven along dusty roads to a region of the island known as Roca Agostinho Neto where the race would start the following day. We arrived in a botanical garden and our accommodation was a huge old empty building amongst the trees. After finding a space on the floor for my kit, I sat on the steps of the building for the race briefing and afterwards a few of us wandered into the local town where we were looked at with a mixture of caution and smiles. It was obviously not a tourist area and we were something of a novelty. I slept badly under my mosquito net because it was so hot and sticky, but I got up feeling excited about the opening 38km-day of the race.

After the normal rush, having breakfast and getting my kit ready, we walked back into town to the official start line. We were greeted by the President of Sao Tome, more television crews and a group of school children who sang the country's national anthem. I felt like I was at the Olympics. It was an amazing experience and really brought home how big the race was for Sao Tome. After the anthem we got started, opening with a loop out and back through the town leading on to a long stretch of beach and the scenery was fantastic. It was extremely hot, but I was running at my own pace and got into a good rhythm. I arrived at the foot of a steep hill that climbed through the jungle. I had a quick chat with a lovely lady called Lynn who is proudly vegan, and fosters dogs in Turks and Caicos as well as being a part-time mermaid!

I started marching up the hill and into the jungle, using my walking poles. Just over the brow of the hill, something dropped out of a tree and landed a couple of metres away from me on the path. My first thought was, 'Why has a car tyre fallen out of the tree?', but then I realised I was looking at a Black Cobra snake. I had read about them and knew they were the deadliest snake on the island and as it stared at me, I took the decision not to stick around and introduce myself. I made my way around the snake as it raised itself preparing to strike, but I managed to keep a very safe distance and kept going. After a couple of minutes, I suddenly remembered Lynn was behind me and I had visions of her walking straight into the snake and I would never have forgiven myself if she had been bitten. I made my way back to the snake which was still sitting there, so I waited until I saw Lynn and another lady coming up the path. I shouted at them to walk towards me on the outside of a bend and when they saw the snake, I think they were extremely grateful for my warning.

The rest of the day was somewhat uneventful after the Black Cobra excitement. I ran through various villages along dusty trails, reaching the finish line at a school in Monte Café, the island's largest coffee plantation. I was hot, tired, and sweaty but felt good. I ate my dehydrated meal in the school and went into the village with Simon (my roommate from the hotel) and had a drink at the local bar. I say bar, it was really just shabby wooden seats and tables in one of the village huts, but we were made to feel very welcome and it was nice to have a drink after a long day. We spent the night on the school floor and the second day of the race was 31km through more villages and jungle, and past run-down colonial buildings. It started raining after 10km and it didn't stop for the rest of the day. It made the conditions tough, as the trails turned to mud, but we eventually finished at an old, abandoned, rundown hotel called the Pousada Bombain, which was our accommodation for the night. I was soaking wet, covered in mud and the roof of the hotel had holes in it which meant finding a dry spot to dump my kit was crucial. After settling myself down, I looked after Simon, who was feeling ill, and tried in vain to dry our kit in the humid conditions.

The third day started in the rain and my already wet kit got even wetter. Thankfully, the weather slowly improved and eventually the sun came out, which was a relief. I continued to mix running with walking as I made my way through villages and thick jungle. My body felt good and I got through the 29km route relatively unscathed. I arrived at the finish, which was by the sea in a small fishermen's village. Our campsite had been laid out in the middle of the village, surrounded by huts that were home to the fishermen and their families. We were made to feel very welcome and I went for a swim in the sea and took in the landscape. The vista was so beautiful, the kind of thing that you would see in a nature documentary; I half expected David Attenborough to appear from behind a palm tree. Spending the night in the village was the sort of experience I had been hoping for and I was loving being part of this unique race.

The following morning, I had my breakfast watching the sun come up over the village and set off on the 59km 'long day'. It was hard work, running on dirt roads and through dense jungle, with a couple of steep climbs. Just like Cambodia, I found myself scrambling through thick foliage, following paths that had been cut by the organisers using a machete. It was hot, sticky, tiring work, but I was being sensible, running the flat stretches and walking the hills. For much of the day I could see the Pico do Cao Grande, which is a needle-shaped volcanic rock, that towers 2,000ft over the jungle canopy. It is also known as 'Big Dog Peak' and climbers come from all over the world to test their skills on it. At one stage I had to cross a fast-flowing river near the edge of a waterfall. The rocks were slippery and the current was trying to knock me over, but thankfully Stefan had arranged for support crew to hold our hands if we wanted help. I thought back to the time I helped Lloyd over the jebel on the MDS, pleased that someone had been thoughtful enough to care about us getting across safely. I certainly had no qualms about someone's hand saving me from a full soaking followed by a 30ft drop!

I reached the finish at Praia Grande, which is a village on the beach, and I was delighted to have completed the 'long day'. After resting in my tent with Simon, I stayed up late into the night watching and cheering other runners over the finishing line. Many of the slower runners had struggled to find the trail in the pitch-black night so were doubly pleased to cross the finish line and see friendly faces.

I woke up on my 55th birthday and had my breakfast on the beach looking at the Pico do Cao Grande. Ever since my diagnosis, each birthday is an important landmark for me and this one was made extra special when everybody sang 'Happy Birthday' to me on the start line. I headed into the jungle facing a 28km day and although shorter than some days it was an extremely hard route which included crossing a river, followed by a steep climb that nearly finished me. I had to scramble up a slope, pulling myself over logs and fallen branches. It was horrendous and I was exhausted when I reached the top, but it was worth it. Once I got my breath back, the views of the island were breathtaking. The finish was at another beach called Praia Piscina and this was genuinely paradise, with sandy beaches and palm trees. There was a rumour that some of the Bounty adverts had been filmed there and I spent a lovely afternoon swimming in the sea and resting on the beach. In the evening, Stefan thoughtfully gave me a large birthday cake to share with everyone. Afterwards, I sat on the beach, with a beer, 55 years old, having survived another year of cancer and one day away from ticking off another ultra-marathon.

The final day was only 16km and it was certainly different. After 10km of dirt tracks and jungle, I reached a beach. They effectively stopped the clock and I had to catch a boat to take me to a small island called Ilheu das Rolas. After a ten-minute boat journey, I arrived at a tiny dock. They started the clock again and I ran another 6km around the island on paths that were covered in thousands of fallen coconuts. Not great for your ankles at the end of a gruelling race! I climbed a steep hill and arrived at the finish, which was on the line of the equator on a huge map of the world laid out in a clearing. I got my Union Jack flag out of my backpack and had my photograph taken. It was an amazing place to finish an ultra-marathon and the first time I had ever been in the Southern Hemisphere. I was delighted to have got through the race and I was proud of myself as I sat cheering all the slower runners over the finishing line.

We all followed Stefan as he led us to our hotel for the night and it was paradise. It was five-star accommodation, on a tropical island, an incredible place to celebrate running 250km. I shared an air-conditioned chalet with Simon and spent the afternoon lounging by the hotel swimming pool. The awards dinner was in the evening, where all the finishers were presented with a locally hand-carved wooden bowl and I spent the rest of the evening at the bar having a few beers.

Despite being knackered and a little hungover, I got up the next morning and ran back to the equator, which was a couple of kilometres away, because of course I still had to carry on my running streak. After breakfast, we packed our kit and were driven back to Sao Tome International Airport for our flight home. After a short stopover in Lisbon, I arrived back in England and as always was delighted to be back with Sarah and Ollie and proud to have run the first ever Sao Tome ultra-marathon.

On my first day back at work, I was sitting at my desk and started to get this awful itching on the top of my head and shoulders. Big lumps started appearing and I remembered on the first day of the race feeling what I can only describe as hot pin-pricks, coming through my hat and my shirt. I took myself to the London School of Tropical Medicine because I was worried that I had been bitten by a deadly insect! They did several tests and thankfully it was nothing serious. After a few days, the lumps and itching disappeared, but to this day I still don't know what took a liking to me in the jungle. Other than the bites, my body was tired and sore but felt ok and I continued running every day. By now, there was far more discussion about Coronavirus on the news and in the papers and, as we all know, everything changed in March.

At the start of the month, I received an email from the organisers of the Marathon des Sables, saying the race had been postponed until September because of Covid. I was obviously disappointed, and I couldn't see the race being able to go ahead in September either with everything I was reading about the pandemic. Because of my cancer, I did wonder if I would get the chance to run the MDS again as I had no idea what the state of my health would be like once it was safe to go back to the Sahara. I started to think about what I could do instead of the MDS, because I felt fit and strong. The news about Covid was getting worse every day and the word 'lockdown' started to be mentioned, so even doing a challenge in England was looking increasingly unlikely.

On 23 March, Boris Johnson announced the first 'national lockdown' with the 'stay at home' message. I also had the issue of whether my cancer would put me at a higher risk of ending up in hospital if I contracted Covid, so I contacted the always receptive Professor Parker. He explained that I was at a higher risk because of the daily steroids I was taking, but my fitness negated this and meant I was no more susceptible than anyone else. This of course was good news as I didn't fancy the idea of shielding for a prolonged time. I took the attitude that 'what will be, will be' when it came to my cancer and Covid.

I was determined to prove you could find a way to do things during lockdown if you wanted it enough, so I decided to run the Marathon des Sables in my back garden. With the GPS from my watch, I measured a 0.06km route along the perimeter of the garden, down the side of the house and on to our small driveway. I was going to run that route for the equivalent number of kilometres for each day of the race, including the 'long day'. I decided to wear all my kit for the opening day, but opted not to sleep in a tent in the back garden. As always, I was running to raise money for Prostate Cancer UK and this time the National Emergencies Trust Coronavirus Appeal as well, because the bank was supporting them and it just felt right at that time.

I realised what I was attempting was probably unique and because it was at the start of lockdown, not many other people were taking on challenges. I messaged BBC journalist and newsreader, Sophie Raworth, on Twitter, who I had met on the 2018 MDS, and told her what I was attempting. She told me I was mad, but nonetheless arranged for a researcher from the BBC to ring me and next thing I was booked on Saturday's *BBC Breakfast* for an interview, the day before I was to start the challenge. So, on the last Saturday of March I was live on the BBC from my back garden to explain to the world how I was running the Marathon des Sables in Ewell. After the interview, I looked at my phone and saw that my sponsorship page had increased by £12,000 in 15 minutes, which was amazing and showed the interest that people had in what I was attempting for great causes.

The following morning, I started the MDS in traditional fashion with 'Highway to Hell' blaring from a small speaker and the weather was perfect. The first day was 472 laps. Sarah had counted out 472 pebbles and each time I completed a lap I took a pebble from one pot and dropped it into an empty bowl. Every hour I went on Facebook Live and the response was magnificent. The first day took six hours, which seemed too long for the distance and I mentioned this on social media. A mate of mine called Graham dropped a surveyor's measuring wheel on my doorstep and when I measured the route again, it came out at 0.09km. I had done an extra 6km on day one and that was why it had taken me longer than I had expected: so much for the accuracy of GPS watches when doing small laps around buildings!

The rest of the week was amazing, including the 'long day' which was 956 laps of the garden and I was blown away by the support I received. I think I was one of the first people to do a challenge of this kind during lockdown and because of that the press really got behind me, including more interviews on the BBC and a feature in the *Metro* newspaper. When I finished, Sarah had made me a medal and I was extremely proud of what I had done in adversity. Despite the lockdown, I had managed to raise £32,000 and generated publicity for Prostate Cancer UK and the National Emergencies Trust. During my week of the 'back garden MDS', another gentleman started his challenge, proving you can always make things happen if you want it enough. His name... Captain Sir Tom Moore.

Chapter 16

Virtually running the Arctic

RUNNING MY back-garden Marathon des Sables gave me a real buzz. I was blown away by the support I received, and it made me feel people cared about what I was doing as a campaigner and fundraiser. I realised that this had become my mission in life. People were really buying into what I was doing and this was inspiring them to get out there and achieve their own goals and dreams. On top of that, many had started to fundraise for Prostate Cancer UK too, which was very humbling.

On the last day of my back garden MDS, I got messages from lots of people saying they were walking laps of their gardens to support what I was doing. A friend from the actual MDS sent me an envelope full of sand to put in my shoes to make it feel more like the desert and he also made a significant donation to the charity. Our local scout group, where I had been a member myself in my youth, did laps of their gardens and I felt my efforts were inspiring others to make a difference.

People have used the word 'inspirational' to describe my journey since my diagnosis and at the start it was not a word I was comfortable with. Whilst the word does not sit well with me, I do realise that people have changed their approach to many things in a good way because of me, which is something I am proud of. The back garden MDS was the first time I had seen my efforts make an immediate impact and influence people on such a scale. Every time I did my Facebook Live updates, so many people were tuning in and I felt I was making a connection with them and that gave me an enormous sense of worth.

I wanted to take on more challenges like the back garden MDS, to show people that organising your own event can have as much impact as running across the Sahara or walking across the Arctic. Whilst my efforts then were prompted by the Coronavirus lockdown, I also wanted to broaden people's attitudes for times to come, whatever their personal restrictions were, be they health, geography or cost.

Big events proved that anybody could achieve the impossible but to most people, running round the back garden was a far more realistic goal and just as important. I am a realist and, looking at what was happening with Coronavirus around the world, I knew in my heart that 2020 was going to be a write-off in terms of organised ultra-marathons. My focus went on finding a way to continue fundraising and campaigning during lockdown and giving myself things to look forward to. I was still going to the hospital for blood tests, but I was being given my results on the phone, which I hate. Due to the doctors' packed schedule, the calls are very rarely on time and whenever they are late, I always think it is going to be bad news. I have always imagined the worst whenever things don't go to plan and my mind goes back to the room where I was first diagnosed. Even though the calls will hopefully keep telling me my PSA scores are where they should be, if the call is late, to this day, that feeling of dread creeps up on me until the phone rings and I hear the, so far, reassuring words.

Towards the end of May was my ten-year wedding anniversary with Sarah. Arguably every year is special but there is something about an anniversary that ends with a zero being extra special. Covid restrictions meant we were unable to celebrate anywhere exciting, but actually, being at home, together, was just as special.

The bank had told us to work from home for the foreseeable future and even though I missed going into the office and seeing the team, lockdown gave me the opportunity to spend more quality time with Sarah and Ollie, which was fantastic. The weather was great, I was with my family and I had accepted the fact it was going to be a long journey out of Covid. The Bhutan ultra-marathon in May and the Al Andalus Ultimate in July were both cancelled, which was sad but inevitable.

My life got into a rhythm of Zoom calls with the bank and online presentations, offset by the luxury of spending more time with Sarah and Ollie around the house. Covid meant companies and charities needed to do something different in their meetings and I regularly found myself being asked to speak about my cancer journey, which I was more than happy to do from the comfort of my kitchen. I presented to a couple of major pharmaceutical companies and I found speaking 'virtually' far more relaxing than having to stand up in front of a room full of people. One of the many side-effects of the cancer drugs I take are hot flushes and because I get nervous giving presentations, I sometimes end up looking a sweaty mess and feeling self-conscious. Sitting behind a computer screen at my kitchen table is far less stressful. I really enjoyed, and still do, chatting to all sorts of people and companies and hoping in some small way that I have made a difference.

During the summer, lockdown restrictions were slowly eased which meant I could travel a bit farther for my runs and I was enjoying the simple life. I was fit and strong thanks to running every day and my friend Hayley, who I knew from the MDS and 6633 Arctic Ultra, became my 'virtual' personal trainer.

By July, the 'rule of six' had been introduced and I took the opportunity to travel to see lots of my friends and go running with them. I went to the Peak District and ran with Mark, who I had shared a tent with in Albania. I ran with Simon, my roommate from Sao Tome and my friend Perry from the Ibiza ultra-marathon and the marches with Jeff Stelling. Then there was a fab couple of days with my MDS 2019 tent-mate Matt who has a home in the beautiful village of Hope on the Devon coast. Spending time with him running along the South

West Coastal Path was definitely a highlight of that summer's running and finally I caught up with Maggie and Pete, who I knew from the Al Andalus Ultimate in Spain, and ran with them too. Like everybody in the country, I was enjoying seeing my friends again.

One special journey I made was to see an artist called Cliff Collins. Back in November 2019, I had an email from Cliff, explaining he had read my cancer story and had been inspired to paint a picture of me running using only photos he had found of me on the internet! Sadly, Cliff also had advanced prostate cancer and we had organised to meet in person, but those plans had been put on hold because of lockdown restrictions. During our conversations, Cliff mentioned that he wanted to do something to help Prostate Cancer UK. I had looked at his website and saw an amazing portrait of David Bowie that he had painted. I asked him if he would be prepared to paint another one of Bowie for me to auction for charity. He loved the idea and I think just like me he felt an extra sense of worth doing something that would help others. Finally in August, I travelled to Birmingham and met Cliff properly. After months of chatting on the phone, it was lovely to meet in person, hear Cliff's story and pick up the paintings, both of which were fantastic. The Bowie painting eventually sold for several thousand pounds, a testament to the quality of Cliff's work and the generosity of people who know me.

By now, all the races I had entered for the year had been cancelled. It would have been time for the Hangman Ultra in Hampshire and because we could travel outside our area, I got in touch with my mate Andy, who I first met at the Gatliff race in Kent, and asked him if he fancied running the route with me. As ever, he did, so we travelled to Hampshire and ran the 33 miles and did our own unofficial Hangman Ultra. It was a great day and when we finished, I emailed Andy Nuttall, the race organiser, and told him we had just run the fifth Hangman Ultra on our own. I think he was pleased we had made the effort to do his race despite Covid, which was a testament to the quality and beauty of the course.

Life carried on and I ran a couple of virtual races, which were becoming popular, including the Great North Run in October. I ran with a lady called Zeph in Bedgebury Forest, completing a half-marathon, and it was nice to spend the day with her and her friends. The following week, I embarked on my own personal challenge of running 100 miles in 24 hours. On my Just Giving page, I had called the challenge 24 Heures de Kev and it was another way of raising some money for Prostate Cancer UK and keeping my campaigning going during the pandemic. I had planned a three-mile loop on the streets around my house and I had a strategy for the run that was carefully planned. I put a table on my drive with snacks and drinks on it, Sarah invited some friends to come and sit at a social distance and cheer me on and I had let everybody know what I was attempting in my blog. I planned to set off at 10am on Saturday morning and keep running until 10am the following day and I was excited about taking on the challenge. The weather was lovely, but 20 minutes before I set off, I got a text from a friend called Colin, telling me my 'cancer twin' Lloyd Pinder had died. I was devastated because Lloyd and I had shared so much of our cancer journeys together and now his was over. He had two beautiful young children and all I could think about was them and his wife and what they must be going through. I was an emotional wreck and almost didn't run but knew I had to because it was the right thing to do for Lloyd.

I set off at 10am and I don't mind admitting I was crying when I started because all I could think about was Lloyd. My focus wasn't on my running and after an hour and a half I suddenly thought of Jeff Stelling because he knew Lloyd really well from his Marches for Men and often gave him a shout-out on *Soccer Saturday* on Sky Sports. I couldn't bear the thought of Jeff saying something without knowing that Lloyd had died, so I stopped and texted him with the awful news. On the next lap, I was joined by my best mate Jim and my mood slowly lifted, but I knew I was running too quickly and wasn't drinking enough on a hot day.

Other people turned up one at a time to do a lap or two with me: Rob, Bob, Anita and Colin all appeared at various stages through the day, which gave me a real boost.

I kept going and as I hit the 50-mile mark after nine hours, I turned into my road and all my neighbours were stood on their driveways, clapping and cheering me on. I was blown away and very emotional but as the evening wore on, the pace

I had been running at came back to bite me. I was with another mate called Rob and it was getting tougher and tougher to keep going. Rob had run the MDS the year before and we had become friends. He is a better runner than me and I thought would be a great pacer to get me through the last 12 hours or so. After 78 miles of running, I hit the wall at two in the morning. I tried to keep going but I was cold, my foot was hurting, and I told Rob I had to stop and go into the house to have something to eat and try and warm up. I collapsed in a chair, Rob went to make me a coffee and Sarah came down to see me. I was feeling nauseous, went to the toilet and started vomiting. I was in bad shape and knew I was done, having pushed myself to the limit. I slowly made my way up the stairs to bed, feeling I had let Lloyd down, but it was the right thing to do because the following morning I was still being sick.

I had managed to run 78 miles in 17 hours, a great achievement for me, but I still felt sad when my original finish time of 10am arrived. I slowly started to feel better and in the early evening Sarah told me to come to the front door. I was greeted by the amazing sight of 40 or so of our neighbours who had decided to continue the challenge for me by each running a socially distanced mile to complete – and as it turned out, exceed – the 100 miles I had set out to run. I was so touched and proud that my silly challenge had brought our road together and raised a few more quid for Prostate Cancer UK.

The next day I was sent a video clip from the charity of Jeff Stelling on *Soccer Saturday* paying an emotional tribute to Lloyd, which was a wonderful thing to do. I knew he would have been touched by Jeff's words and delighted that his beloved Sunderland had won. I was still on my running streak, so had to hobble the worst 2km of my life because my foot was agony and I still felt ill. Over the next week, I slowly began to feel better, my foot recovered and I started running longer distances again.

Monday, 5 October was Lloyd's funeral. I travelled to Leeds, on the way picking up Gary from Prostate Cancer UK who, like me, had made a personal connection with Lloyd. It was understandably an emotional day. Due to Covid restrictions, Lloyd's family had invited people to a pub where we would be able to watch a live streaming of the funeral on tables of six, socially distanced. Lloyd was obsessed with trainers and his wife, Tina, had asked everybody to wear their brightest pair, so I was in my suit and on my feet were bright lime green Inov-8 trainers. Hundreds of people in dodgy trainers lined the road from Lloyd's house as the hearse left for the church. I stood with Gary and Jeff Stelling, who had come to see Lloyd go past on his final journey. I don't mind admitting that I cried as the hearse went past and, selfishly, I couldn't help thinking about my funeral and how much longer I had until that horrible day inevitably arrived. I watched the funeral in the pub, and it was a beautiful service. I miss Lloyd every day, I am proud that he was my 'cancer twin' and that we shared and supported each other in some good and bad times together.

A week after Lloyd's funeral, I ran my first proper race since Covid started. Fortitude is a race in Sussex where you can choose to run either five-mile, four-mile or three-mile laps of the course. You have an hour to complete each lap and you must run ten laps. If you complete a lap in over an hour, your race is over, and your medal is awarded for the shortest lap you completed. The race was organised in accordance with government restrictions and I ran with my friends Perry and Rob. We decided to try to complete the four-mile race but after five laps I told the other two we would have to drop to three-mile laps otherwise I wouldn't finish. It was a tough day, but I managed to finish each of my ten laps in the allotted hour and it was great to see so many familiar faces, even if sadly from a social distance.

During the race I had let Perry and Rob into a little secret. Back in May I was informed that I had been awarded the British Empire Medal for services to charity as part of the Queen's Birthday Honours list. Unfortunately, because of Covid the official announcement had been delayed. Normally, you have to keep your award secret for a month, but I hadn't been able to tell anybody, apart from Sarah for five months and I was bursting to tell someone. I told Rob and Perry because the official announcement was the next day and I didn't think spilling the beans a day early would be too much of a problem. To be included in the Queen's Birthday Honours list and be recognised by the nation was an incredible honour. I found out Paula at my work had been the one who had started the nomination process and, being a patriotic bloke, I was incredibly proud when the announcement was made. Thank you, Paula! Once life gets back to normal, the Lord Lieutenant of Surrey will present me with my medal and that is a day I am looking forward to with immense pride.

At the start of November, the country went back into lockdown, but I continued giving presentations and running every day. I celebrated the sixth anniversary of my diagnosis with Sarah and Ollie and I was proud and delighted that I was still alive and hopefully making a difference. I was invited to be a guest at a virtual ceremony for my mate Nick Butter, who had run a marathon in every country in the world and was being awarded the Freedom of the City of London for his amazing effort. At the virtual gathering I chatted to the Lord Mayor of London, told him my story and later in the day I received a call from the Chamberlain of the Court. He told me the Lord Mayor wanted to award me the Freedom of the City of London as well, because of all the work I had done for Prostate Cancer UK. I couldn't believe it and was delighted to accept the award, having worked in London for most of my adult life. The ceremony would normally take place at the Guildhall, but Covid meant, like Nick's, it would take place by a video call. I was joining a list of names that includes Captain Sir Tom Moore, Sir Winston Churchill and Sir Michael Caine. One of the privileges that comes with the award is apparently the historic right to drive sheep across London Bridge and I look forward to taking this up as soon as I have my own flock!

I was now running a couple of marathons a week as part of my 'streak' and I took part in a virtual race to Uganda with ultra-race organisers XNRG, who also organise the Pilgrims Challenge. They were raising money for disadvantaged children in Uganda and anybody could enter and run as many miles as they wanted from the start of December until Christmas Day. The aim was that the cumulative mileage achieved by all participants would total the distance from the UK to Uganda. This fitted in well with my running streak as a little extra motivation, so I of course entered. I really pushed myself every day and ran 250 miles towards the total, which had almost been double the original target by Christmas Day.

Another ultra-racing company called Ultra X, who organised the ultra-marathon in Jordan, approached me with an idea to do a virtual race along the same lines as the one to Uganda. They wanted to call their race Run Around the World with Kev and the idea was to get people to run or walk any distance they wanted on one particular day. If enough people entered, they hoped the distance would add up to around 40,000km, which is the circumference of the earth! After a couple of Zoom calls, I convinced them the race should be run on New Year's Eve. According to my research, when New Year's Eve starts in parts of Oceania, which are the furthest ahead in the world's time zones, it is 10am on 30th December in the UK. The last place in the world to see in the New Year is American Samoa at midday UK time on 1 January. That, I surmised, would give people three days or 50 hours to run the distance they wanted as the world celebrated the arrival of 2021. Ultra X kindly said that all the entrance fees would go to Prostate Cancer UK. I committed to running a marathon on each of the three days to lead from the front and started publicising the race on my blog and social media channels.

Like everybody, we celebrated Christmas in our family bubble, but Sarah started feeling unwell on Boxing Day and had a Covid test which unfortunately turned out to be positive. We all went into isolation, but a couple of days later I lost my sense of taste and also had a Covid test on 29 December. I had committed to doing a marathon a day for Run Around the World With Kev, so on 30 December, New Year's Eve and finally at a minute after midnight on New Year's Day I ran a marathon in my back garden (I knew the route from my virtual MDS!). The support for the race was brilliant and we had 1,600 people in total 'running around the world with Kev'. Overall, the entrance fees donated by Ultra X and sponsorship money from some of the participants raised over £12,000 for Prostate Cancer UK. Even though we fell slightly short of the target of 40,000km, I was so proud of everybody who took part and managed to get us almost round the world.

On 2 January the results of my Covid test finally arrived and they were positive. Thankfully, the only symptom I had was a loss of taste, so I spent ten days in isolation and ran every day in the back garden. When I was running my three marathons over the New Year, I did some research on exercising with Covid. Everything I read was telling me not to run because of the damage Covid could do to your heart, but as I was still waiting for my results at that stage, I ignored it. When my test came back positive, I was feeling tired and lacked energy, but it didn't feel like I had done any permanent damage to myself, so I just kept running. I did wonder if I might be the first and only person to run three marathons with Covid.

Later that month, Prostate Cancer UK asked me to record a couple of adverts for a campaign they were running that would be played on the Planet Rock radio station. I wrote the scripts for myself and Sarah, which we recorded at home, and I sent them to the radio station. I didn't think any more about them until a few weeks later when my phone started buzzing with messages from family and friends saying they had just heard me on Planet Rock. I was pleased because I hadn't told anybody about the adverts, so I was being recognised because of my cancer story and that proved I was still making an impact on people.

In early February, I was officially awarded my Freedom of the City of London. As I mentioned, because of Covid, I couldn't go to the Guildhall, so my ceremony took place via a Zoom call as I sat in the kitchen at home with Sarah. The Lord Mayor of London conducted the ceremony and I was incredibly proud to be officially awarded the Freedom of the City. When I was a child, one of my favourite books was *Dick Whittington*. Everybody knows the story of the boy who went to London to make his fortune, buying a cat, leaving when it all went wrong but being drawn back to the city when he heard the bells of Bow church urging him to, 'turn again Whittington, thrice Lord Mayor of London'. His story resonated with my cancer journey, when there have been so many times I have felt like giving up but have kept going and pursued my dreams. Speaking to the Lord Mayor of London, which of course Dick Whittington became, was very special and a real privilege. My name will forever be in the history books: that means a huge amount to me.

I celebrated my 56th birthday at home and, as I have already explained, each birthday is an important milestone since my diagnosis. On 19 February I should have been flying to Canada for my third 6633 Arctic Ultra. I had entered the long race, but understandably it had been cancelled due to Covid. The organisers announced there would be a virtual race instead and I spoke to them and asked if they would consider using the virtual race to raise money for Prostate Cancer UK. They agreed to give a minimum of £5 from every entry fee and any profits from the race to the charity, which was fantastic. The number of entries was high because they had given everybody the month of March to run or walk either the 120- or 380-mile races, plus you didn't have to go to the Arctic! I decided to treat the 380 miles like a race and attempt to complete it in the nine days allowed if I had been in the Arctic. That meant running and walking 42 miles a day, which I wasn't sure I was up to, but I was determined to give it a go. I took over the front room of our house and used it as my base for kit, medicines and snacks. I decided against trying to recreate the full Arctic experience so mercifully wouldn't be sleeping in a tent or pulling a sledge.

On the first day, I set off at 6.30am and didn't have a set route in my head. I ran some trails near my home and my aim was to complete a marathon in the morning, come home for a sandwich and do 16 miles in the afternoon. The first day went well and after 11 hours I got home feeling tired. My feet were sore, so I had a hot bath. Sarah made dinner, I posted on Facebook, put my feet in a bucket of ice and went to bed at 9pm. I couldn't get to sleep because my leg muscles kept twitching, which happens all the time on ultra-marathons, but it made me feel like I was in a proper race and I perversely enjoyed the feeling.

After a broken night's sleep, I set off again at 6.30am, running and walking the same route and completing another 42 miles. It was a tough day and there were a couple of moments when I found myself questioning whether I was going to be able to do nine days, but I managed to push through. After my bath, food, bucket of ice and Facebook post, I was in bed at 9pm again, feeling exhausted. On day three I changed my route after discovering a traffic-free, off-road, three-mile loop on Epsom Common that enabled me to switch off, but I was still exhausted when I got home, having hit the 120-mile mark. I sat in the bath and remembered the third day of any race is often the hardest and hoped the toughest part was over. The following day, I did my loops of Epsom Common, combining running and walking. Mentally, I had got through the barrier of thinking I wouldn't be able to do the race in nine days. By day six, however, everything started to hurt. My right foot was painful, and bruises were appearing on my calf which was a concern, but I decided to keep going and ignore the discomfort.

Robin, a friend from my old rugby club, joined me on the morning of day seven, and it was great to have some company. Robin had signed up for the 120-mile race, which he had already completed, finishing fourth, which he was chuffed about. Robin met me at Epsom Common and we had an enjoyable morning doing the three-mile loops together. In the afternoon, my neighbour, Mike, joined me and I ticked off another day. On the penultimate day, I did my marathon in the morning and Mike joined me again for the afternoon. I got home that night and my body was in pieces, but I was getting some wonderful messages from people and the total on my sponsorship page kept going up, which gave me a massive lift. I got a message from my mate Pete, who you might remember had got in touch with me on the Camino de Santiago to tell me his dad had been diagnosed with prostate cancer. Sadly, his father died from the disease in 2020 and Pete's message said he wanted to do something with his sister in memory of his dad, so they donated an extremely generous sum of money and I was really touched. Not for the first time in the last six years I was running with tears in my eyes.

I set off on the final day of the virtual 6633 Arctic Ultra and my ankle was in a dreadful state, but I knew I was going to complete the 380 miles in nine days and that was a good feeling. I got through my morning marathon and in the afternoon, Sarah joined me to walk the final seven miles together, which was lovely. Sarah has always supported me, and I felt like I was supporting her because she had entered the 120-mile race and was able to tick off some of her miles.

When my watch told me I had done my 34 miles for the day, it meant I had completed the 380 miles of the long race and it was an emotional moment. I was proud of myself but more importantly I was pleased for all the people who had supported me, not just over the nine days of the virtual race but over my entire cancer journey. My family and friends, Prostate Cancer UK, the people who have sponsored me, the people who have messaged me and the bank who have enabled me to chase my dreams. I had proved anything is possible if you put your mind to it and want it enough.

The bloke with terminal cancer had taken on another challenge, completed it, raised a few more quid and hopefully inspired some more people to get out there and make a difference. Not bad for a dead man running.

Chapter 17

Some final thoughts

SO THAT'S my story so far. I have tried to describe my cancer journey without any sugar-coating, and I hope it has made you stop and think. There is no doubt that my mind may have played tricks on exact times, people and the odd location, but it is honestly how I remember everything (apologies to anyone who may have been offended by any error: that was never my intention) and when I look back at my journey it is always with a smile and a sense of pride.

If you had said to me on that dark day in 2014 when I was told that I might only have two years to live, that I would still be here over six years later and have done all that I have for Prostate Cancer UK and others, I would not have believed you. Equally, I would not have believed that I had it in me to train for and complete so many incredible and challenging races in so many amazing places and countries. It just goes to show, you should never stop dreaming and try to live your dreams every day.

'So, Kev, what are you going to do next?' is a question that is always in my mind. The short-term future is as certain for me as it is for everyone because we could all be hit by the number 17 bus tomorrow or have some other life-changing event happen through no fault of our own. And that is why we must all make the most of every single day by doing what we are able to do, whenever we are able to do it.

In terms of running, in 2021 I have entered the multi-day ultra-marathon races in Spain, Bhutan, the Sahara (the MDS for the fifth time) that you have read about and hopefully they will all go ahead if safe to do so but if Covid gets in the way again, so be it, I am sure I will find things closer to home. Beyond this year, I intend heading back to Canada in 2022 for the 380-mile 6633 Arctic Ultra to see if I can actually finish it and I really want to go back and run in Cambodia because I fell in love with the place. After these races, there are so many challenges that I want to take on and I have high hopes for the future, but having already had more time that I ever expected in 2014 I can't be upset if some or all end up not to be.

Before I was ill, if you had asked me to stand up and speak to an audience about anything, then I would have tried my hardest to get out of it. Today I still don't think I am a great speaker and I often read my script, but I hope sharing my story has made an impact on people over the past six years. By taking people on my journey and increasing the awareness of prostate cancer, I hope people see the opportunities that are out there to do something good and the fun you can have making a difference. Hopefully, this book can also make a difference in some small way to people's lives.

Then there is the fundraising. My aim is still to be responsible for raising £1 million for Prostate Cancer UK. I have some way to go, but with what I have already raised and the amazing support of others who have joined me and been inspired to do their own fundraising, I know I can get to that target. I'm already threequarters of the way there. In some ways, my quest to reach a million quid is selfish. Realistically, I know it is too late for there to be any major breakthroughs in prostate cancer research that will make a significant difference to me. But I do believe that breakthrough could be made by the time my sons are 40. If mine and other people's fundraising efforts can be used to further understand how prostate cancer turns from benign to being a killer, then a cure can be found and all the money I raise is potentially saving my sons' lives. Whilst that reason is the main driver for raising money, it will also help save my male relatives, friends, colleagues, perhaps your friends, your relatives, your colleagues, maybe even you, and that would help to keep families together for longer. I cannot think of a better reason to keep running, talking and fundraising, even if I am probably repetitive. It's a record I don't want to change until the happy day when it's no longer required.

Finally, and most importantly, I dearly want to be here to witness and contribute to the simple things in family life. Seeing my children get older would be a massive bonus. Fingers crossed, there will be weddings, grandchildren, exam success, jobs and fun. And I want to be around to enjoy it all. I also desperately want to spend more time with my wife Sarah. The saddest thoughts I have tend to focus on the emotional mess that I may create when the drugs stop working and I get really ill. I know one day my cancer will kill me (unless the bus gets me first!) and I think an awful lot about how my family will be without me. It doesn't seem fair that Sarah, who chose to marry me for the rest of her life, will one day be left on her own. Whilst prostate cancer is not my fault, I do feel guilty about putting Sarah and my family through this journey. Sarah is amazing, but the thought of her being on her own and having no one to make her coffee in the morning breaks my heart.

I don't know how you will feel having got to the end of this book. Maybe my skills as an author mean you haven't got this far, but I hope the words on the pages have been enjoyable to read. As I said, I have tried to be honest and my biggest hope is that my story has potentially been life-changing for you in some small way. If it makes you live every day a little bit more and if you make happy, lasting memories by doing more for others, then I will be a happy man. Life is for living today and every day, so please get out there and make the most of it.

Thank you.

Kevin

Postscript: Sadly, just as I finished this book, my friend, the artist Cliff Collins, died with prostate cancer. I had managed to see Cliff a couple of weeks before he was taken as he was keen to sign 20 prints I had produced of his Bowie painting, to be auctioned in the future to raise funds for Prostate Cancer UK. He knew his time was short but that was the mark of that incredible man. RIP Cliff.

If you or anyone you know is worried about any unexplained changes to your body, don't delay, go and see a doctor as it may just save your life!

2018 MDS #3
Sandstorms didn't
make it any easier
but I do love a
challenge

2018 In the
Cambodian jungle
being attacked by
ants (again)

2018 Global Limits Cambodia finished in front of the amazing Angkor Wat

2018 Lloyd came to meet me for an emotional reunion whilst on my solo seven marathons in seven days March 4 Men

2019 The Northern Lights on my failed attempt of 380 miles on the 6633 Arctic Ultra, worth it just to be there though (Weronika Murray)

2019 An amazing month walking the Camino de Santiago with my brother Ian, priceless

2019 MDS #4
heading off into the
sunset on the long
day
(Ian Corless)

2019 With Chris and
Nick from MDS tent
105 running Nick's
196th marathon in
Athens for his world
first

2019 Finishing another March 4 Men and getting a hand shake from the late great Ray Clemence who sadly died of prostate cancer just over a year later

2019 Live with Matt Smith from BT Sport after another solo March 4 Men

2019 Live on BBC radio with Mark Church at the Oval

2019 Proud Dad with my family at Hayley's graduation

2020 The locals loved our checkpoints in the jungle racing in Sao Tome

2020 Global Limits Sao Tome finishing on the Equator, my first steps into the Southern Hemisphere and last overseas race before Covid

2020 Not really MDS #5 but 2,600 laps of this equalled 230k and was the best I could do in a Covid lockdown (Peter Macdiarmid/London News Pictures)

2020 The talented Cliff Colins giving me his Bowie portrait to auction for Prostate Cancer UK, sadly Cliff died with prostate cancer aged just 57

Reflections on Kev

My Wife, Sarah

Where do I start?! Life before cancer? Of course, we had a life but a very different existence. The usual work/life imbalance peppered with plans for the future. When we retire, we should…

Then came the first trips to the doctors. I had absolute belief that Kevin was overreacting. There were so many other possible explanations and he was far too young to have prostate cancer! Of course it would be ok and even if it was cancer (which it couldn't be) they would have caught it early enough. An eminently curable cancer. Except it wasn't.

I don't really remember a lot of the specifics of the first few weeks after the diagnosis. It's mostly memories of the emotions. Disbelief, despair and the utter gut-wrenching, heart-breaking, soul-destroying day we had to tell the children. But then a kind of clarity. We're all going to die one day, but actually having a time-frame brings everything into sharp focus. No more woolly plans of what might be but definite plans of what should and could be.

It became vital that special memories were made. Memories that would keep us all going long after the ability to make more had ceased. Kevin could have, and do, anything and everything that would make whatever time he had happy and fulfilling. Fortunately for us and the world he didn't choose fast cars and a room-sized tv. He chose to make a difference.

That first Marathon des Sables was terrifying. I had no idea what effects of the cancer, the chemo or the ongoing treatment would have on putting his body through the race. Then I realised that wasn't what I was afraid of. I was afraid he wouldn't finish. But, of course, he did and I've never been afraid since.

Don't get me wrong, life isn't all hurrahs and high fives. Monthly testing and medication side-effects that drive mood swings are constant reminders for both of us. Someone who knows their time is limited isn't always concerned with the minutiae of life (housework mostly!) and that can be a 'challenge' sometimes. Kevin's amazing dedication to the cause can be hard to live with and live up to sometimes, but it really is only sometimes and the balance is still very much weighted in favour of the absolute pride we have in everything he does.

We have no idea what the future will hold for any of us. The only thing I do know is that Kevin is doing everything he can to make sure it will be the best future it can be and for that he has my eternal support, thanks and love.

Sarah Webber

My Kids, Ollie, Hayley and Ben

Sixteen, fourteen and nine: those were our ages when the future we thought we had with our dad changed. The day, Remembrance Sunday 2014, is forever ingrained on our brains: sitting in the back room of the house, whilst Dad and Sarah prepared lunch, and we all waited to hear whatever it was that Dad wanted to tell us. Ben and I knew it was going to be bad news when we all sat down for lunch, although we thought it would be about our grandad not our dad. Bertie, one of our cats, was on the coffee table and Dad was stroking him whilst trying to come up with the right words to explain the news. And then he told us. He had cancer, prostate cancer to be precise. I was the first to cry because I realised what was about to happen and what Dad's news meant, and that life would never be the same again. Then we were all crying. I think of that moment every Remembrance Day during the two minutes of silence and dread the month of November until the 11th has passed.

I do not think any of us children initially realised what diagnosis Dad had been given. During that Sunday lunch, Dad did not tell us the doctor's prediction of the number of years he had left to live and the fact that prediction was dependant on the drugs working. Dad, Ben, and Ollie went to play football in the park after lunch and I stayed to do revision for my A-level mock exams with Sarah. She asked how I was feeling, and I told her I was okay. I told Sarah something Dad had said to me about my grandad when he was diagnosed with prostate cancer. Dad had said that, 'Most men die of something else before the prostate cancer takes over.' Sarah replied that she did not know if that would be the case for Dad and that was the moment I realised how bad it must be.

Within a month or so his treatment started. The chemotherapy, the radiotherapy, and the drugs. Dad did well and as far as we are aware only had minor side-effects from his gruelling treatments. He decided he wanted to run the Brighton marathon whilst on chemotherapy and we were all proud of him for doing that.

Thinking about Dad and his diagnosis took over a large part of my life in that first year. Google is not a friend when your dad has cancer and you are busy researching any drug you hear about to find out more about it and see whether it might help.

After the first year, things have got better to a large extent. Dad does not look sick and as I always said to my friends from school who knew Dad and asked how he was doing, you would not know he has stage four cancer, from looking at him. And you definitely wouldn't know he had cancer from the activities that he took up after that first year. The first ultra-marathon he did was the Marathon des Sables, which at the time seemed an unnecessary risk. Dad was travelling to a country without access to his doctors if something went wrong, taking his medications in ridiculous temperatures and running/walking long distances when his body was already weakened from the cancer and treatment. It scared and angered me.

A lot of the races Dad does still stir those two emotions because whilst I am happy and proud that he is raising so much money and awareness for prostate cancer, I am scared that something bad will happen to him in a foreign country away from us. It reduces the amount of time we get to spend with him and particularly when I was younger that used to really bother me, but now I am used to it.

I found the news about Dad's cancer hard to take and I also thought about Ben and Ollie and how they had taken the news. Here is how Ollie remembers that Sunday when Dad told us he had cancer.

At nine years old, finding out your dad has cancer didn't seem as bad for me as it did for everyone else, because I didn't really know what it meant for the long term. I knew it was bad, but I didn't really know how bad it was at first. I knew it meant I could spend more time with my dad because he wasn't working as much, and it also meant he could walk me to school, which was something that almost never happened before. Seven years later, I understand what it all means, not only for the short term but for the long term as well.

As Ollie says, I think we all understand what Dad's cancer means for us as his children. When you are given a ticking clock and you know you are living on borrowed time with your dad, it is frustrating that he goes on runs for weeks at a time. For Ben and me, when we were at school, that was difficult as we already had our time with him limited to one day a week and suddenly even that wasn't guaranteed anymore. Now we are adults and have other things going on in our lives, it is not as noticeable when Dad goes off to do his runs and races. The Coronavirus lockdown has made it difficult as we have only seen him sporadically when the rules have allowed it. Christmas was very different during lockdown because we couldn't celebrate together, which was hard because we enjoy the tradition of having our Christmas together on Boxing Day.

Ollie, Ben, and I are grateful for every day that we have with our dad because we have had more time than we or he ever thought we would after that Sunday in November almost seven years ago.

Thank you to anyone who is reading this and that has ever donated to Prostate Cancer UK or Cancer Research, as your money has developed the drugs that mean our dad is still here.

Hayley, Ben and Ollie Webber

My brother, Ian

When Kevin told me he had terminal cancer it was a shock. I am five and a half years older than Kev and you don't expect to get told that news by your younger brother.

I am amazed by everything Kevin has done since his diagnosis. When he first started running on chemotherapy, I honestly thought he would just do the Brighton and London marathons and completing those was an incredible achievement. But he decided he was going to do something even bigger and I couldn't believe it when he said he was going to run across the

Sahara Desert. That's the thing with Kev. He keeps reinventing his challenges, including running the Marathon des Sables in his back garden, and what he does is phenomenal.

Spending time with Kevin when we walked the Camino de Santiago gave me a real insight into how he operates. Walking together gave us time to talk, share memories and we became closer, which I think our parents would have liked.

Kevin has a death sentence, but he has not let that stop him inspiring an awful lot of people. He has definitely inspired me not to take life for granted. I am in awe that he continues to get out there and do his races, give his speeches, and raise money for Prostate Cancer UK.

I also think he is a complete nutter. Regardless of being ill, most people would not do what Kevin does in terms of running and there are times when I do wonder if he is being sensible, putting his body through the training and races. He has always been headstrong, and I think his attitude has helped keep him alive alongside the brilliant medical support he has received.

Sometimes you forget he is ill, which is wrong, but it's because he keeps going out there and achieving his goals, no matter how he is feeling.

Mum and Dad would have been incredibly proud of Kevin and how he has dealt with his illness, the challenges he has set himself, his achievements, and the money he had raised. And I think they both would have been especially proud of Kevin being named in the Queen's Birthday Honours list and being awarded the British Empire Medal.

Kevin's journey has been incredible and as his older brother, I am very proud of everything he has done and continues to do.

Ian Webber

My Oncologist, Professor Chris Parker

In my job, I see lots of men who present with advanced prostate cancer, but most of them are well past retirement age. So when Kevin walked in to my clinic, I was struck by the fact that he was just 49 years old: as it happened, the same age as me. I was also struck by the fact that, despite having just been diagnosed with a life-limiting illness, he already seemed to have accepted his situation and was ready to make a plan.

For the previous 60 years, treatment of advanced prostate cancer had been with hormone therapy alone. However, just a few months earlier, a trial in the US had suggested that the addition of chemotherapy improved survival. Kevin was one of the first patients to receive early chemotherapy, outside of a clinical trial. I am sure that it cannot have been easy for him, but he seemed to sail through the treatment. Indeed, to this day, I sometimes tell patients who are worried about the prospect of chemotherapy that one of my patients managed to run two marathons while on chemo!

It was disappointing, but not entirely surprising, when his PSA started to rise again about a year later. Once again, Kevin was able to get a new treatment, abiraterone, that had just become available on the Cancer Drugs Fund. Typically, abiraterone works for around 18 months, but in some men it can work for much longer. At the time of writing, Kevin has been on abiraterone for nearly five years, and continues to have a fantastic response.

It is always a real pleasure to see Kevin in the clinic, and to hear about his latest athletic exploits. I have no idea why his cancer has responded so well to treatment, but I can't help but wonder to what extent his running might have contributed. Not all of us can manage ultra-marathons, but we can take inspiration from Kevin's remarkable example.

Professor Chris Parker

My work colleague, Neal

Kevin is a character. We've worked for the same organisation for a long time and when I first became aware of Kevin it was clear that he was a singular personality and prepared to voice his thoughts.

At a time of considerable change in the bank, Kevin became one of my team and it was clear very quickly that he was a popular member of the team. He'd led a life, without doubt, and socially was engaging and always ready with a story, some of which he might prefer not to re-tell now, but he is always so entertaining.

Professionally he had faced a number of challenges, but as far as the role he performed in my team was concerned, he was hugely knowledgeable, professional and worked hard to add value to his customers and provide them with good advice on how to further their respective businesses. Kev was an active member of our team – sometimes challenging but always because he wanted to deliver to a high standard. As a line manager, I always respected his counsel.

The emergence of his extreme diagnosis came a time when I was transitioning into a new role and to some degree I watched from afar, shocked at such stark news for a young and fit guy. After the extremes of chemotherapy and other debilitating treatments, Kevin appeared to emerge from a new cocoon and it became obvious that it was a challenge he was going to meet, head on, with the usual determination that we had come to know.

What we have seen over the intervening years is truly remarkable. From those early forays into running, his challenges have gradually became more and more extreme. He introduced us to events such as the Marathon des Sables, that many of us had never come across before and we could not imagine the extremes that one would have to put oneself through to complete. Was it not enough to run a marathon whilst undergoing chemotherapy we wondered?

One particular highlight for me was joining Kevin on one of his Jeff Stelling/Prostate Cancer UK walks and it was there that you could witness just how Kevin has grown in confidence and as an ambassador. He has certainly inspired so many people within our organisation by being prepared to turn up and talk candidly about his illness and how he is addressing a new paradigm. Through this activity, he has won so many friends within our organisation and far, far wider.

Kevin is so confident now with all forms of media and he is using them to push men to think seriously about their health and for those that are struggling he provides evidence of what can be achieved with such a positive outlook. His blogs are epic, and we all look forward to hearing the tales of what he is up to next.

Coronavirus has just been one of those bumps in the road that have seen him change his approach to what he sees as his mission in fundraising and he continues to inspire.

The award of the British Empire Medal was just desserts. All his colleagues were so delighted that he was recognised with the medal.

I look forward, post Coronavirus, to spending time in Kevin's always entertaining company. I'm pleased to count him as a friend.

Neal Graham (Head of Business Delivery, Commercial and Business Banking at NatWest Bank)

My charity mate, Gary

Six years ago, in the build-up to the 2015 London Marathon, I'd chatted to an enthusiastic fledgling fundraiser several times on email. I vividly remember reading his first-ever email to the charity, back in January of that year, when he talked of completing the Brighton marathon when on chemotherapy. I was blown away by the sheer audacity to achieve the seemingly impossible and, with my journalist's nose going into overdrive, reacted immediately.

Learning he was a runner of some distinction as we continued to converse, we chatted about my own marathon training and plans, and he was as selfless as you'd expect with his advice. Indeed, his very first sentence to me warned me not to overdo it.

Fast forward to April, and some 19 or 20 miles into the London Marathon, and around the Docklands area, I was struggling slightly. My shoe was tight, and I slowed down and stopped to adjust my lace. It was then I received a tap on the back and heard someone say, 'Come on, Prostate Cancer UK.' I looked up and it was an uber-positive, lanky chap in similar blue and black colours with 'Kevla' emblazoned on his chest. And so it goes that was my first-ever meeting with the most incredible man I've ever met – one Kevin Webber.

We ran together that day, chatting like old mates, and since then we've been inextricably connected as I've been his inside man.

When Kev thanked me for bringing him into the Prostate Cancer UK fold at one of our all-staff away days, it was one of the most humbling experiences of my life. Then, and now, I'll always say it should be me thanking him on behalf of our organisation and I know a raft of colleagues past and present would agree.

To list all of Kev's exploits would, quite frankly, take up all of my allotted word count. But it would be remiss to ignore his astonishing accolades. Needless to say, he's absolutely smashed it, navigating sand dunes, snowstorms, volcanoes, hills, jungles and tundra across the globe, always brilliantly branded in 'club colours' with our 'Man of Men' logo consistently in view. And when the pandemic shattered life as we know it, he circumnavigated his own back garden hundreds and hundreds of times. As you do.

Since our initial interaction back in January 2015, Kevin has run marathons, ultra-marathons, realised his dream of crossing the Sahara, and also marched across the UK with his mate Jeff Stelling, strolled alongside banking colleagues new and old, and ploughed on solo through the heartlands of non-league football.

As well as raising more than a quarter of a million pounds – and influencing so many others to boost their own fundraising – Kev has been the face of Prostate Cancer UK in direct marketing appeals, powerful videos and his incredible story has helped us win corporate pitches. Oh, and he's a pretty good public speaker too, spreading the gospel to all and sundry and educating so many about the dangers of the most commonly diagnosed cancer in the UK.

His tireless work has saved countless lives. And his story has stunned and inspired thousands upon thousands more.

We are proud and honoured he's part of our family at Prostate Cancer UK, and it's hard to imagine a life without him bending my ear about his next wacky adventure. Which is why my heart still breaks about what he goes through on a regular basis. Indeed, sometimes, amid all the joy and craziness, it's easy for even me to forget Kev is a man living with incurable prostate cancer.

Back in 2014 his expiry date, as he puts it, was put around two years. Yet here he is, six and a half years on, never complaining, and showing no sign of slowing down. I know one day he will. But, like him, I'd rather not dwell on that.

As a sports journalist, the word legend is used far too often for my liking in my field. But that is the perfect description of this stubbornly selfless and heroically humble guy from Epsom.

Answering that email was one of the best things I ever did. For sure, it has benefitted Prostate Cancer UK and the people we represent in immeasurable ways. But it's also earned me a great mate, confidant, sounding board – and occasional chauffeur.

Thanks for everything, Kev. You've changed my life.

Gary Haines (Prostate Cancer UK)

My best mate, Jim

I became mates with Kevin (Kevla) through my wife Jo being friends with his wife Sarah. We met at a Year 2 school quiz night and have never looked back.

He told me he liked to run to keep fit, and before I knew it, he suggested I took up running as well. Seemed like a good idea at the time, but we soon moved on from a 10k run to a marathon, followed by an ultra-marathon (London to Brighton).

We share the same sense of humour, having watched *The Life of Brian* together far too many times. And we have a mutual love of crisps and beer!

When Kevin got the news, the year we completed the London to Brighton Ultra, that he had terminal prostate cancer, it was hard to hear. I remember him texting me at work to ask me to pop in on the way home. I knocked on his door, and he said to me, 'let's go for a walk'. We did, up to my house, and on the way, he dropped the bombshell.

Since that day, our friendship has got stronger and since the bombshell, life has continued almost normally, which was a surprise to me, all things considered. We have had many great days out: concerts, cricket matches, football matches (watching his beloved AFC Wimbledon play), and shared family holidays, from sleeping in yurts to Spanish villa vacations, with a trip to Morocco in between.

Kevin never ceases to amaze me with his positivity. I have never heard him moan once about his illness. Instead, he is normally excited to tell me about his new plans. They could be for another ultra-marathon, which he is going to run in challenging conditions somewhere in the world to raise more money for Prostate Cancer UK. Or, he could be giving another inspirational talk to promote awareness amongst men of this terrible form of cancer through his journey. The thing about Kevin is, he never stops planning.

For me, losing out on a year of doing with Kevin the things we had planned, due to Covid, saddens me. As great as socially-distant walks with Kevin have been, I feel we have missed out on so many other experiences. Time is a precious commodity in Kevin's situation. Putting my sadness to one side, Kevin has somehow once again remained upbeat and positive throughout, which is a credit to him.

Kevin is a hero to so many people, offering support to other sufferers of cancer, not just prostate cancer. He is a loving husband and father to his wife Sarah and his three children. However, to me, as well as being a hero, he will always be Kevla, my mate, who I can sit and listen to either *Soccer Saturday* or The Stylistics with (not many people will know he likes them!), whilst drinking a pint and eating crisps. We have enjoyed many a curry night, followed by cheese and biscuits (there is a lot of food consumed in our get-togethers) as well as laughter.

Bottom line is that he is my buddy, my best friend, Kevin Webber. Long may that continue.

Jim Walker

My coach, Rory

I've coached over 1,000 people, including celebrities such as Sir Ranulph Fiennes, for the Marathon des Sables, but Kevin's phone call to me in August 2015 really excited me. Being of a similar age we instantly clicked and I enjoyed his no-nonsense attitude to life that being terminally ill with prostate cancer obviously brings. Instead of someone running in the desert to find out how valuable life is, which is the norm, here was someone who knew the value of life but valuable time was running out to fit in as much living as possible into whatever life they had left.

Of all the people I had running at the race that year, it was vital that Kevin finished.

I felt a huge sense of care towards him and his family to get him to the finish line and made sure that he was in my tent, positioned right next to me, where I could keep a watching eye over him. I wasn't quite sure what to expect from someone with his condition, but I'd coached Sir Ranulph, who had recovered from prostate cancer, and Kevin told me that unlike other cancer sufferers he felt okay as he'd been through all the treatments available to him.

With that in mind, I continued training Kevin just like anyone else. With Kevin's banking mind, even on our first run together he analysed my business as well as my coaching methods to form his own route to the race and put me straight on my business – I liked that. I totally got that he was running the race for the experience and not to be bogged down in the minutiae of carrying as little kit as possible for the week, like most people. His rucksack was like a magician's hat and even on the last day he could offer tea and energy bars to all seven of us in the tent to mark the day!

Of course, he finished the 2016 Marathon des Sables with ease and had the huge satisfaction of the ordinary guy doing something extraordinary that everyone feels after running 250km across the Sahara Desert. But then life threw me a curveball just like it had for Kevin. A week after my return from the race, I came down with Guillain Barre Syndrome, a rare neurological condition that paralysed me from the neck down for five months – a very serious, but luckily not terminal life-changing condition, that turned my whole world upside down just as cancer had for Kevin.

Using the 2017 race as a recovery goal, and knowing that Kevin was running again, I made sure he was again next to me in my tent. Not so that I could keep a watchful eye on him, but so that he would be there for me as I was still in a very wobbly stage of my recovery and as a payback for my help in 2016, he'd do anything, even carry my rucksack, to get me to the finish.

This was something exceptional from a person with limited time left to live. Being prepared to sacrifice some of that precious time to help me, made me feel very special, but that's Kevin all over, isn't it?

We were both there again in 2018, side by side, and who knows where he'll stop – I just hope he continues to motivate and raise awareness for prostate cancer for as long as 'Super-Humanly-Kevin-Possible'.

Rory Coleman (15 Marathon des Sables, 1,082 marathons and 255 ultra-marathons. Business, sport and lifestyle coach)

My race director mate, Steve

I first met Kev in 2016. I had previously spoken to him on the phone when he was trying to understand what he had committed to do when he signed up for the Marathon des Sables, 'The toughest footrace on earth', 250km in some of the most hostile conditions on the planet, with daytime temperatures regularly tipping over 50 degrees Celsius, carrying everything (other than water) that he would need for the six gruelling days whilst running approximately a marathon a day, with one day when he would be running two marathons. The challenge is of course physical, but that is far from the whole story. We say that the MDS is 90 per cent mental. The other ten per cent is in your head.

After I had finished explaining that with proper training, nutrition, foot preparation, mindset and hydration protocols, he should have no problem completing the challenge, he said to me, 'Thanks, but I should tell you that I have terminal prostate cancer and have been given 18 months to live.' I remember thinking that I couldn't have heard the last bit correctly and didn't want to ask him to repeat what I thought he had said, so we talked about his treatment and I sat speechless. What do you say to someone who is counting down their days? What do you say to that person when they want to do something so monumentally challenging? As it turns out, you say the same as you do to everyone else who has a lifetime target this enormous.

Roll on to April 2016 and here is Kevin in camp in the Sahara before the start of the race. He certainly doesn't look ill (as if I would know what that looks like). He is excited: not the nervous excitement that most runners have, he obviously cannot wait to do this. He is more like someone ripping open a wrapped present in anticipation of the gift of a lifetime. The reality of the difficulty of the race seems almost irrelevant to him. He is smiling and chatty and really pleased to be here.

I ask him if he would like to meet Patrick, the founder and race director of the MDS for the previous thirty years. There is nothing that Patrick hasn't seen in this time and he has a natural charm and air of accomplishment about him; he really likes meeting runners and always has a word of encouragement for everyone. I made the introduction in French and English and explained to Patrick the situation, saying that Kev was fulfilling a dream within the confines of his life expectancy and illness. Tears were starting to run down Patrick's cheeks behind his sunglasses. Kev leaned towards me and said, 'I didn't want to upset this guy, what have you said?' After explaining to Patrick that this was a moment of great joy for Kev, he gave him one of his legendary gallic hugs, which he repeated on the finish line a week later when Kev made it across, looking a little more dazed but with a huge grin on his face that stayed there right up to when we disappeared up the steps of the flight home.

As you may guess, I was expecting that news of Kev would not be great from that point and he would fight the fight and travel the journey described by the men in white coats. When I answered the phone to Kev again in the summer of 2016, his words – 'I would like to do the MDS again, could you find me a place? I am doing this again for Prostate Cancer UK' – were like a symphony of joy. How is this possible? Have you told your wife and family about this? Of course, the answer was positive and has been every year since. Kevin has defied the men in white coats and he talks about their ever so slight air of disappointment every time he has his tests and the diagnosing consultant tries to make sense of Kev's homemade treatment plan that involves doing the opposite of what most do after the word 'terminal' is dispensed.

So not only has Kev done the MDS every year since 2016 (including doing an epic version of Captain Tom and staging a full MDS replica around his garden during the 2020 Covid-19 lockdowns) but he has done a whole raft of other challenges that put him right at the front of endurance events, despatching the few failures with the same aplomb as his numerous successes and seemingly growing in stature, confidence, fitness and form after each.

His appetite and success with ultra-races, pale into insignificance against his achievements in bringing awareness (and funding) of prostate cancer and his evangelical calls seem to land pretty much every time with audiences responding to his achievements, goals and unrelenting commitment to the cause.

Every year, we put on an Expo, a prestigious event that marks the start of serious preparation for the next year's Marathon des Sables. A few years ago, I asked Kev if he could come and say a few words to open the event and his words resonated brilliantly. He talked in real world terms about challenges, finding your own version of success, with fundraising commitments being the key to never giving up, even when your world is tumbling around you and you cannot find the light you need to shine towards your way forward.

Kevin is both known and loved in equal measure in the ultra-running world, and do you know the best bit of all of this for me? Kev's friendship has become a valuable part of my life that I will always treasure.

Steve Diederich – Organiser of Marathon des Sables UK

My tentmate, Jeff

Rory Coleman chose my tentmates on the 2016 Marathon Des Sables, and he chose extremely well.

I have remained friends with all of the seven other runners that shared that sandy experience, running through the Sahara Desert, and is my life richer for it? Hell yes, it is.

Kev and I ran the MDS together, we shared a speaking stage together as another member of our Tent 105 embarked on his journey running around the world, and drank too much together in Athens when global runner Nick finished his amazing challenge in 2019.

We have also grown closer as we have got to know each other, and both share the same love for life, living in the moment, and serving others.

Kev's philanthropy is off the scale, and I hope by reading his book he inspires you to do whatever you can to be the best version of you; I know he would love that, and so would I.

I am very honoured to be asked to write something for his book, and to use Kev as my inspiration, I would sum up by saying don't count the days, make the days count.

Jeff Smith

My mate, Jeff Stelling

Whoever told Kevin Webber he had two years to live when he was diagnosed with prostate cancer clearly did not know Kevin Webber. He is a man of steel.

I first met Kevin when he did the last of my ten walking marathons on my 'March to the Arch' from my hometown Hartlepool to Wembley. The 260-mile trek alongside Russ Green – then the chief executive of Hartlepool United FC – was to raise funds for, but, more specifically, awareness of, prostate cancer. I didn't know it at the time but Kevin was near the start of his cancer journey and didn't know if he would even manage to complete that one marathon as he was injured. Suffice to say he did though!

When we did 15 marathons in 15 days the following year, Kev was still with us and planned to do them all, although I still didn't really know much about Kevin. I would amble along in the middle of the group trying to pass the time by chatting to as many people as possible. Kevin was almost always at the back of the group, encouraging, cajoling and helping anyone who was struggling in any way. You are doing this, he would tell them, to save the lives of my two boys. Powerful motivation!

In the middle of it, though, a personal crisis meant he had to return home. But Kevin was determined he would still complete the 15 marathons. So, on the three days he was away from the group, he did solo marathons in his home town. He then came back to join me on the last few, effectively also doing

15 in 15 days like me! By the time we had finished the final leg I had some idea of the mindset that makes him the most remarkable person I think I have ever met.

He is driven by a desire to make the most of every day he has on earth. I will never forget his mantra. If you have a bad day, make bloody sure the next day is a good day.

I was proud to be asked to present the award when Kevin was named Endurance Fundraiser of the Year in 2018. Winning awards is not his motivation, but I knew how much it meant to him as, surrounded by his family who have made so many sacrifices of their own, he came to the podium and made a powerful motivational speech. Well, what would you expect? It was Kevin after all. For me he was more than fundraiser of the year. He was Man of the Year. As he was in 2017. And 2019. And 2020 and 2021 and ...

Jeff Stelling

My mate, Vassos Alexander

The Athens Classic Marathon route is mainly unremarkable and mostly uphill. And yet when I recall running those dusty suburban streets with Kevin, I sound like someone from *The Great Gatsby...* What a joy! Such a treat! What fun!

I went to Greece with some pals from our south-west London running club, Barnes Runners, to run the marathon that began it all in 500 BC. That's when the Ancient Greek messenger, Pheidippides, dashed from Marathon to Athens with news of a vital victory in battle. You run essentially the same route today. And then the finish is truly epic, in the all-marble Panathenaic Stadium, venue for the first modern Olympics in 1896. If you're a fan of marathon running, you can't *not* run this race.

Our plan was to tick off the 26.2 miles as fast as possible, then reconvene for some well-earned Mythos beers in the shadow of the Acropolis.

I chatted to Nick Butter on the morning of the race and he invited me to run with him and Kevin. I declined. I preferred to start at the front – get this done quickly, and go play! But three miles in, on a whim, I decided to stop and wait for them. I'm so pleased I did.

Kevin has a gravitational force field around him, effortlessly inspirational. He's frequently mentioned in running circles, and with good reason. What he has achieved is nothing short of incredible, and I'm well placed to judge: I know how hard some of those races are, and I don't have a cancer diagnosis hanging over me. I was thrilled to meet Kevin in person.

The group I joined that day was among the happiest and most jocular I've ever experienced during a race. You could almost taste the euphoria. We stopped for photos, interviews, chats, and always ran at the pace of the slowest runner. This was not a race to Athens; this was a celebration. Almost the exact opposite of Pheidippides' original dash 2,500 years previously. He needed to deliver the message from the battlefield as quickly as possible. We would simply arrive when we arrived, and make the most of every mile along the way.

When I'm asked to give talks before races, I frequently advise anyone listening: 'Don't let your time ruin your time.' I use the quote, but largely ignore it when it comes to my own races. Indeed, this was the first marathon when I didn't even glance at my watch.

That's Kevin's doing. He is an extraordinary human being. Inspiring, uplifting, cheerful, resilient, determined. Thanks, Kev. I can't wait to run some miles with you again one day.

Vassos Alexander

Acknowledgements

THERE ARE so any people without whom I would never have got this far both physically and mentally and there are sadly not enough pages to mention every single one of you. But please believe me when I say, each of you has given my life a huge sense of worth. If you have ever run with me, organised an event I have been part of, sponsored me, messaged me, read my blog, been a supportive friend, colleague or family member, you know who you are and I hope you realise the impact you have made on my life over the last six years.

Having said that, I must single out three organisations that have been the foundation blocks of my journey, because without them, I would never have made the impact I believe I have.

Firstly, my employer, NatWest. From the first moment I suspected I was ill, through diagnosis, treatment and living with my death sentence, they have been nothing but supportive in everything I have ever attempted to do. Many times, I have pushed the boundaries and they have always understood that I am trying to make a difference and supported me on every step of my journey.

Next, we have the incredible doctors and nurses at the Royal Marsden Hospital. From the moment I started diagnostic tests they have only ever been sympathetic, understanding, and honest about my situation. My oncologist Professor Parker has shared my six-year journey with me and has used his knowledge and instincts to give me a path of treatment that has kept me alive. Even though he could never guarantee success, I have always trusted his instincts and I would never have achieved everything I have without his knowledge and understanding.

And finally, there is Prostate Cancer UK. At the start of my journey, they provided me with information and a forum that was my lifeline. From the first time I spoke to Gary in 2014, the charity has made me feel I can make a difference. The love and support from the CEO Angela, her husband Ian and key people I have worked with such as Seren, Dan, Amy, Jon, Phil, Seb and Ellie to name but a few, has given me a reason to keep getting up in the morning and put that first step outside my door. Whether I am running, walking, or speaking, the backing of the charity has enabled me to prove to other people in my situation that you should never give up until it's physically impossible. Nobody at the charity sees their role as 'just a job' but rather as a labour of love and every single one of them gives me my purpose in life.

Turning to this book, my heartfelt thanks go to Mark Church, who stupidly one day said he would help me write the story of my journey. Mark has written the book for no reward other than hoping it might help others in times of trouble to pick themselves up and keep moving forward. The hundreds of hours of recording my words and writing them have all been done with a smile and without Mark this book might have remained a pipe dream. So, if you don't like the book, blame him!

My thanks to Paul, Jane, Alex, Duncan and especially Katie at Pitch Publishing, who believed there was enough of a story to back the book and publish it. Whilst many of the photographs in the book are mine, thank you to all the professional photographers who gave me free use of their creative genius and allowed their pictures to go with my words.

And thank you all of you that have given personal reflections about my journey. I know this was not easy for some of you and, for my family, dragged up some sad memories, but I hope that you all realise how important your contributions are to the book.

My final thank you is to my wife Sarah, who has been my constant support throughout the journey and the book. Without her, I am nothing.

Also available at all good book stores

9781785314537

9781785313301

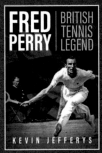

9781785312908

9781785314452

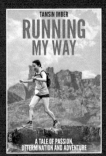

9781785314544

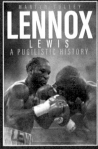

9781785313295

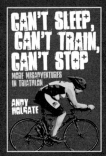

9781909178335

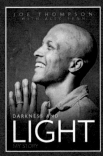

9781785314513

9781785312298

2017 Northern Lights at the end of the long day on Fire and Ice. (Fire & Ice)